ISLAM IN A
CHANGING WORLD
Europe and the Middle East

Edited by
Anders Jerichow
and
Jørgen Bæk Simonsen

CURZON

First published in 1997
by Curzon Press
St John's Studios, Church Road, Richmond
Surrey, TW9 2QA

© 1997 Anders Jerichow and Jørgen Bæk Simonsen

Typeset in Sabon by LaserScript, Mitcham, Surrey

Printed in Great Britain by
Biddles Ltd, Guildford and Kings Lynn

British Library Cataloguing in Publication Data
A catalogue record for this book is available from the British Library

Library of Congress in Publication Data
A catalogue record for this book has been requested

ISBN 0–7007–0508–2 (hbk)
ISBN 0–7007–0509–0 (pbk)

Contents

Conference Organizers

Special editorial acknowledgement to **Steven Rubin.**

The organizers of the Conference *Islam in a Changing World – Europe and the Middle East* were:

Svend Aage Christensen, Director, Department of Analysis, DUPI

Henriette Rald, Conference Coordinator, DUPI

Trine Mogensen, Student of Political Science, DUPI

Michael Zilmer-Johns, Deputy Head of Department, Ministry of Foreign Affairs

Ole Neustrup, Deputy Head of Department, Ministry of Foreign Affairs

Dorthea Damkjær, Head of Section, Ministry of Foreign Affairs

Anders Jerichow, Foreign News Editor, Politiken

Birthe Hansen, Associate Professor, University of Copenhagen

Jørgen Bæk Simonsen, Associate Professor, University of Copenhagen

Co-sponsored by the European Commission

List of contributors

R. Hrair Dekmejian is Professor of Political Science at the University of Southern California since 1986 and Professor at the International Business and Education Program since 1992. He has written extensively on active political Islamic groups in the Arab Middle East and on political Islamic groups in Egypt in particular. Professor Dekmejian is often used as a commentator on World Affairs and as a consultant for US and international organizations.

Saad Eddin Ibrahim is Professor of Political Sociology at the American University in Cairo. President of Cairo's Union of Social Professions. Trustee of the Arab Thought Forum, Jordan, Chairman of the Board of the Ibn Khaldoun Centre for Development Studies. He has taught at several universities in the United States and in the Middle East. Professor Ibrahim has been advisor in the Arab League and commented on politics.

Shahram Chubin is Executive Director of Research at the newly founded Geneva Centre for Security Policy. He has worked out comprehensive and multi-dimensional studies of Middle Eastern politics in the areas of co-operation as well as conflict. A specialist in security problems in the Middle East, Mr Chubin has been a consultant *inter alia* to the US Department of Defence, the Hudson Institute and the United Nations.

Ahmad S. Moussalli is Professor of Political Science at the American University of Beirut. He received his PhD from the University of Maryland, USA. He has written more than eight books including *Radical Islamic Fundamentalism*, which was selected by CHOICE (Journal of current reviews of academic books in the USA, 1994) as Outstanding Academic Book, and another book *Islamic Fundament-*

alism and World Order, which was selected as a bestseller during International Book Exhibition in Beirut, 1993.

Mir Zohair Husain is Professor at the University of South Alabama, Political Science Department since 1986. He was born in Karachi, Pakistan. Professor Husain received a PhD in International Relations from the University of Pennsylvania, Philadelphia. He has acted as a guest speaker for the World Affairs Council of Philadelphia.

NematAllah Adel Guenena is Director of the Socio-economic Development department at Environmental Quality International (EQI) in Cairo since 1991. She holds an MA in Sociology/ Anthropology and a BA in Middle East studies from the American Univerity in Cairo. Professor Guenena has specialized in regional development issues and special emphasis placed on socioeconomic developments in the Middle East.

Anders Jerichow is Foreign News Editor at the Danish daily 'Politiken'. He has written extensively on Middle Eastern political and cultural issues and authored several books on political development and democratization in Muslim nations. He is a member of the board of Danish PEN.

Juan Prat is Acting Director General for External Relations. Responsible for Southern Mediterranean, Middle and Near East, Latin America, South and Southeast Asia as well as North–South Co-operation of the Commission of the European Communities. He joined the Spanish Diplomatic Service in 1968. Holds the rank of Minister Plenipotentiary.

Ellen Margrethe Løj is Permanent State Secretary of the South Group in the Danish Ministry of Foreign Affairs. She has been stationed around the world through the Danish Ministry of Foreign Affairs. Most recently she was the Ambassador to Israel. Ms Løj has also been Counsellor to the Permanent Mission to the EU and secretary to the Permanent Mission to the UN, New York.

Niels Helveg Petersen is Minister for Foreign Affairs in Denmark, appointed in January 1993. Mr Petersen has a Law degree from Copenhagen University. He has been an elected member of the Danish Parliament in two rounds (November 1966–September 1974 and February 1977–), representing the Social Liberal Party.

Henriette Rald is Conference Coordinator, DUPI, Copenhagen.

Introduction

Though the world changes constantly, it *evolves* only belatedly. Such has been the case for Islam, and Western perceptions of Muslim traditions, values and societies. However inter-related the Christian West and the Muslim East may be, stereotypes often tend to overshadow reality, just as enemy projections are inclined to overrule mutual interest.

With these thoughts in mind, an impressive number of leading international scholars and representatives from various Arab-Muslim institutions and movements, assembled, in mid-June of 1996 in Copenhagen, to develop a dialogue, and subsequently, further an understanding of Islam's place in the modern world. The conference, which was hosted by the Danish Institute of International Affairs (DUPI), and sponsored by the Danish Foreign Ministry, received widespread attention from both the public and the media.

The focus of the forum concerned itself with the multiple faces of Islam, and dealt specifically with the triangle between populism, Islam and civil society in the Arab world. It raised the question of unity versus fragmentation, and looked into the current dilemmas of pluralism, human rights and fundamentalism.

Introducing the debates were six international scholars – Hrair Dekmejian, Saad Eddin Ibrahim, Shahram Chubin, Ahmad S. Moussalli, Mir Zohair Husain and NematAllah Adel Guenena – all of whom accepted invitations to prepare an essay on various issues for this publication. While the issues themselves were selected by DUPI, all titles and ideas, including the use of technical terms and their mode of Arabic and Persian transcription, belong solely to each writer individually.

A seventh chapter, written by the Foreign News Editor, Anders Jerichow, has been included as a personal reflection on the subject of religious interpretation and political pluralism.

Furthermore, a special annex submits the official texts of two speeches from the conference, given by Juan Prat, EU Commission General Director for External Relations, and Ambassador Ellen Margrethe Løj, Danish State Secretary, as well as a chronicle originally published for the Danish newspaper, Politiken, written by Niels Helveg Petersen, Danish Minister for Foreign Affairs.

Finally, Conference Coordinator Henriette Rald reproduces a sampling of Danish newspaper illustrations from the time of the conference which, in their own right, may serve to represent the prevailing perceptions of Islam.

Anders Jerichow, Jørgen Bæk Simonsen and *Henriette Rald*

Chapter 1

Multiple faces of Islam

R. Hrair Dekmejian

In the fourteen centuries of its existence as a universalist faith and civilization, Islam has assumed a variety of forms and modalities of expression. In keeping with the pattern followed by other world religions, successive generations of Muslims have understood and practiced Islam in different modalities depending on their historical milieu, social status and spiritual requirements. Indeed, the varieties of Muslim belief, social thought and practice that emerged throughout history were foreshadowed by a Prophetic tradition inherent in the manifestation of seventy-three sects (*firaq*) within the Islamic community (*umma*).[1]

The contemporary crisis milieu

The multiplicity of contemporary Islamic groups and movements represents a reaction to the legacy of the past as well as to the problems faced by the Islamic community in the modern world. In the last three centuries, the Islamic world was buffeted by powerful external and internal forces. It witnessed the decline of Ottoman and Persian power in the face of European imperial might and cultural hegemony. This decline of Islamic power gave rise to ethnic nationalist movements among the Turks, Persians, Arabs, Kurds and non-Muslim minorities. Within the Arab sphere, a Pan-Arabic nationalist movement emerged in the 1950s as a reaction to both the establishment of Israel and Anglo-French-American hegemony over the region. This movement, which sought to unite the Arabs under Egypt's Gamal 'Abd al-Nasser and/or the Syrian Ba'th Party, was defeated by rivalries among the Arab leaders as well as by Western interventionism and defeat by Israel in the June 1967 war.

The failure of secular Pan-Arabism, along with abortive experiments with state socialism, set the stage for a protracted and intense crisis which ultimately led to a search for an alternative venue for both identity and social and political action, i.e., Islam in its fundamentalist expression.[2]

Six interactive clusters of catalysts characterize the crisis conditions besetting the contemporary Arab world: 1) identity crisis; 2) legitimacy crisis; 3) elite misrule; 4) class conflict; 5) military impotence; and 6) culture crisis.[3] Each of these attributes of crisis have resonated throughout Arab society and have evoked responses and solutions from among the different proponents of Islamist ideology and their secularist opponents. The result has been a proliferation of Islamist political ideologies, associations and movements which have all had a powerful impact on shaping the social, spiritual and political life of the Arab countries. While some of these ideologies constitute new forms of Islamic discourse, others represent beliefs and trends that hark back to the early centuries of Muslim history.

Tables 1.1, 1.2, 1.3 and 1.4 represent the major Islamic ideological tendencies and organizations that have emerged as responses to the contemporary crisis milieu of Arab/Islamic society.

The Islamic spectrum: an analytical framework

Table 1.1 is a general overview of contemporary tendencies and movements that characterize the different facets of Islam and its revivalist phenomenon in their social, spiritual and political manifestations. These tendencies can be subsumed within the following categories.

Islamic secularism

Islamic Fundamentalism – the movement back to the roots of Islam – has become a pervasive phenomenon throughout the Arab world and the Islamic orbit, affecting the beliefs and lifestyles of all socioeconomic classes to different degrees. Within this comprehensive Islamic effervescence, commonly known as 'Islamism,'[4] there are important segments of secular nationalists (*'Ilmaniyyun/Wataniyyun*) who persist in pursuing modern lifestyles despite the pressures from their Islamist environment. This secular constituency includes Westernized elites, journalists, bureaucrats and intellectuals who retain a Muslim identity within a modernized framework.

Table 1.1 The Islamic spectrum

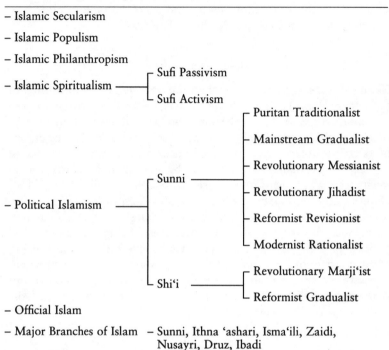

– Islamic Secularism

– Islamic Populism

– Islamic Philanthropism

– Islamic Spiritualism ⎯⎯⎯⎯ ⎡ Sufi Passivism
⎣ Sufi Activism

– Political Islamism ⎯⎯⎯ ⎡ Sunni ⎯⎯⎯ ⎡ Puritan Traditionalist
⎢ ⎢ – Mainstream Gradualist
⎢ ⎢ – Revolutionary Messianist
⎢ ⎢ – Revolutionary Jihadist
⎢ ⎢ – Reformist Revisionist
⎢ ⎣ Modernist Rationalist
⎣ Shi'i ⎯⎯⎯ ⎡ Revolutionary Marji'ist
⎣ Reformist Gradualist

– Official Islam

– Major Branches of Islam – Sunni, Ithna 'ashari, Isma'ili, Zaidi, Nusayri, Druz, Ibadi

Islamic populism

The amorphous revivalism of the masses is characterized by a deep social and spiritual fervor. Islamic populism is evidenced by regular and conspicuous observance of religious rules and practices. Despite a general political passivity, this mass constituency, may be known to turn volatile in times of social turmoil or serve as a recruitment source for radical Islamist groups.

Islamic philanthropism

Within the inchoate crucible of popular Islam, certain organized forms of Islamist expression have proliferated to provide social services as benevolent societies – *al-jama'at al-khayriyya*. These organizations are a response to the existing crisis milieu and the vacuum left by the state's inability or unwillingness to help the needy.

As such, these benevolent organizations are building 'alternative societies' at the grass-roots level, and have become a clear and growing long-term challenge to the authorities.

Islamic spiritualism

Islam has had a rich spiritualist tradition, reflected by the profusion of Sufi orders (*turuq*) since early times. The Sufi orders provide a haven for mysticism, a withdrawal from mundane affairs into an esoteric (*batini*) milieu for spiritual comfort and salvation. The Sufi traditions of doctrinal tolerance, esoteric practices and distinctive modes of worship (music/dance) are opposed by most Sunni Islamist movements such as the Muslim Brethren (*Ikhwan*) as well as the Ahl al-Hadith and their Salafiyya offshoots. Most Sufi orders refrain from opposing those in power and do not share the Sunni Islamists' intolerance toward the Shi'a and the West. Despite a tradition of political passivity, some Sufi orders have entered the political arena in recent years in order to prevent the establishment of Islamist regimes which they consider a threat to their existence. Among the Sufi groups that oppose political Islamism are Al-Ahbash of Lebanon and the large Naqshabandi order (Table 1.2).[5]

Political Islamism

The rise of political Islamism constitutes a response to the legitimacy crisis facing most Arab regimes. As an ideology, political Islamism has filled the ideational vacuum that developed after the decline of secular Pan-Arabism and socialist statism. As such, political Islamism has

Table 1.2 Islamic spiritualism – Sufi

Sufi Passivist	Over 70 Sufi Orders (*turuq*)	Arab World
Sufi Activist	Ahbash	Lebanon Arab World Europe
	Khatimiyya	Sudan
	Naqshabandiyya	Arab/Muslim World
	Bushisiyya	Morocco

provided a new identity for the multitudes experiencing crises of individual and collective identity. Similarly, Islamist groups and movements have come to occupy the "public sphere" left empty by the state's growing incapacity and retreat from effective governance.

The general objective of political Islamist movements is to establish an Islamic Order (*al-Nizam al-Islami*), or at least to reform the existing Arab polities by applying Islamic precepts. Thus, the political Islamists seek to transform the sociopolitical order of the Arab countries, regardless of their form of government, i.e., monarchies, single-party nationalists, military oligarchies or limited democracies. The degree and modalities of the prescribed regime transformation would depend on the particular ideology of an Islamist group and its relations with those in power.

Both the Sunni and Shi'a branches of Islam have given rise to movements of political Islamism. However, among the Shi'a, only the Twelvers (*Ithna 'ashari*) have manifested a strong propensity toward political Islamism, as evidenced by the success of Iran's Islamic Revolution and its impact on Arab and other Islamic countries. Political Islamism has not found a high degree of resonance among the Isma'ilis (Seveners), Zaidis, Nusayris, Ibadis and the Druz.

Table 1.1 sets forth the major ideological trends associated with both the Sunni and Shi'i branches of political Islamism. Within the Sunni Islamist framework, six major and minor ideological currents can be identified (Table 1.3).

Puritan traditionalist

The most conservative and traditionalist segment of the Islamist constituency is the Ahl al-Hadith, who are followers of the traditions of the Prophet's exemplary life (*sirat*) and his sayings and deeds (*athar*). Their quest for pristine authenticity centers on Muhammad's traditions (*ahadith*) and is the core element of Saudi Wahhabism and its Hanbali antecedents. In Saudi Arabia, as in other Arab and Islamic countries, the Ahl al-Hadith call themselves al-Salafiyyun – followers of the pious ancestors (*Salaf al-Salih*) – as distinct from al-Usuliyyun (legalist-fundamentalists). The Ahl al-Hadith are led by Shaykh 'Abd al-'Aziz Ibn Baz of Saudi Arabia. His support of the Saudi regime, however, alienated some of his younger disciples and triggering a protest movement in the 1990s which was led by young radical Salafiyyun who opposed the monarchy and its economic and defense ties to the United States and its Western allies.[6]

Table 1.3 Political Islamism – Sunni

Ideology type	Organization	Country
Puritan Traditionalist (Salafiyya)	Ahl al-Hadith (Wahhabi)	Saudi Arabia Gulf
	Salafiyyun	Saudi Arabia
	Ansar al-Sunna al-Muhammadiyya	Egypt Sudan
Mainstream Gradualist	Ikhwan al-Muslimun	Egypt Arab World
	Islah al-Ijtima'i	Kuwait
	Harakat al-Nahda	Tunisia
	Jama'a al-Islamiyya	Lebanon
Revolutionary Messianist	Takfir wal-Hijra	Egypt
	Al-Ikhwan	Saudi Arabia
Revolutionary Jihadist	Tanzim al-Jihad	Egypt
	Jama'a al-Islamiyya	Egypt
	Hizb al-Tahrir	Arab World
	Hamas/Jihad al-Islami	Palestine
	Ikhwan al-Muslimun	Syria
	Jabha al-Islamiyya lil-Inqaz	Algeria
	Jabha al-Qawmiyya al-Islamiyya	Sudan
Reformist Revisionist	Ikhwan al-Jumhuriyyun	Sudan
	Hizb al-Umma	Sudan
Modernist Rationalist ('Asriyyun 'Aqlaniyyun)	Individual Thinkers, Scholars and Groups	

Mainstream gradualist

The Society of the Muslim Brethren – Jama'a al-Ikhwan al-Muslimun – has come to occupy the mainstream of the Islamist constituency. The Muslim Brotherhood (MB), more than any other organization, has become the ideological and institutional epicenter of Sunni Islamism in the Arab world and beyond. Founded in Egypt by Hasan al-Banna in 1929, MB's militant stance in the 1950s and 1960s led to its repeated suppression until the organization's reemergence in the 1970s with the support of President Anwar al-Sadat. In view of its painful past, the new MB eschewed militancy and adopted a gradualist approach focused on building an Islamist society from the grass-roots through the use of preaching and social action.[7] Despite MB's eventual alienation from Sadat and its harassment under President Mubarak, the organization has persisted in spreading its mainstream creed dedicated to peaceful Islamization (*al-Wasatiyya*) throughout the Arab countries, where its affiliates have emerged under various names as proponents of political Islam.[8] However, MB's strategy of evolutionary Islamization was rejected by a younger generation of Islamists in the 1970s and 1980s, which led to the formation of many radical groups dedicated to revolutionary challenges to the state.[9]

Revolutionary messianist

Among the young radical Brethren who chose a revolutionary path was the Society of Muslims, later known as al-Takfir wal-Hijra. It was led by Shukri Ahmad Mustafa who believed in separating his followers from the sinful (*jahili*) society and its members and against whom he leveled the charge of "unbelief" – *takfir*.[10] Thus, Mustafa sought to establish a compact community of true believers patterned after the Prophet's *umma*. As an autocratic *amir*, Mustafa was regarded as the *mahdi* (messiah) by his followers. These followers would desist from waging *jihad* until they first strengthened themselves as a piously militant community, as the Prophet had done. This strategy was aborted when the Egyptian security forces arrested more than four-hundred Takfir members in the killing of a former minister of religious affairs; Mustafa and four others were executed in March 1978.[11]

Another separatist group with a messianic belief, Al-Ikhwan of Saudi Arabia, took over the Holy Sanctuary in Mecca on 20 November 1979 – Muharram 1400 AD – in the belief that a *mahdi* would appear at the turn of the Islamic century. Al-Ikhwan were led by Juhayman al-'Utaybi, whose brother-in-law, Muhammad ibn 'Abdalla al-Qahtani, declared himself as the *mahdi*, only to be killed by the Saudi National Guard in the ensuing fighting to secure the Grand Mosque. While Juhayman's Al-Ikhwan had originated from Shaykh Ibn Baz's Ahl al-Hadith, their alienation from their elder teacher had led them to believe in separatism and *mahdism*, and ultimately to challenge Saudi legitimacy by the Grand Mosque takeover.[12]

Revolutionary Jihadist

Since the 1970s, a growing number of militant Islamist associations have risen to challenge the Arab regimes, which they consider *jahili*, and thus Islamically illegitimate. In contrast to the Takfir wal-Hijra and Al-Ikhwan, these revolutionary groups do not have a strong messianic orientation, nor do they practice social and spiritual separation from society. Instead, they are committed to perpetual armed Jihad against the authorities in order to establish an Islamic Order, thereby rejecting the gradualist strategy of the Muslim Brotherhood and its affiliates. During the Sadat era, over a dozen militant groups emerged as offshoots of the Muslim Brotherhood, three of which became notable in terms of their violent impact on society: Tanzim al-Jihad (Jihad Organization); Jama'a al-Islamiyya (Islamic Society) and Hizb al-Tahrir al-Islami (Islamic Liberation Party). The Jihad Organization assassinated President Sadat in October 1981 and, despite its repeated suppression, continues to fight the Egyptian regime. Its spiritual guide, Shaykh 'Umar 'Abd al-Rahman, was tried and imprisoned in the USA in 1995 for the charge of inciting violence in New York City. The Palestinian-led Islamic Liberation Party was suppressed in Egypt after its attack on the Technical Military Academy in 1974. Its cells remain active in several Arab countries, including Syria, Libya and the Palestinian territories. More violent and persistent is the Islamic Society, known in Egypt as "al-Gama'a" which reemerged in the 1990s as the Mubarak government's implacable foe by targeting Coptic Christians, officials, police, and tourists. Members of these groups, along with other Islamists, fought in the US-supported Afghan civil war as Holy Warriors (*Mujahidin*), only to return as experienced fighters to destabilize pro-American Arab regimes.[13]

Several radical affiliates and offshoots of the Muslim Brotherhood have sought to change the status quo in the Palestinian territories, Syria and Algeria respectively. In the West Bank, Gaza and Israel, two groups of Palestinian Islamists – Hamas and Islamic Jihad – have fought the Israeli authorities through suicide bombings since the late 1980s. The Muslim Brotherhood of Syria, along with smaller Islamist groups, precipitated a losing war in 1976–82 against President Hafiz al-Asad, whose legitimacy they reject as an idolater (*mushrik*) because he belongs to the 'Alawi sect.[14] In Algeria, the government's cancellation of the 1992 elections that favored the Islamic Salvation

Front, led to a virtual civil war between the regime and several militant Islamist groups.[15]

Unlike the success of the Islamic Revolution in Shi'i Iran, no Islamist movement has taken power in the Arab/Islamic countries through mass revolutionary action. A partial exception is the Sudan, where the Islamic Nationalist Front led by Dr Hasan al-Turabi, emerged out of the Sudanese Muslim Brotherhood to take power in 1989 with the help of a military *coup d'état* under General 'Umar al-Bashir.

Reformist revisionists

While most political Islamists are committed to strict legalism and scripturalism based on the Qur'an, the Traditions (Sunna), and the Shari'a, several reformist thinkers have attempted to revise the 'cannon' against all odds. Mahmud Muhammad Taha, the leader of the Sudan's Republican Brothers (*Ikhwan al-Jumhuriyyun*), advocated a liberal reinterpretation of Islamic law based on the primacy of the Prophet's Meccan revelations over those revealed in Madina. In 1985, Taha was charged with heresy and hanged by Ja'far al-Numayri's regime.[16] Another Sudanese exponent of Islamic liberalism is al-Sadiq al-Mahdi, the grandson of the Mahdi Muhammad Ahmad who overthrew the British-led Turko-Egyptian regime in 1885. As a former prime minister, al-Sadiq al-Mahdi remains under detention by the Islamist government in Khartoum.

Modernist rationalist

The Islamic revivalist movement has produced a plethora of important thinkers who have attempted to reinterpret Islamist ideology in order to strengthen its contemporary relevance and applicability to the complex problems of today's society. Among the thinkers who have made significant contributions to Islamist thought are such modernist-rationalists as Rashid Ghannushi, Malik Bin Nabi, Hasan Hanafi, Muhammad 'Imara, Tariq al-Bishri, 'Abdalla al-Nafisi, Fahmi Huwaidi, Ahmad Kamal Abu al-Majd, and others.[17]

Shi'i political Islamism

The Islamist movement among the Arab Shi'a has been fueled by their generally inferior sociopolitical status *vis-à-vis* the politically dominant Sunnis. In addition, Ayatulla Ruhalla Khomeini's Islamic Revolution has had a powerful impact on the Shi'i revivalist movements in the Arab world (Table 1.4). Within the context of the Lebanese civil war, Khomeini's revolutionary ideology, combined with Iranian military and financial support, contributed to the creation of Hizb Allah and its radical affiliates. Emerging from Imam Musa al-Sadr's Amal movement and the Da'wa Party, Hizb Allah constituted a militant response to Israel's occupation of South Lebanon as well as to the inferior sociopolitical status of the Shi'a, Lebanon's largest sectarian group. Since 1982, the Hizb Allah and its affiliates have waged war against Israel and its American and European allies, both inside and outside Lebanon.[18] Several other revolutionary organizations tied to Hizb Allah have fought the Sunni governments of Iraq, Saudi Arabia and some Gulf countries. In Iraq, Saddam Hussein's Ba'thi regime, supported by the Sunni minority, has been repeatedly challenged by the majority Shi'a since the 1970s. Repeated Shi'a insurrections led by the Hizb al-Da'wa al-Islamiyya, and its offshoots, have led to large-scale repression and massacres by the Iraqi regime.[19] In Bahrain, the island's majority Shi'a community has sought a return to the constitutional order of 1975 through violence and popular demonstrations against the Sunni government of Shaykh 'Isa Al Khalifa. In Saudi Arabia, the Shi'a minority of the Eastern Province has sought to change its inferior status, fueled by the doctrinal opposition of the dominant Wahhabis to Shi'ism. Recent negotiations between the Kingdom and the Shi'i leader Hasan al-Saffar appear to have produced a tentative accommodation.[20]

All of the foregoing Shi'a Islamist groups follow the teachings of Ayatulla Khomeini, who preached revolutionary action against 'unIslamic' monarchies and military regimes. In keeping with Khomeini's concept of *wilayat al-faqih*, the Shi'a Islamist organizations are led by top *mujtahids* or *marj'is* – experts in Islamic law. In contrast to the Sunni Islamist groups, the principle and practice of clerical leadership is a hallmark of the Shi'a organizations.[21] In recent years some Shi'a Islamists have adopted a reformist strategy. In Kuwait, after years of opposition and oppression, the Shi'a minority won parliamentary seats in the 1992 elections under the rubric of I'tilaf al-Islami al-Watani. A similar reformist tendency has emerged among the Bahraini Shi'a in the form of the Freedom Movement (*Haraka al-Tahrir*), which eschews violence in favor of peaceful political change.

Table 1.4 Political Islamism – Shiʻi

Ideology	Group	Country
Revolutionary Marjiʻist	Hizb Allah	Lebanon
	Hizb al-Daʻwa al-Islamiyya	Iraq Gulf Lebanon
	Jihad al-Islami	Lebanon
	Jabha al-Islamiyya li-Tahrir al-Bahrain	Bahrain
	Munazzama al-Thawra al-Islamiyya lil-Jazira al-ʻArabiyya	Saudi Arabia
Reformist Gradualist	Iʻtilaf al-Islami al-Watani	Kuwait
	Haraka al-Tahrir	Bahrain

Conclusions

The Islamist movement and its political exponents have sought to influence Arab and other Muslim governments through a variety of methods with considerable success. While Islamist revolutionary takeovers have generally not succeeded, except in the Sudan, clearly the ruling elites have been placed on the defensive by the political Islamists. Through preaching and political pressure, the Islamists have forced both secular and monarchical rulers to adopt some Islamist precepts and practices in most Arab/Muslim countries. As a result, the Muslim Brethren and other Islamist groups have strengthened the roots of Islamism as well as contributed to its persuasiveness. Despite this success, the Islamist movements remain dissatisfied because they insist on the *total* implementation of Shariʻa law, not its selective incorporation into the existing legal systems of Arab and other Muslim countries. However, it should be understood that the Islamist insistence on such a comprehensive change also entails their demand to take part in governance – the assumption of power. Thus, the struggle for power between the Islamists and the ruling oligarchies constitutes the crucial determinant of the evolution of the Arab countries and the Islamic world.

Notes

1 Abd al-Rahman bin Mu'alla al-Luwayhiq, *Al-Ghuluw fi al-Din fi Hayat al-Muslimin al-Mu'asira*. (Beirut, 1992) p. 205.
2 R. Hrair Dekmejian, *Islam in Revolution*, 2nd edn. (Syracuse: Syracuse University Press, 1995), pp. 23–25.
3 Ibid., pp. 23–32.
4 For different meanings and labels given to Islamic fundamentalism, see ibid., pp. 4–5.
5 A. Nizar Hamzeh and R. Hrair Dekmejian, "The Islamic Spectrum of Lebanese Politics," *Journal of South Asian and Middle Eastern Studies*, Vol. XVI, No. 3, Spring 1993: 25–42; and A. Nizar Hamzeh and R. Hrair Dekmejian, "A Sufi Response to Political Islamism: Al-Ahbash of Lebanon," *International Journal of Middle East Studies*, 28 (1996): 225–27.
6 R. Hrair Dekmejian, "The Rise of Political Islamism in Saudi Arabia," *Middle East Journal*, Vol. 48, No. 4, Autumn 1994: 627–43.
7 Dekmejian, *Islam in Revolution*, pp. 74–79.
8 Ibid., pp. 213–19, 223–47.
9 Ibid., pp. 84–102.
10 Ibid., pp. 84–96.
11 Ibid., pp. 57–63, 91.
12 Ibid., pp. 133–37.
13 Ibid., p. 32.
14 Ibid., pp. 108–12, 116–18.
15 Ibid., pp. 205–08.
16 Ibid., p. 188
17 Ibid., pp. 117–81.
18 Hamzeh and Dekmejian, *The Islamic Spectrum*: 35–41.
19 Dekmejian, *Islam in Revolution*, pp. 121–29.
20 Dekmejian, *The Rise of Political Islamism*: 642
21 Dekmejian, *Islam in Revolution*, pp. 123–25, 165–70.

Chapter 2

The troubled triangle: populism, Islam and civil society in the Arab world

Saad Eddin Ibrahim[1]

Introduction

The six months between the end of October 1995 and the end of April 1996 encapsulated in the most dramatic way the promises and perils deeply stored in the Arab/Middle East region. The six month drama opened up with the glorious Amman Economic Summit (30 October 1995) attended by 63 countries and over 3,000 leading businessmen, intellectuals, statesmen, and several heads of states, including King Hussain of Jordan and Prime Minister Yitzhak Rabin of Israel. In the days and weeks ahead, it was followed up by the tragic assassination of Yitzhak Rabin (3 November 1995), the clean and hopeful presidential elections in Algeria (16 November 1995), the disappointingly sad legislative elections in Egypt (29 November), the indecisive elections in Turkey (24 December), and the euphoric maiden presidential and legislative elections in Palestine (20 January 1996). Throughout these events, deadly salvoes between Israel's MOSAD and Palestinine's Islamic Jihad and Hamas were being issued Backstage in the region, the Iraqi "Republic of Fear" continued to horrify the world with brutalities, which were becoming intra-familial among Saddam Hussain's own clan. In Qatar, a son staged a palace *coup d'état* against his own royal father, only to see the father, exiled in a neighboring country, attempt his own counter *coup d'état* to restore his throne from the incorrigible son. Palestinian Islamic Hamas performed three successive suicide bombings in the heart of Israel (in Jerusalem and Ashkelon on 25 February, and in Tel Aviv on 3 March), killing and wounding some 100 Israelis while much of the world sympathized and responded to Egyptian President Mubarak's hurried invitation for a World "Summit for Peacemakers," attended by some 30 heads of state including US President Clinton and Russian President Yeltsin (Sharm

El-sheikh, 13 March). With pending elections in Israel itself, and amidst charges by the opposition that Israel's Prime Minister was too weak to deal with the Arabs or to lead Israel in peace and war, Shimon Peres put on a show of brutal force against Palestinian civilians in the occupied territories, and an even more brutal one in neighboring Lebanon to the north (11–27 April 1996).

Thus, there was no moment of boredom in the midst of this despotic brutal confusion. Nor was there a loss of hope. Even during the height of bombing and killing in Lebanon, the Palestinians and the Israelis were carrying out earlier mutual pledges for peace: first the Palestinian National Council (PNC) removed from its Covenant the clause calling for the destruction of the Jewish state (24 April) and a day later, the ruling Israeli Labor Party removed from its political program the articles of commitment banning it from allowing the establishment of a Palestinian state (*Time*, 6 May: 45–46).

Even the tragic assassination of Israeli Prime Minister Rabin came as a shock not only to peoples of Israel, but also to the rest of the Arab world and the Middle East. It evoked diverse and contrasting feelings of sadness, fear, vindictiveness, and joy. But the soul-searching event also had implications and ponderings for civil society and democratization in a new Middle East.

For the first time since its creation in 1948, Israel had experienced a full-blown Jewish-Israeli act of assassination of its top leader. It was an act incited by a protracted, profound and intense political divisiveness in Israel over the peace process. The Arabs in general, and the Palestinians in particular, have all known and experienced first-hand Israeli acts of violence and brutality of all kinds – e.g., at the hands of the Israeli army, police, intelligence, and civilians. Occasionally, Israelis have also used violence against each other. However, the Israelis had convinced themselves and the rest of the world (i.e. outside the Middle East), that they were far more "civil" than their Arab neighbors. With the assassination of Rabin, a kind of "moral parity" was suddenly established. Neither Israelis nor Arabs have a monopoly on acts of political violence; neither side has a monopoly on the "moral high-grounds."

For the first time in the one hundred years history of the conflict, we saw Arabs genuinely and publicly grieving an Israeli leader. Obversely, we saw Jews in Israel and in New York genuinely and publicly rejoicing over the same event. To be sure, there were Arabs who equally rejoiced, especially the pro-Islamic Jihad movement whose leader, Fathi Shakaki, had been assassinated in Malta a week earlier (presumably by the

Israeli MOSAD). The point here is that grief and joy were deeply and widely cross-cutting Arabs and Israelis alike.

For the first time, dozens of top Arab officials were seen on Israeli soil in an Israeli funeral, fully exposed to the full-blown Israeli society with all its stresses, strains, and advances. It was surely a brief moment of such exposure for many of them, akin to that first American step on the moon – a small one for human beings, but a giant one for the region. From the moment of Rabin's assassination to that of his burial, there were many other "firsts" for Arabs and Israelis during those two days of November. Many words were said and written about those forty-eight hours, but for the purpose of this chapter, it is the "civil" dimensions of the tragedy which concern us here.

These events, along with many others, testify to the dynamism and profound dialectics in the region: from the new quest for peace and economic co-operation *vis-à-vis* the old patterns of hostility and isolation; to the fledgling civil society and democratic drive *vis-à-vis* entrenched primordialism and oriental despotism. This chapter is an update of an earlier effort (Norton, 1995: 27–54) examining the regional dynamics bearing on the topic. A special mention of Egypt, Algeria, and Jordan should elucidate the democratic/despotic and the tolerance/intolerance dialectics currently raging across the entire region. In all three cases we observe a three-way conflict among the authoritarian impulse of the state, the democratic impulse of the fledgling civil society, and the relentless quest for power by Islamic activists.

Revisiting the concept of "civil society"

As late as the 1985 revised edition of the *Social Science Encyclopedia* (Routledge: London and New York, 1989), there was no entry for the concept of "civil society." The concept goes back to the seventeenth century, and was widely used, especially by the "Social Contract" theorists. It was still being used in the early decades of this century. But none of the 450 authors from among the twenty-three social sciences and humanities who wrote up the Encyclopedia, felt that the concept was important enough to deal with in the 1985 edition.

It is only in the late 1980s and 1990s that the concept of "civil society" has forcefully been incarnated. The collapse of the Berlin Wall, coupled with totalitarianism in Eastern Europe and the former USSR, coincided with its powerful comeback. But there have been other factors as well: the weakening of the nation-state, the failure or

dismal performance of several development paradigms, the proliferation of multinational corporations, the mushrooming of non-
governmental organizations (NGOs), and the sprouting of democracies in all corners of the globe. The concept "civil society" is now so
often in use, and so overloaded, that there is a serious theoretical
threat to its sharpness and utility.

A working definition

Of some seventy-six definitions this author has encountered in recent
social science literature, the following seems to capture the most:

> Civil Society is the totality of self-initiating and self-regulating
> volitional social formations, peacefully pursuing a common
> interest, advocating a common cause, or expressing a common
> passion; respecting the right of others to do the same, and
> maintaining their relative autonomy *vis-à-vis* the state, the
> family, and the market.

The term "civil society" has emerged as an over-arching concept
linking "democracy," "development," and "peaceful management of
conflict". The associational component of civil society encompasses a
wide range of organized collective action, e.g., PVOs, NGOs, clubs,
trade unions and political parties. But it is equally the normative
component which adds to the appeal of the concept, i.e., civility in
dealing with others, respect of differences, and a tacit or explicit
commitment to peaceful management of conflict.

Both the associational and normative dimensions of it have made
many scholars postulate a close link between civil society and
democracy. Both are rooted in the "equality of citizenship," respect
for the "rules-of-the-game," and "peaceful management of conflict".
The 1990s literature on civil society has listed its attributes to include:
tolerance, respect and protection of human rights, transparency, a
check on state power, rule of law, accountability, promotion of
citizenship and practices of democracy (Norton, 1995: 4–24).

Correlates of civil society

By the same token, many social scientists now equate "civil society"
and "social capital." Robert Putnam defines "social capital" as those
"features of social organization which improve the efficiency of
society by facilitating coordinated actions – such as trust, norms, and

networks" (Putnam; 1993: 167). The title, sub-title, and contents of Putnam's book, *Making Democracy Work: Civic Traditions in Modern Italy*, highlight the "holy trinity" of civil society, democracy and development. Putnam's twenty years of painstaking empirical research concludes that it is civic associations which have made the difference between "development" and "underdevelopment," "democratic" and "non-democratic" practices in Italy.

Retrospectively, it seems clear that civil society emerged organically out of modern socioeconomic formations, e.g., classes, occupational categories, and other interest groups. In the West, this process unfolded simultaneously with the processes of capitalization, industrialization, urbanization, citizenship and the nation-state. While the ultimate loyalty of citizens was supposedly held to the nation-state as the natural sovereign embodiment of all society, sub-loyalties were to follow interests, i.e., focused on class, occupation, and residential community. Volitional associations emerged and expanded around the saliency of the many interests of the citizens, e.g. political parties, trade unions, professional associations, clubs, and community organizations. While loyalty to the supreme sovereignty of the state was emotive, abstract, and only occasionally invoked, solidarities of volitional associations were interest-based, concrete and more frequently invoked. While loyalty to the state was supposedly universal and consensual among all citizens, solidarity in a volitional association was particularistic and variable in intensity and duration. That is to say, while citizens hardly change their belonging to a nation-state, they frequently do so with regard to volitional associations – such as class, occupation, status, and residence change due to vertical and horizontal mobility. With competing, or even conflicting interests of various socioeconomic formations in the same nation-state, governance would gradually evolve along participatory politics – e.g., "democracy." Some socioeconomic formations were more conscious of their interest and quicker than others in organizing their ranks to retain, seize, or share political power within the state. The less conscious and less organized formations would, over time, learn by emulation the art of associational life. Thus, the organs of civil society in the West have multiplied in numbers and organizational sophistication.

Civil society in the Middle East[2]

Some Middle East area observers have contended that the lagging democratization of the Arab World is due to the absence or stunting of its civil society and its corresponding political culture. Some orientalists and ethno-centric mongers may go as far as to totally dismiss even the potential for the evolution of an Arab civil society and hence, any prospect of genuine democratization. Propagators of this point of view often forget the long, arduous, and occasionally bloody march of civil society and democratization in their own Western societies. It was more than seven centuries between the issuance of the Magna Carta (1215) and granting suffrage to women (1920) in Great Britain. What Huntington calls "waves of democratization in the West" during the last two centuries, were followed by counter waves of authoritarianism in several European countries (Huntington, 1992:17–21). At any rate, the assertions made about the inhospitality of Arab society and culture to democratization will be examined in both pre-modern and contemporary Arab realities to argue a counter proposition: that despite noted distortion and time lags, the Arab World is currently going through civil society building and democratization. The relationship between the two processes is essentially the same: as modern socio-economic formations sprout and take shape, they create their civil society organizations, which in turn strive for participatory governance. The two volumes edited by A. R. Norton (1995) and its accompanying primer edited by Jillian Schwedler (1995) elaborate and examine this relationship closely in several Middle Eastern countries.

Resilient traditional Arab civil formations

Pre-modern society in what is now called the Arab world was fairly ordered around a political authority (Rizk, 1993) whose legitimacy was derived from a combination of conquest and/or religious sources. But the public space was immediately shared by *ulama*', merchants, guilds, *Sufi* orders, and sects (*millets*) (Halperin, 1962; Gellner, 1988; Harik, 1990: 1–28). Outside this first concentric zone, the public space was populated by peasants and tribes. Political authority asserted itself most clearly in the first concentric zone of that public space. Outside the first zone, its assertion varied markedly. In most cases it was hardly felt. Other collectivities, especially the tribes, were quite autonomous from, if not outright defiant of the central authority (Ibn Khaldoun, 1980; Gellner, 1988).

Even in the first concentric zone, often within city walls, various groups coexisted and interacted with a great deal of autonomy. Guilds, religious sects, and ethnic groups ran most of their own internal affairs through elected or appointed leaders. The latter were accountable to both the political authority and their own communities. Tension, no doubt, existed within each category but was of low intensity. Equally, tension may have existed between or among two or more of these communities, but was often resolved inter-communally; or occasionally warranted the direct intervention of the political authority (Rizk 1993: 40–48).

Leaders, elders, and notables of the above traditional formations performed several functions in the overall governance of pre-modern Arab society. Beside running intra-communal affairs and managing inter-communal conflicts, they acted as councillors and advisors to rulers. They were called "Solvers and Binders," *Ahlu al-Hal wa al-akd*, the important among them were the *"ulama,"* learned men of religion. In this capacity, Solvers and Binders (SAB) reduced the absolutist nature of the pre-modern Arab Islamic state. They spoke for the people in general and for their respective constituencies in particular. SAB equally mediated and legitimated the ruler's decisions regarding such constituencies.

This traditional equilibrium of governance was maintained by a multitude of mechanisms – i.e., clear hierarchies, occupational and residential aggregation, and autonomous resources (mostly from *Awkaf* or *Hobous* religious endowments). Social solidarities existed along primordial, occupational, religious, and ethnic lines. Central authorities collected taxes, administered justice through the *Shari'a*, maintained public order and defense, and occasionally patronized arts and sciences. Social services and direct economic functions were not expected obligations of the "state", but mostly left to local communities. In this sense, traditional Arab society not only knew the equivalent of civil formations but also survived through them. Individuals relied on these formations for their identity and much of their basic needs. They insulated them from direct dealing with political authority (Rizk 1993: 141–42). In the traditional equilibrium, the public space, in which civil formations interacted, coincided with the physical space in which they lived and worked.

The new Arab state and civil society: expansion and retreat

The birth of the new Arab states was midwived by Western colonial powers (Ibrahim, 1988: 45–78). They bore numerous deformities, ranging from the artificialities of their borders to the internal weakness of their institutions. Right from the start, they faced severe problems and challenges from within and from without. Initially, the new states neither tapped the reservoir of traditional wisdom of pre-modern civil formations, nor adequately allowed enough public space for new ones to sprout and flourish autonomously. As a result, for the first four decades of independence, the new Arab state found itself embattled on many internal and external fronts (Harik, in Luciani, 1996: 1–28).

The Arab World shared some, but not all, of the processes that had accompanied the emergence of the modern state and civil society in the West – e.g. the erosion of traditional equilibria, rapid population growth and urbanization. But the processes of capitalization and industrialization lagged far behind. Hence, the new socioeconomic formations which are the backbone of the modern state and civil society, have not grown progressively or evenly.

The Arab World witnessed a phenomenal socioeconomic growth in the four decades following the Second World War, the birth period of most independent Arab states. But the growth was erratic or sluggish, resulting, among other things, in a distorted stratification. The bearing of this distortion on the development of Arab civil society were detailed by this author elsewhere (Ibrahim, 1988, 1992, and 1995). The most pertinent for this paper was recently summarized by Jillian Schwedler (1995: 37–38), which is excerpted below:

Four variables – socioeconomic formations, the articulation of civil society, the state, and external factors – have been acting upon each other to produce a mini-wave of democratization in the Arab world. The interplay varies from one Arab country to another, which accounts for the degree of democratization empirically observed in each at present.

Civil society in the Arab world has revitalized itself in the last two decades due to internal, regional, and international factors. Internally, new socioeconomic formations have been growing steadily, as the autocratic and/or populist regimes have no longer been able to accommodate or completely suppress. Regionally, protracted armed conflicts have weakened the state, exposed its impotence in managing such conflicts, and drained its resources. Meanwhile, other regional developments have unwittingly empowered new and old constituencies within each Arab state. Internationally, the patron–client relationship between Arab regimes and the two superpowers has either ended or been greatly altered. The global wave of democratization has also had its marked demonstration effect on the expanding Arab middle class.

Sprouting civil society organizations in the Arab world have pressured for greater liberalization to atone for the state's failure in meeting socioeconomic needs by tending to itself and, later, for its reluctance to respond to their political quest for participation. The sluggish performance of the state *vis-à-vis* these demands has led many disenfranchised young people of the lower middle class to espouse Islamic militancy as a mode of protest. Table 2.1 shows the profile of Islamic militants in Egypt between the 1970s and 1980s. They are getting younger and being drawn more from small towns, slum areas, and small towns. This changing profile signifies the ever-widening alienation and social discontent. While we do not present, here, comparative data from Algeria, the sociological story there, is essentially the same (Willis, 1996: 5–26).

During the 1980s and early 1990s, the Arab world has witnessed a three-way race to maintain or seize power among autocratic regimes, Islamic activists, and civil society organizations. In some Arab countries, one variant of the race has been the squeezing of civil society out of the public arena by autocratic regimes on one hand and by Islamic activists on the other hand. In another variant, both the autocratic regimes and Islamic activists have attempted to win over or appropriate civil society organizations. The first variant is what the public opinion in the Arab world and in the West associates with the violent Islamic militants in Algeria, Egypt and Palestine.

Palestine: Islamists' fear of democracy

Earlier in this chapter we alluded to the Palestinian Hamas and Jihad, who have been carrying a lethal fight against Israel and to a lesser extent against their own Palestinian opponents – e.g., Yasser Arafat's PLO, and later, Palestinian National Authority (PNA), in an attempt to derail the peace process. Their argument is that Arafat is too weak to negotiate an honorable peace with the Jewish Zionist state, i.e., he will sell out or compromise Palestinian historical rights.[3] Palestinian Islamic militants had an opportunity, in January 1996, to put forth this argument to a test in the first Palestinian presidential and legislative elections. But they did not.

They warned the rest of their people to boycott the elections and stay away from the polling stations, but they failed. Some 85 per cent of the eligible voters went to the polls; Yassir Arafat received over 87 per cent of the vote. The whole democratic exercise in Palestine was a mark of success for one of the Arab world's strongest civil societies.

Table 2.1 Socioeconomic profile of Egypt's Islamic militants, 1970–90 (%)

Profile dimensions	1970s	1980	1980s
A. Age categories			
1. Less than 20 years	5	11	23
2. 20/25 years	28	31	48
3. 25/30 years	61	53	24
4. Over 30 years	6	5	5
B. Formal education			
1. Below secondary		5	9
2. Secondary	8	12	29
3. Junior college	11	24	42
4. College and post-grad	79	59	20
5. Elite majors	51	27	11
C. Community of residence			
1. Villages	0	7	18
2. Shanty towns	8	16	36
3. Towns	37	43	31
4. Large cities	55	34	15
Total	100	100	100

Source: Guenena (1996). *Changing Face of Egypt's Islamic Activism.* A research project in progress. Cairo: Ibn Khaldoun Center for Development Studies (ICDS).

The latter had sprouted during many decades of Jordanian authoritarian rule (before 1967), and nearly three decades of Israeli occupation (after 1967). The absence of a national state of their own meant that the Palestinians had to rely on their civil society organizations. Hundreds of new NGOs sprouted in the occupied territories, along with old professional syndicates and welfare associations (Abu-Amr, 1995).

Algeria: state fear of democracy

The Algerian case is somewhat different in that the Islamic activists, symbolized by the Front Islamique de Salut (FIS), had accepted the challenge of democratic politics and ran for both the municipal elections in the spring of 1990 and the Parliamentary elections at the end of 1991. Their performance in both was so impressive, especially in the latter, that the Algerian Army, which could not bring itself to accept the Islamists in power (i.e., forming a majority government), rushed to take over power in its own hands and forced the then

President Shazli Ben-Jadid to resign (the rest of the story is too well known to recount here; it is a case of an authoritarian regime unwilling to play by the rules of the democratic game).

The Algerian FIS felt, therefore, justified in resorting to violence since state violence was used to rob it off its electoral victory. The country was plunged in a massive armed internal strife. Some 6,000 Algerians are estimated to have been killed in the clashes between FIS and GIA (Groupes Islamic Armé) on one hand, and the Algerian Army and security forces on the other hand. Another 30,000 have perished between 1992 and 1995 (Willis, 1996: 5). The irony in the Algerian bloody tragedy is that most of the casualties were civilians – journalists, teachers, and women activists in Algerian budding civil society.

Four years after the bloodshed began, the Presidential election alluded to earlier was held in mid-November, 1995. Algeria's Islamic militants warned their fellow countrymen not to participate. But most Algerians were not intimidated. Al-Amin Zeroual, the incumbent president, was re-elected by a 61 per cent majority in an election judged by international observers as "fair and honest" (*Civil Society*, December 1995). This act of democratic politics enhanced the regime's "legitimacy," and morally isolated the more militant Algerian Islamists (who are now quite splintered). Algeria in 1996 is a far cry from that of 1992. Civil society advocates may still have serious misgivings on the Algerian state; but they are working closer with each other against forces of violence and anarchy than ever before.

Egypt: the sterile triangle

The Egyptian case is even more complex as far as the triangulated conflict is concerned. Egypt was one of the earliest Arab and Third world countries to resume its second democratization process in 1976, after a quarter of a century of non-democratic rule (since the 1952 Nasser's revolution). However, several counter forces have impeded the process. Among these are the inertia of the authoritarian legacy (1952–76), and the continued restrictive law of associations (namely Law 32 of 1964), which stunt the flourishing of Egyptian civil society. The former has ingrained into the executive branch of the government the practice of election rigging in favor of the ruling party (NDP). The latter has in effect meant that the political parties would have weak cadres and political infrastructure, both of which can only be best assured by a robust civil society.

In contrast with a host of socioeconomic problems bedeviling the Egyptian society at large, and the middle class in particular, Islamic activism has been one form of potent opposition force to the regime (Ibrahim, 1988B: 632–57). One wing of the Islamic movement in particular, the Muslim Brotherhood, has, since 1971, opted for peaceful means in pursuing its objectives, i.e., instituting an Islamic sociopolitical order, and has achieved results. Through teaching, preaching and grass-roots work in service provision, the Muslim Brotherhood has in fact created new organizations of civil society, and penetrated or taken over many already existing ones. In the 1980s for example, the Muslim Brothers managed to take over some of the major professional associations through democratic, peaceful means (Ibrahim, 1988B: 637–47) such as the Medical, Engineering and Lawyers associations.

The other more militant wing of the Islamic movement opted to use violence to destabilize the regime or overthrow it altogether. These militants have not only engaged the state but also symbols of civil society, i.e. killing policemen and officers, other governmental officials as well as intellectuals and journalists. The government attitude, in turn was mixed. As the confrontations with the militants escalated (e.g., 1992–93), the government sought the support of civil society organizations. As soon as it regained the initiative or the upper hand over the militants, the government often turned its back on secular organizations of civil society and harassed the more peaceful Muslim Brothers.

With the domestic situation well under government control in 1994 and 1995 (see Table 2.2), it fell back into the same authoritarian practice: rigging elections (ICER, 1995), arresting Muslim Brothers; and alienating many forces of civil society. The 1995 parliamentary elections were potentially the most promising: an unprecedented 4,000 candidates competed for 444 seats, two-thirds of whom were independent, including some 100 women and some 60 Copts. President Mubarak repeatedly assured "clean elections" (Al-Ahram, 30 November 1995). Most Egyptians took the elections quite seriously. However, the elections turned out to be the worst in modern Egyptian history, i.e., since the first such elections in 26 November 1996. Many candidates and their supporters, sensing or observing governmental unfairness, took the law into their own hands. Clashes broke out on a large scale and some seventy-one persons (including a candidate) were killed, with at least three times as many were reported seriously injured (ICER, 1995: 179–222).

Table 2.2 Scoreboard of political violence: Egypt, 1992–95

Year	Security			Militants			Civilians			Total killed	Total wounded	Total casualties	Arrested suspected
	Killed	Wounded	Total	Killed	Wounded	Total	Killed	Wounded	Total				
1992	23	38	61	38	83	122	32	107	139	94	228	322	3773
1993	120	181	301	111	252	363	101	341	442	332	774	1106	17785
1994	93	112	205	159	30	189	52	213	265	304	355	659	6812
1995	108	95	203	217	15	232	90	95	185	415	205	620	4119

Source: Guenena, Nemat, 1996. *Changing Face of Egypt's Islamic Activism*. A research project in progress. Cairo: Ibn Khaldoun Center.

It is not at all surprising, therefore, that after two years on the defensive, Islamic militants have begun to strike out in the heart of Cairo and Upper Egypt. In the first four months of 1996, killings have included two police Generals, scores of other policemen and officers, as well as some thirty Greek tourists (18 April). This was essentially the same pattern after the lopsided 1990 parliamentary elections, which were boycotted by all major opposition parties because of governmental refusal to allow a complete judiciary supervision of the elections.

The Islamic militants took advantage of the mass alienation resulting from the government's attitude and struck back at the state symbols, starting with the Speaker of Egypt's People's Assembly (November 1990), ushering in the longest period of intense confrontations within the state and civil society.

Conclusion

Another reading of the above account of Palestine, Algeria and Egypt is that the middle classes and other socio-economic formations have a legitimate quest for participation in the public affairs of their societies. If they are not allowed to do so peacefully, they force their way into the system, or against it – violently. Islam, in this case, provides a mere culturally legitimate idiom permitting this. Kings Hussain of Jordan and Hassan II of Morocco, as well as the ruling Prince of Kuwait, Sheikh Jabber, understood this fact and acted accordingly. Other populist authoritarian regimes have been either unable or unwilling to understand or to act accordingly. The price for this delayed understanding and subsequent reluctance to act has often been a heavy "blood-tax" paid by both Islamic dissidents and the security forces (both of whom, by the way, come from the same social background, i.e., lower middle class).

This second variant contains the greatest promise for civil society and for the democratization process. Importantly, it has provided ample bargaining power for civil society organizations when they deal with the state in attempts to gain concessions of a sociopolitical reformative nature. It also has had a moderating effect on several Islamic activist groups. In Jordan, Kuwait, Yemen, and Lebanon this promise has actually been unfolding. In each, Islamists have accepted the principle of political pluralism, participating alongside other secular forces in national elections. Islamists are currently represented in those countries' parliaments. In Lebanon, Yemen, and Jordan for instance, women have been elected for the first time and the Islamists did not march out in protest.

So long as religious-based parties and associations accept the principle of pluralism and observe a modicum of civility in behavior toward the different "Other," then they can expect to be integral parts of civil society (Ayoubi, 1995: 100–01; Goldberg, 1991: 3–4). In this respect, even the Islamists may evolve into something akin to the Christian Democrats in the West or the religious parties in Israel. There is nothing intrinsically Islamic that contradicts with the codes of civil society or democratic principles. This point was argued by Zubaida (1995) in his rebuttal of Gellner's theory of Muslim Society (Gellner, 1983, 1988 and 1992). Zubaida contends that social and political forms evolved by Muslims could be conducive to modernity and progress, for "Islam is a development ideology" (Zubaida 1995: 184).

The responses by Arab regimes to their civil societies indicate as many prospects for further democratization as against it. The modernizing monarchies, namely of Jordan and Morocco, have impressively engineered a smooth transition toward more democratic governance. Their example may tilt the balance toward greater democratic prospects in the entire region; prospects that promise to enhance the peaceful settlement of some of the region's protracted conflicts while also growing in strength from such settlements.

Notes

1 The author is grateful to Ms Nemat Guenena and her assistants in the project on, "Changing Face of Egypt's Islamic Activism," Ibn Khaldoun Center, Cairo, Egypt, for allowing me to use some of the project data for this paper.

2 This section of the paper is excerpted from an earlier article, "Civil Society and the Prospects of Democratization in the Arab World," (see Norton, A.R. ed., 1995, pp. 28–32).

3 Not surprisingly, this is the same argument used by Jewish extremists, including Yigal Amir, the confessed assassin of Israels Prime Minister Yitzhak Rabin.

Bibliography

Abu-Amr, Ziad (1995) *Civil Society in Palestine* (Arabic). (Cairo: Ibn Khaldoun Center.)

Ayoubi, Nazih (1995) (ed.) "Rethinking the Public/Private Dichotomy: Radical Islam and Civil Society in the Middle East," in *Contention*, Vol. 4, No. 3, Spring 1995: 79–105.

Binder, Leonard (1988) *Islamic Liberalism: A Critique of Development Ideology*. (Chicago and London: Chicago University Press.)

Boulding, Elise (ed.) (1994) *Building Peace in the Middle East: Challenges for States and Civil Society*. (Boulder and London: Lynne Rienner.) See an article by the editor, "Hope for the Twenty-First Century: NGOs and People's Networks in the Middle East", pp. 319–30.

Civil Society: Democratization in the Arab World. A Monthly Newsletter, Cairo: Ibn Khaldoun Center. Vol. 4, No. 12 (December).

Entelis, John (1995) "Civil Society and the Authoritarian Temptation in Algerian Politics: Islamist Democracy vs. the Centralized State", in *Civil Society in the Middle East*. Vol. 2, A.R. Norton, ed. (Leiden, the Netherlands: E. J. Brill Publishers.)

Gellner, Ernest (1983) *Muslim Society*. (Cambridge: Cambridge University Press.)

—— (1988) *Plough, Sword, and Book: The Structure of Human Society*. (London: Collins.)

—— (1992) *Postmodernism, Reason, and Religion*. (London: Routledge.)

Goldberg, Ellis (1991) "Smashing Idols and the State: The Protestant Ethics and Egyptian Sunni Radicalism," in *Comparative Studies in Society and History*, 33, pp. 3–4.

Halperin, Manfred (1962) *The Politics of Social Change in the Middle East and the Arab World*. (Princeton, New Jersey: Princeton University Press.)

Harik, Ilya (1990) "The Origins of the Arab System," in Luciani, G., ed. *The Arab State*. (Berkeley: University of California Press), pp. 1–28.

Huntington, Samuel (1991) *The Third Wave: Democratization in the Late Twentieth Century*, (Norman: Oklahoma University Press.)

Ibn Khaldoun (1980) (Arabic). *Al-Mukaddima*. (Baghdad: Al-Muthanna.)

Ibrahim, Saad Eddin. et al. 1988A. *Society and State in the Arab World*. (Arabic), Amman: The Arab Thought Forum.

—— (1988B) "Egypt's Islamic Activism in the 1980s," in *Third World Quarterly*, Vol. 10 (2), April: 632–57.

—— (ed.) (1992) *Civil Society and Democratization in the Arab World*. (Arabic), (Cairo: Ibn Khaldoun Center.)

—— (1995) "Civil Society and Prospects of Democratization in the Arab World" in Norton, A.R. ed. 1995. *Civil Society in the Middle East*. (Leiden, New York, Koln: E.J. Brill), pp. 27–54.

—— (1996) "The Changing Face of Egypt's Islamic Activism," in Aliboni, Roberto et al. (eds.) *The Security Challenges in the Mediterranean*. (London: Frank Cass), pp. 27–40.

ICER (1995) *Final Report of the Egyptian Independent Commission on the 1995 Parliamentary Elections* (Arabic). (Cairo: Ibn Khaldoun Center.)

Luciani, G. ed. (1990) *The Arab State*. (Berkeley: University of California Press.)

Maghraoui, Abdesalam (1992) "Problems of Transition to Democracy: Algeria's Short-lived Experiment with Electoral Politics," *Middle East Insight*, VIII, No. 6.

Norton, August Richard (ed.) (1995) *Civil Society in the Middle East*. (Leiden, New York, Koln: E.J. Brill.)

Putnam, Robert (1993) *Making Democracy Work: Civic Traditions in Modern Italy*. (Princeton, New Jersey: Princeton University Press.)

Rizk, Y.L. (1993) *Civil Egypt.* (Arabic). (Cairo: Tiba.)

Tester, Keith (1992) *Civil Society.* (London and New York: Routledge.)

Willis, Michael (1996) "The Islamist Movements of North Africa," in Aliboni, R. et al. *Security Challenges in the Mediterranean Region.* (London: Frank Cass), pp. 5–26.

Zubaida, Sami (1995) "Is There a Muslim Society? Ernest Gelnner's 'Sociology of Islam,'" in *Economy and Society.* Vol., 24, No. 2, May 1995, pp. 151–88.

Chapter 3

A pan-Islamic movement – unity or fragmentation?

Shahram Chubin

Islam is dynamic and growing rapidly, with approximately one billion adherents spread over three continents. In the fluid, shrinking world of few certainties and questionable values, people everywhere are finding more solace in religion. Perhaps nowhere is this more the case, than in the Islamic Middle East. Whether and to what extent a revival of interest in religion will be translated into political unity or co-operation among Moslems in the Middle East, is the issue discussed in this paper.

My basic thesis is, perhaps, rather commonplace and predictable: I do not foresee any perceptible movement toward Pan-Islam; the trend, rather, is towards continued fragmentation. Why should this be so when there are evident trends making for a "return to Islam" throughout the region? It is precisely *because* of the increasing importance of Islam in the politics of many/most Middle Eastern states, that I see further fragmentation. This resurgence is taking place in the context of existing structures, notably the nation-state. It is a response to, and operates in, local conditions; it is a manifestation of a local situation and takes its form and shape from the specific conditions pertaining to its surroundings – its state, society, political economy and historical legacy. The "revival of Islam" which has taken place in parallel throughout the region, illustrates the two faces of "unity."

On the one hand, the Islamic world is united, by sentiments and concerns; events in one Islamic country, the fate of Muslims everywhere, are of genuine interest to others. On the other, the Muslim world is diverse and the local conditions of Muslims varies, as does their response to it. The very fact that Islam is an increasingly important factor in the politics of Muslim states, as a source of legitimization, as a focus for opposition, as a currency of discourse, will – indeed already has – served to increase fragmentation among Islamic states. Given the primacy of the nation state, and national interest, Islam is and will continue to be appropriated to serve national or regime ends, resulting in what one observer has called "Islamo-nationalisms".[1]

In this short chapter I schematically address three questions:

1 What has been the impact of the 'revival' of Islam on unity *within* Muslim nations?
2 What impact has it had on unity (or co-operation) *among* states?
3 What are the prospects for Pan-Islam versus continued fragmentation?

Islam has become more salient in the politics of states as other ideologies (Arab Nationalism, Pan-Arabism, Arab Socialism, etc.) have been found wanting. Most regimes have failed to establish solid institutions, gain legitimacy, tackle the problems of modernization, or to be accountable to its people. Disoriented, alienated, and frustrated, many people have sought "Islam as a solution" to their problems, trusting, rather than inquiring, what the nature of the solution might be. Islamic movements have appeared to many the only credible alternative to the discredited and bankrupt governments in power. The similarity of the problems faced by Muslims in the contemporary world, however, may have concealed essential differences.

Islam provides little specific guidance to the myriad of problems faced by modern society. It is more specific about what it is opposed to. It has proven successful in mobilizing the populace rather than providing political answers. Necessarily, opinions will differ as to the best response. Islamic groups, while agreeing on the need to establish an Islamic society, have differed among themselves as to the details involved: primacy of Sharia, certainly, but what of rule by clerics? The role of women? The position of minorities? Or the question of whether to seize power from above or reform society from below. It is difficult to give operational meaning in specific contexts to general slogans.

From its inception, the Muslim Brotherhood split into factions over the position of evolution versus revolution, reform or seizure of power. The differences between the Muslim Brothers in Egypt and the Gama'a Islamiyya, in the tactics that each pursues – social welfare networks versus terrorism and assassination, are still pertinent today. Islamic organizations today cover the spectrum from those who seek to influence the state and are (allegedly) willing to work in a multiparty democracy (Egyptian, Jordanian Brothers, Ghannoushi's Renaissance Party [E-Nahda]), to those that reject anything but the seizure of power, like the various Islamic Jihads, the Islamic Liberation Organization, Salvation from Hell and other fringe groups. It is worth noting that these last are a distinct minority. Less reassuring, the mainstream Islamic organizations like the Muslim brothers, or the FIS and others, act more as associations than parties and appear to contain a wide diversity of persuasions. There is also the gap between declaration and action; between posturing before acquiring power and actions afterwards (Hassan Tourabi in Sudan exemplifies both tendencies), and a "division of labour" tendency in which contradictory statements are made to accommodate the widest spectrum of adherents.

For our purposes the question remains: does the injection of Islam, into the politics of these countries, act to unify them? As noted, there are similar conditions responsible for the discrediting of existing regimes: a failure to deliver a better life or a sense of participation and belonging, and a failure to instill a sense of indigenous values and social justice. Eroded legitimacy and discarded slogans litter the political stage, leaving it empty with the Islamist organizations ready to walk into the limelight, make an entrance and take a bow. Then what?

Whatever else they do, Islamist groupings entering the political arena do not generate unity. Not only do they differ among themselves on programmes, tactics, and often concrete ends, but also in personalities (consider Sudan Tourabi's and Sadeq al-Mahdi's differences or on another level, differences of the approach and competition between Hezbollah and Amal in Lebanon). They tend, also, to exacerbate existing, and create new, cleavages in societies: first they create problems for minorities or confessions (consider Sudan's war in the south, Islamic Iran, Algeria and the Berbers, and the Copts in Egypt); second, they polarize society between Islamists and Secularists, those seeking an Islamic state and religious control, and those merely seeking more Islamic content in society (Algeria); and third, in seeking to give content to their aspirations, differences emerge within their own ranks.

Islamic Iran serves as an illustration. Secularists have been banished. Within the revolution's ranks, major differences persist on first principles as well as on tactics or emphases such that some have talked of a "crisis of legitimacy" for that country, for example, there exist differences on whether or not there ought to be political parties.

The question of clerical rule is controversial and divisive. Sunni Muslims in Iran have felt neglected and marginalized and have expressed their discontent in recent years. The entire concept of *velayate faghih*, more or less invented by Ayatollah Khomeini, was rejected by the senior grand ayatollahs (though they were powerless to prevent it). The entire question of succession to the leadership among the Shi'i, the Marja'yya, remains open and controversial. Central to that controversy is whether the leader ought to be chosen on scholarly grounds or on the requisite skills as statesman. Another issue is whether Shi'i leadership should be Iranian, a "by right" or open to candidates (and nationalities) from other centres of learning, notably Najjaf in Iraq.[2] One scholar pertinently concluded: "The debate over the Marja'yya demonstrated the difficulties of uniting around a single vision of Islam, even for the one-tenth of all Muslims who were Shi'is."[3]

In Iran, practical questions facing the society have been endlessly postponed or fudged because Islam provides no definitive, or at least no uniformly accepted formulae, e.g. the question of private property versus social justice and private property versus the role of the state. In revolutionary Iran the legitimacy of the Constitution is based on the popular will, not solely on the Sharia. Although the Assembly of Experts designate the Rahbar (the Assembly itself is elected through universal suffrage), this has not ended the problem of whether the leadership is in the gift of the populace or whether the Rahbar or Spiritual Leader is to be popularly elected, like any politician, or appointed. Because of a continuing debate about such issues, Iran's senior clerics are having to confront them. The Head of the Iranian Judiciary[4] recently addressed the issue:

> When people elect someone to govern, be it as a deputy in the Majlis, as the president of the executive branch or into indirectly elected posts, their vote is only one source for determining the right of the ruler.
>
> However, there is another source; the divine revelation which limits the first one . . . In essence, the guardian, as appointed by God, has nothing to do with the issue of representation . . . Does the belief in the guardianship [of the jurisconsult] boil down to a vote or is it a belief in God's appointment? There is an essential difference between the two.

Islam does not provide an unequivocal answer to the problems of society so much as a framework or set of principles. These have to be translated into the context of quite a variety of conditions and societies that are different in terms of ethnic, tribal and sectarian configurations, historical experiences and economic endowment and potential. Even within any one society, Islamic groups are united at only the highest level of generality, viewing goals and means differently. In Iran, a society where Islam is in power, there are persistent, and arguably growing, differences on a host of issues relating to leadership and accountability, programmes, competence and costs. Islam provides a rallying point for opposition to government but such unity is temporary and deceptive. It furnishes little in the way of an alternative programme, cannot transcend the cleavages that exist in each society (and may exacerbate them), or provide a painless alternative to politics, which requires debate, compromise and trade-off. Even within societies, the appeal of Islamic solidarity is insufficient to overcome these differences.

Has the renewal of Islam in politics increased regional co-operation and unity among states? A quick survey would suggest the contrary. While the use of Islam in public rhetoric and posturing has increased, and the most unlikely states now use it for additional insurance or legitimization, divisions persist and may alas, have increased. Sudan and Iran seem to suggest that relations with neighbours and comity are not enhanced by the coming to power of an avowedly Islamic state.

The Iran–Iraq war was, in Iran's view, "imposed" on it. Iran then sought to "Islamize" the conflict: encapsulated in the slogan "the road to Jerusalem lies through Baghdad". Saddam Hussein sought to "Arabize" it, depicting Iraq as the dyke against Persian hordes that would otherwise spread their revolutionary Shi'ism throughout the Persian Gulf. The war divided the Arab world although most supported Iraq. Iran's alliance with Syria was dictated by national interest, as were those of Iraq with Egypt and Saudi Arabia. The upshot of the eight-year conflict was to deepen the chasm between Persian and Arab, Shi'i and Sunni. Iran had avoided war for nearly a century. Was it a coincidence that its first modern conflict was after an Islamic revolution which possibly helped spark it?

Admittedly, Saddam Hussein helped. By the time of the second Gulf war, Saddam, too, was using Islamic imagery and rhetoric to garner wider support and to demonize the opposition. Both Egypt and Saudi Arabia, in turn, were seeking religious authorities to authorize their decision to assist the United States while most Moslem Brotherhoods were opposing this decision. The secular PLO also sided with Iraq. Iran, torn between hostility toward Iraq and the US, adopted a formally neutral stance. Arab populations, notably in the Maghrab and elsewhere supported Saddam while their governments, impelled by *raison d'état*, did not.[5] The Muslim world came out of the war divided. In seeking to insure against a recurrence of the aggression, the Gulf states preferred to rely on their Western allies rather than their Muslim/Arab Damascus Declaration brothers. Islam did not unite Arab public opinion.

Palestine, which Sunnis and Shi'i depict as a Muslim (rather than merely Arab) issue, surely should have generated more unity. Certainly since 1987, the Islamic resistance groups have scored points in their effectiveness contrasted to their secular counterparts. However, Hamas (like Hezbollah in Lebanon) is not only a resistance force; it is also active in community welfare. The two "Islamic" groups are alike in other ways as well.

While both may take funds from foreign sources, they have their own agendas. Hezbollah accepted the Ta'if accords (brokered by Saudi Arabia) in 1989 thus renouncing the establishment of an Islamic state as its goal. It has since mutated into a political party with twelve deputies, the largest block in a fragmented parliament of 128 members. Its leadership has observed that its ties with Iran are largely based on religious affiliation and sentiment, rather than politics.[6]

Hamas, too, is not what it appears to some Westerners. It was originally an offshoot of the Muslim Brotherhood. Its appeal is limited to the occupied territories. While emphasizing its Islamic credentials, it is in essence a nationalist phenomenon. Its criticism of the PLO and Arafat are not that they are insufficiently Muslim but that they are ineffective.[7] Its rhetoric is inconsistent. Some leaders insist that it rejects secular nationalism: "Our strategy is to establish a pan-Islamic state everywhere, not just in Palestine."[8] At the same time Hamas offers to co-operate with the PLO and other leaders argues that the time is not right for an Islamic state and that democracy and the popular will can choose.[9] In reality, Hamas contains many tendencies, united by a concern like Hezbollah, to regain control of their land and using the ties, references and slogans best guaranteed to motivate and unite the people in this enterprise. Beyond that there is no agreed programme.

Where Palestine is concerned, states too have different goals. Iran uses the issue to polish its Islamic credentials and widen its appeal beyond its narrow, Shi'i constituency. Since 1992 it has done this by supporting Sunni rejectionist movements like Hamas. Hamas in turn has no difficulty in reconciling funds from this source with those flowing from Tehran's rival, Saudi Arabia, which supports the peace process. By taking a strong stand on Palestine, Iran curries favour for its steadfastness and equally important, undermines other states aspiring to leadership of the Muslim world. To deflect such criticisms the Saudi leadership attempts to legitimize their stance by having the head of their religious establishment, Shaykh ibn Baz, issue a ruling that peace with Israel would be legitimate "if it is useful to the Muslims and permits the Palestinians to establish their state, delivering them from harm and oppression." Iran's ensuing criticisms were matched by those of the majority of Muslim Brothers (in Egypt, Jordan, Pakistan, Kuwait and the Gulf) as well as all Palestine Islamist movements.[10] As Camp David showed earlier, and the various bilateral agreements continue to demonstrate, states are moved by their specific interests, not by some abstract, notional or general interest. Apart from the status of Jerusalem, to the extent that Islam makes Palestine a religious issue, it makes it less susceptible to compromise and harder to settle. In so doing, it does not in any case bring the Muslim states closer together.

Indicative of this is the status of Turkey. The only explicitly declared secular state, limiting the role of the Sharia, Turkey is also the only Muslim state with a functioning democracy. It also has a strong and growing Islamist party, the Refah (Welfare). Refah is currently the strongest party and supports multiparty democracy while advocating closer relations with other Muslim states. Turkey's immediate neighbours do not share this sense of fraternity. Other issues apart, they are critical of Turkey's co-operation with Israel. Iranian clerics castigate Arabs and Turks alike:

> There was a day when they [Arab leaders] used to say those things about Israel [i.e. "Death to Israel"] and today they sign agreements with them. Turkey today is permitting Israel to enter . . . Why do Islamic countries betray Islam and Muslims in this way? Why do these countries not value religion, people and people's beliefs?"[11]

While Iranian clerics find this a convenient stick with which to beat Turkey, it is doubtful that the Turks as nationalists are convinced that Iran or Turkey's other neighbours are in a position to dictate to them their interests. The use of Islam as a criterion for judgement of national interest in such issues devalues it. Certainly the "Islamic content" of Turkey today is higher than in recent memory, but this has not brought it to share the views of some other Muslim states on Palestine, or made Muslim unity any closer.

In the Gulf it is the same story. Iran and Saudi Arabia share a common antipathy toward Saddam's Iraq. Each purports to represent Islam in its political conduct, domestically and externally. Yet relations between these two states have never been as bad.[12] Iran, in its view, represents populist, revolutionary, "true" Islam, while Saudi Arabia represents establishment, "American" Islam. The Shi'i/Sunni[Wahhabi] factor looms large not simply as a matter of doctrine but as a matter of state security. Some 75 per cent of the Gulf's population is Shi'i (though not all are Iranian). Large numbers of Shi'i in Iraq, Bahrain and Kuwait have been the target of Iranian blandishments and such communities are now distrusted by the Arab states because of their (assumed) potential for subversion.

Iran and Saudi Arabia's different versions of Islam have been one of the principal new causes of division rather than amity. Iran's hostility to the West (especially the United States) is matched by Saudi Arabia's reliance on it. Iran insists on the right to protest US/Israeli policies during the annual pilgrimage, which Saudi Arabia rejects. Each year since the advent of the Islamic republic of Iran, the *hadj* has been the site for a crisis of varying proportions between these two differing conceptions of Islam. After the loss of life in Mecca in 1987, relations were cut off (April 1988). They were restored in 1991. There is still no agreement on the total number of Iranian pilgrims allowed or on how they should comport themselves once in the Kingdom (Saudi authorities seek to limit the number of Iranians for security reasons and Iran threatens to call into question the Saudis competence to administer the Holy Places).

Territorial issues in the Gulf have not been eased by the fact that two neighbours have Islam in common. Iran's dispute with the United Arab Emirates over one island is an inheritance from the Shah's regime. Surely this should be expendable in the cause of Muslim solidarity? If anything, the reverse is the case. It would appear that territorial issues are imbued with greater significance and are less susceptible to compromise when the parties to the dispute are convinced of their superior rectitude.

In Afghanistan, the Muslim world rallied to evict the aggressor. In so doing though, it revealed the primacy of politics and national interest as well as the persistence and dominance of traditional cleavages in that society. Iran and Saudi Arabia (and Pakistan) competed, as much as collaborated, in their support of different groups in the Afghan resistance. On a strategic level, Iran joined the United States and Saudi Arabia against Communist Soviets. On a tactical level, Iran supported Shi'i factions of the Hazara region, whose traditional links with Iran, competed with the groups supported by the Saudis. Once the Soviets withdrew, the war became less ideological and reverted more openly to the traditional "simple client networks of ethnic and tribal solidarity." Afghanistan reverted to a traditional society based on ethnic nationalism,[13] not Islamic unity. The continuing civil war today reflects this and Islam furnishes no practical basis for transcending these cleavages.

Iran and Sudan represent respectively Shi'i and Sunni states pursuing a radical form of Islam and claiming, like Saudi Arabia (which practices a more conservative variant of Islam), a leadership role in the Islamic world. Have these states co-operated and if so has this brought the prospect of Pan-Islam any nearer? In Afghanistan for instance, Sudan and Saudi Arabia have co-operated in support of the Gilbuddin Hikmatyar grouping which opposes Iran. In his pretensions to leadership, Hassan Tourabi has sought to differentiate Sudan from Iran, and in the process, belittling it as sectarian, isolated and therefore limited in appeal. He has denied the need for clerical rule. Other Sudanese have rejected the notion of the jurisconsult.[14] Iran in turn has snubbed Tourabi's leadership efforts. Tourabi has created an international forum for Muslims, the Peoples Arab and Islamic Conference (PAIC) which, despite a more radical orientation, is in direct rivalry with the Saudi-funded and based Organization of the Islamic Conference (OIC). PAIC met three times between 1991 and 1995. Tourabi used the conference and its communiqués for his own purposes but was unable to achieve anything resembling unity. Islamic groups remained too divided and their leaders were unable to agree on subordinating themselves to the command of one leader.[15]

Iran has created its own groupings like the Islamic propaganda bureau in Qom and has held conferences, often devoted to themes to overcome differences between Shi'i and Sunni, as well as participated in the Saudi-led OIC. Rather than set up a rival grouping, Iran has pursued its rivalry with the Saudis' "American" Islam by using the existing institutions to its ends. It has insisted on its right to host future meetings. It has been active in demanding that Muslim states react to the plight of the Bosnians, itself pledging upwards of US$100 million to that cause, and offering 10,000 peacekeepers towards a Muslim force (1993). Iran has also urged the lifting of the UN arms embargo and taken steps unilaterally to supply arms when this proved impossible. Iran called for an emergency meeting of Foreign Ministers of the OIC during the latest (April 1996) flare-up in Lebanon. Castigating Arab governments that remained silent, Iran's policies appear motivated by genuine concern for the plight of oppressed Muslims in Bosnia and Lebanon (whose fate did not appear to move the West to action). It may also be seen as a way of outbidding the Saudis and embarrassing them about their Western connections, thus demonstrating Iran's willingness to stand up for Muslims everywhere. Either or both interpretations are possible.

Similarly, the proliferation of international conferences held by Muslims can be seen as heralding a new consciousness and solidarity, which in time can be translated into greater unity of purpose and action. Alternatively, it is possible to see these conferences as the manifestation of continuing splits and rivalries within Islam, and specifically as the extension of states' rivalry by other means. Indeed, a case could be made that, with the single exception of the Muslim Brotherhood, which is independent, all the international Islamic institutions are primarily instruments of states' interests.[16]

Islam has a large and growing part in the lives of many people in the Middle East. Signs of its centrality and vibrancy are everywhere discernible in the region; in apparel and appearance, in public discourse and in individual and collective piety. As part of their identity and indigenous culture, Islam plays an especially necessary and comforting role for people in an era of upheaval and disorientation characteristic of modernization. It provides a sense of continuity and a set of immutable values which appear all the more essential and true when measured against the corruption and materialism of existing governments. By providing a feeling of community it fosters a sense of stability in a period of dislocation. Its solidity contrasts with the often senseless rationalizations evoked by local authorities to justify their shifting policies. Recognising the potency of this appeal, governments have increasingly adopted the rhetoric of Islam, especially in their public diplomacy. They have pursued policies of "re-Islamicization" to defend against this trend or to co-opt or confuse opponents and buttress their legitimacy.

Muslims are bound by a sense of oneness given vivid expression in the annual *hadj*. Shared culture, values, and common bonds of sentiment among the *umma* transcend colour, sect or nationality. They are testimony to the solidarity of diverse peoples who require no elaborate institutional apparatus or underpinning. These affective ties, manifest in concern for the plight of Muslims everywhere, are increasingly reflected by governments in their foreign policies. Middle Eastern Muslims care about their co-religionists not just in Kashmir and Palestine but also in Bosnia – not least because they feel that it may be the fact of their religion that has been at the root of their current predicament.

This popular sentiment is not declining and may in fact be growing. It can certainly be described as resilient, having survived despite competition from Pan-Arabism. A survey of eight Arab countries found that students, regardless of sex, ranked religion first in their hierarchy of group affiliation (followed by family and nation-state citizenship). Another survey (of ten Arab states) found that 60 per cent of respondents with at least secondary education emphatically agreed with the statement that "Islamic dimension is a major component of Pan-Arabism" while 36 per cent said they would "prefer Arab unity on an Islamic basis as an immediate goal".[17]

Muslim solidarity is not a recent phenomenon. In the early nationalist period, Islam served as a bond for many developing countries seeking independence from their colonial rulers:

> In the Muslim world, Pan-Islamic movements formed a link between countries as far apart as the Dutch East-Indies, French North Africa and India and facilitated co-operation between different nationalist groups.[18]

Islamic peoples' affective solidarity and its expression in their states' public pronouncements and occasional policies, is testimony to a sense of interdependence. This undoubtedly exists on one level. As Islamists take comfort in the success of Islamic movements in other countries, so too do their governments fear the spillover of Islamic agitation and its imitation by their own Islamists who might be emboldened by developments elsewhere. Observers refer to the "domino-effect" in lending credence to the notion that often, intangible ties and a similarity in societal make-up bind these states security together, i.e., President Mubarak looks at the Algerian leaders' handling of its Islamists and draws his own conclusions about an appropriate policy for Egypt).

Hence, common values and concerns (sometimes translated into co-operation in foreign policy), a sense of kinship and an inter-dependence politically (which cannot be captured by quantitative data) all undoubtedly exist in the Muslim Middle East. Some are clearly on the rise. What does this mean for Pan-Islam?

The Muslim states of the Middle East are very diverse politically in type of regime; republican and monarchical, Islamic and secular nationalist, pro- and anti-western. Their historical experience varies from old states (Iran, Egypt and Morocco) to new states (Jordan) to the stateless (the GCC); from continuously independent (Iran) to colonized (Algeria). In an age of increased communications, political mobilization and rising expectations, their political economies vary greatly (contrast the United Arab Amirates with a population of 1.4 m and per capita income of $15,500 (1992), with Egypt at 55 m people and per capita income of $650[19]). These disparities are growing, not shrinking. There is little intra-regional trade. Economic performance is of growing political salience in all these countries. National performance varies, and interests will continue to be framed and exercised in a national context.

Much of the co-ordination among states on Islamic issues has been more apparent than real. Competition among Iran and Saudi Arabia (Egypt) and Pakistan characterizes their policies in Central Asia. On Afghanistan, Bosnia and elsewhere, policies are similarly driven. Iran's emphasis on Bosnia is itself revelatory, throwing into sharp relief its politically selective indignation and inactivity over Chechniya (a far more flagrant act of commission by one of the erstwhile "great satans").

Greater interaction has not led to more co-ordination on Islamic issues or to greater comity among Muslim Middle Eastern states. No state pursues an "Islamic" foreign policy per se, and none seek Pan-Islam even as a declaratory goal (Iran's use of Islamic groupings against the West in the 1980s was in the service of its foreign policy). The elements of co-operation among Islamic groupings internationally are unrepresentative. Iran's cultivation of the Shi'i in the Lebanon (the Hezbollah, not Amal), is atypical. Even so, while sentimental and instrumental ties have overlapped, they are likely to be severed when the goals of the two parties diverge. Islam as the axis for unity, as a substitute for existing alliances or even as a basis for new ones, appears a very distant goal.

The phenomenon of the "Arab Afghans" veterans of the war against the USSR, testifies to the creation of a network forged in that war.[20] This free-floating group of radical Muslims is under no effective control. They scarcely support the notion of an Islamic international, let alone a force for Pan-Islam. Mobility, migration and a failure to assimilate into the Westernized cities, leaves a core of alienated and potentially desperate people susceptible to manipulation by governments or groups in acts of random terrorism. Such fringe elements are not the expression of, nor likely catalyst for, Islamic unity.

What precisely do we mean by Pan-Islam? A loose expression of it could take the form of greater "*co-operation*" among Islamic states on a wide range of issues. A second possibility is that it could mean a tight Islamic "*bloc or alliance*", effectively united in foreign policy. A third definition is the creation of a "*single state or entity*".

The last variant is clearly the most demanding. It raises important questions about the willingness to submerge sovereignty, to share wealth and the precise terms and conditions under which this would be possible. Islam furnishes no unequivocal or specific answer to such questions, which would themselves generate fresh animosities. Given the wide variation in the conditions and orientations of these societies, unification can be ruled out. A tight Islamic bloc is also unlikely. Just as political Islam has divided groups within states and imperilled regimes, divisions among these Islamic states have grown since the rise of Islam as a political factor in the politics of these states. Governments have been unable to give tangible expression to the greater sense of Islamic consciousness among Muslims by their failure to enhance co-operation with other Muslim *states*. If the Islamic world has "bloody borders", it is primarily because of conflicts among Muslims (rather than *jihad's* against non-Muslims). Greater co-operation among Muslim states, as a loose political bloc analogous to a subdivision of the non-aligned should, in theory, be attainable. If co-operation between and among some states on *Muslim* issues is meant, this is possible. Also likely is greater attention to the appearances of unity and more declaratory policies extolling solidarity. However, unity among Muslims, even on Muslim issues, will prove as elusive as ever.

States will continue to declare themselves in favour of Islamic unity but, at the same time, insist on their right to determine the basis and conditions and to define how to give it meaning. Moreover, modern man has multiple identities. Without denying the "rediscovery" of Islam and its continuing centrality in the Middle East, there are grounds for scepticism on whether it will continue to be the controlling or dominant identity in all circumstances. As state nationalism increases – reflected in the diversity of conditions characterizing Muslim states – the gap between the sense of fellowship with other Muslims and actual policies conducted by states will persist, and may even widen.

The prognosis, then, is for continued, and possibly accelerated, fragmentation rather than meaningful unity in the guise of Pan-Islam.

Notes

1 Olivier Roy, interview *Le Monde*, 6 March, 1996 and *L'Echec de L'Islam Populaire* (Paris: Saint Espirit/Seuil, 1992).

2 For a discussion of some of these issues see, Shaul Bakhash, "Iran: The Crisis of Legitimacy," in *Middle Eastern Lectures*, 1. (Tel Aviv: The Moshe Dayan Centre for Middle Eastern and African Studies, 1995) pp. 99–118.

3 Martin Kramer, "Rallying Around Islam" in Aya Ayalon, (ed.) *Middle East Contemporary Survey*, Vol. XVIII, 1993 (Boulder, Colo.: Westview, 1996), p. 129.

4 Ayatollah Mohammad Yazdi, Friday sermon, Tehran, Voice of the Islamic Republic of Iran, 19 April in BBC Summary of World Broadcasts, ME/2592 MED/25–26, 22 April 1996.

5 For a survey see James Piscatori, ed. *Islamic Fundamentalism and the Gulf Crisis*. (Chicago: American Academy of Arts and Sciences, 1991) [The Fundamentalism Project].

6 Shakyh Hassan Nasrollah, the Secretary General of Hezbollah, thus, unusually, made a distinction between religion and politics. Quoted in Martin Kramer, "The Global Village of Islam," in Ami Ayalon, ed. *Middle East Contemporary Survey*, Vol. XVI. (Boulder, Colo.: Westview, 1994), p. 205.

7 See Olivier Roy, *Le Monde*, 6 March, 1996, p. 2.

8 Dr. Mahmoud Zahar quoted by David Gardner, "From Guns to Soup Kitchens," *Financial Times*, 10 March 1995, p. 21.

9 See the comments by Shakh Sayyid Abu Musamih, excerpted in *Al Quds*, Jeruslaem, 28 April 1996, in BBC ME/2600 MED/19, 1 May 1996.

10 Kramer, "Rallying Around Islam,", pp. 136–37.

11 Ayatollah Ali Akbar Meshkini, the speaker of the Assembly of Experts, Sermon in Qom, 12 April on Vision of the Islamic Republic of Iran, Network 1, 13 April in BBC ME/2586 MED/21, 15 April 1996.

12 For amplification of this with examples and citations see Shahram Chubin and Charles Tripp, "Iran-Saudi Relations and Gulf Security," *Adelphi Paper* (forthcoming, 1996), London: IISS.

13 Roy, *L'Echec de l'Islam Populaire*, pp. 186–87.

14 The interview of Hassan Tourabi in *Al Sharq al Awsat*, London, 21 March in BBC ME/2571 MED/21, 27 March 1996 and interview with Dr Ghazi Salah al-Din Atabani, Secretary General of Sudan's National Congress, in *Al Sharq al Awsat*, 29 April in BBC ME/2600MED/26–28, 1 May, 1996.

15 See the articles by Mouna Naim, "La Conference Islamiste de Khartoum denonce le 'sionisme' et 'l'imperialisme' occidental", *Le Monde*, 1 April 1995 and "La Conference de Khartoum a revele les contradictions des Islamistes," 4 April 1995. For Tourabi's performance in the 1993 conference see Kramer, "Rallying around Islam," pp. 141–46.

16 c.f. Roy, *L'Echec de l'Islam Populaire*, p. 139.

17 Quoted in Emmanuel Sivan, *Radical Islam: Muslim Theology and Modern Politics*. (New Haven: Yale, 1985), pp. 170–71.

18 H.A.R. Gibb, *Modern Trends in Islam*. (Chicago: 1947), pp. 27–28, 32, 36, 119–20. Quoted in Geoffrey Barraclough, *An Introduction to*

Contemporary History. (Harmondsworth, Middlesex: Penguin, 1967), p. 159.

19 Quoted in Brian Beedham, "Not again for Heavens sake," *A Survey of Islam, The Economist* 6 August, 1994, p.4.

20 Kramer writes: "What Qom and Najaf had been to Shi'i radicalism in the 1980s, Peshawar may have been for Sunni radicalism in the 1990s,", in "The Global village of Islam," p. 198.

Chapter 4

Discourses on human rights and pluralistic democracy

Ahmad S. Moussalli

Both Western scholars and politicians, and their Muslims counterparts are exploring the possibility of combining Islam with democracy and pluralism. The difficulty in exploring this possibility is that Islam is posited as essentially opposed to democracy and pluralism and, consequently, any scheme for human rights. However, Muslims have been convening conferences on the need to democratize and liberalize politics, society and thought. One might be surprised to know that the majority of fundamentalist theoreticians are now engaged in developing Islamic doctrines on democracy, pluralism and human rights.

The fall of the Soviet Union focused attention on the legitimacy of democracy, the necessity of human rights and the appropriateness of pluralism to Islamic countries. Now, both secular and fundamentalist thinkers attribute the miserable conditions of economic, social and political life to the real and theoretical absence of democracy and pluralism in the Arab world. A new political process that stresses the importance of political democratization and liberalization is on the rise and is entertained in the media, conferences, universities and other institutions.[1]

Notwithstanding this, the West at large has mostly focused on Islamic fundamentalist dangers, disregarding the unending oppression of the peoples of the area as well as the dialogues and debates that have been going on among diverse political trends about political theories and rights of people. Sensational titles in magazines and newspapers such as "Will democracy Survive in Egypt?" or "The Arab World: Where Troubles for the US Never End" or "The Clash of Civilizations" have further frightened and pushed the West away from the East. While quite a few Western academics concerned with the Middle East deal with the real concerns of the peoples, the West in general prefers to look at these concerns as being negligible insofar as they are indigenously developed.[2]

However, current events in the Muslim world, particularly in Egypt, Algeria, Tunisia, Lebanon and Sudan, as well as in the West, have produced political and academic discussions on the compatibility of Muslim fundamentalist discourses, especially the doctrines of an Islamic state, with democracy, human rights and pluralism as well as the "the emerging world order." This chapter therefore aims at highlighting some of the important debates that have been going on in modern Islamic fundamentalist discourses about democracy, pluralism and human rights.

While a majority of Western media and scholars along with a majority of their Middle Eastern counterparts treat fundamentalism as exclusivist by its nature, and while a few widely publicized fundamentalist groups are truly exclusivist and adhere to the notion of change through radical programs and uncompromising revolutions, most mainstream fundamentalist groups are pluralistic, democratic and inclusivist indeed. Furthermore, exclusion is not limited to Islamic fundamentalist groups and includes the champions of the new and the old world orders. It is only with Islamic fundamentalism that the doctrine of exclusion is transformed into a part of a new theology of metaphysical perceptions and abstract doctrines of belief. Islamic fundamentalism is, however, an umbrella term for a wide range of activist discourses that tends to move from a high level of moderate pluralism, and thus inclusive democracy, to extreme radicalism, intolerant Unitarianism, and thus exclusive majority rule.

In this chapter, I argue that the inclusive democratic and exclusive authoritarian policies of most Middle Eastern states, along with whatever international powers existing at the time reinforce, and in fact create, bring about a dual nature of fundamentalist political behaviour. Fundamentalists in general believe that their governments do not serve the ideological, political or economic interests of their peoples but those of the dominant world powers. Imperialism, colonialism, exploitation, materialism – all these are charges brought against the West. Liberalization, whether economic, political or cultural, as well as social justice, political freedom and democracy are major demands of both radical and moderate fundamentalist groups. Modern national states have been considered by fundamentalists as the link between what is unacceptable and inhumane in both Western and Eastern civilizations, namely Western materialism and Eastern despotism.

This chapter, then, answers briefly the conditions that make a fundamentalist or Islamist theoretician and moves to develop a discourse on, or reject ideological and political doctrines of, pluralistic democracy. It also shows the comparable inclusive or exclusive policies of Middle Eastern states as well as the international order in reinforcing one doctrine or another. Part one of this chapter briefly contextualizes general academic and political discussions centering on inclusion and exclusion, pluralism and democracy in the West – particularly in the USA, – and the Arab world – particularly in Egypt. Part two deals with the theoretical foundations and development of inclusion, exclusion, pluralism and democracy. Then the inclusivist and pluralist discourse of the Muslim Brotherhood in Egypt, is explicated.

The world, pluralism and democracy

Both fundamentalist theoreticians and activists, in addition to Muslim and Western academic and press circles, have discussed the issues of exclusion, liberalism and democracy under the rubric name of "liberal democracy".[3] In *New Perspective Quarterly*, the whole issue of pluralism and tolerance is discussed under sensational titles that make the reader shy away form reading the articles on Islam; thus for instance, who wants to travel "From Beirut to Sarajevo . . . " to fight "Against Cultural Terrorism" or to witness "Galilee Meets Allah."[4] However, the editor of the journa, Atbar S. Ahmad, puts his concern in the following way:

> Islam, alone in a plural world, remains monotheistic in faith as well as, in many places, in practice. In today's globalized cultural space, Islam will inevitably be faced with a host of challenges that will pit *"the word"* not only against the mere *language of Western literature*, like Salman Rushdie's novel, but also against non-dogmatic, for example, of Hindu beliefs, not to speak of *the radically free style tolerance of Europe and America* that so riles the mullahs. Faced with these challenges, will Islam turn toward pluralism and the West back toward faith? [Emphasis added][5]

"No", says Ahmad

> "for in the main, only one civilization, Islam, will stand firm in its path. Only the Muslim world, poised both to implode and

explode, offers a global perspective with a potential alternative role on the world stage. Islam, therefore, appears to be set on a collision course with the West."

For while the West is based on secular materialism, the scientific reason of modernity, and the absence of moral philosophy, Islam, argues Ahmad, is based on faith, patience, pace and equilibrium. He puts up a picture of non-conciliation between Islam and the West: when he states it is "a straight-out fight between two approaches to the world, two opposed philosophies."[6]

Ahmad's exclusionary idea is not just Islamic, but has its equivalence among prominent Western intellectuals such as Samuel Huntington, who argues that the future will witness the clash of civilizations. In his *The Islamic-Confucian Connection* as well as his more celebrated article "The Clash of Civilizations", he considers the conflicts that took place since the peace of Westphalia in 1648, up until the Cold War, as "Western civil wars." Now the "cultural division of Europe among Western Christianity, Orthodox Christianity and Islam has re-emerged. Today the most significant dividing line in Europe may be that identified by the British scholar William Wallace – the eastern boundary of Western Christianity in the year 1500."[7]

Disregarding any diversity in his interpretation of Islam, as well as disregarding its historical schools and modern different tendencies in religion and politics, Huntington, who served at the White House under President Carter in security and planning for the National Security Council and witnessed both the collapse of the Iranian regime under the Shah and the establishment of an Islamic state, proclaims that Islam is a militant religion in which there is no distinction between what is religious and what is secular. The idea of "render unto Caesar's what is Caesar's, render unto God what is God's" is totally antithetical to Islam. This theocratic proclivity makes it extraordinarily difficult for Islamic societies to accommodate non-Muslims. It makes it very difficult for Muslims to easily fit into societies where the majority is non-Muslim.[8]

In addition to showing very little knowledge of Islamic history and philosophy, he disregards the compatibiliy of Islam with other religions, which, though they look at politics and religion as Islam does, nevertheless are included in the Western, and not the Eastern culture.

In general, the Islamic world has been included, but only negatively, that is by military force employed originally by the colonial powers in the past and now by dominant world economic powers that use the threat of economic sanctions and sophisticated weaponry. Why then do not these powers try to include the Islamic world economically, morally and philosophically, especially if one of the features that distinguish the West is its inclusive pluralism? Or is the non-Islamicity of Muslims the condition for being included?

Judith Miller advocates a non-democratic exclusivist attitude towards the Muslim world since Islam is incompatible with the values of pluralism, democracy and human rights. This means that Western policy-makers should not support democratic elections since they might bring about radical Islamic fundamentalists to power. She exhorts the American administration and others to reject any sort of conciliation with, or inclusion of, radical political Islam:

> Western governments should be concerned about these move-ments, and, more importantly, should oppose them. For despite their rhetorical commitment to democracy and pluralism, virtually all militant fundamentalists oppose both. They are, and are likely to remain, anti-Western, anti-American and *anti-Israeli*. [Emphasis added]

She further rejects indirectly Edward Djerejian's distinction between good and bad fundamentalists. Accepting Martin Kramer's idea of the non-compatibility of militant Islamic groups with democracy insofar as they cannot be by nature "democratic, pluralistic, egalitarian or pro-Western" and Bernard Lewis' argument that liberal democracy and Islam are not bedfellows, Miller concludes along with Lewis that autocracy is the norm and postulates:

> Islamic militancy presents the West with a paradox. While liberals speak of the need for diversity with equality, *funda-mentalists* see this as a sign of *weakness*. Liberalism tends not to teach its proponents to fight effectively. What is needed, rather, is almost a contradiction in terms: a liberal militancy, or a militant liberalism that is unapologetic and unabashed. [Emphasis added][9]

Fortunately, not all American thinkers, policy-makers and diplomats think similarly. Edward Djerejian, former assistant Secretary of State and US Ambassador to Israel, puts the matter differently. He states that "the US government, however, does not view Islam as the next 'ism' confronting the West or threatening world peace. That is an overly simplistic response to a complex reality." He goes on to say:

The Cold War is not being replaced with a new competition between Islam and the West. It is evident that the Crusades have been over for a long time. Indeed, the ecumenical movement is the contemporary trend. Americans recognize Islam as one of the world's great faiths. It is practised on every continent. It counts among its adherents millions of citizens of the U.S. As Westerners we acknowledge Islam as a historic civilizing force among the many that have influenced and enriched our culture. The legacy of the Muslim culture which reached the Iberian Peninsula in the 8th century, is a rich one in the sciences, arts, and culture and in tolerance of Judaism and Christianity. Islam acknowledges the major figures of Judeo-Christian heritage: Abraham, Moses, and Christ.[10]

The US differs, according to Djerejian, with those groups that are insensitive to political pluralism, "who substitute religious and political confrontation with engagement with the rest of the world and who do not accept the peaceful resolution of the Arab-Israeli conflict and pursue their goals through repression."[11]

Some scholars on the Middle East and the Islamic world go beyond this general statement. Augustus R. Norton in his "Inclusion Can Deflate Islamic Populism" argues that democracy and Islam are not incompatible since it is the demand of the people of the area to be included in the political system. While skeptics deny the usefulness of democracy for the people, because the regimes are inefficient and suffer from legitimacy claims and the fundamentalist political movements are anti-Western, anti-Israeli and anti-democratic, Norton pins down the claims against the skeptics by saying that "to argue that popular political players are irremediably intransigent and therefore unmoved by tenets in the real world is at best naive and, at worst, racist."

So long as the fundamentalist movements are given no voice in politics, there can be no surprise that their rhetoric will be shrill and their stance uncompromising. In contrast, well-designed strategies of political inclusion hold great promise for facilitating essential political change.[12]

Norton concludes his article with a sober reflection:

The rulers have no intention of stepping aside, but they must be encouraged to widen the political stage and to open avenues for real participation in politics. For the West, and especially the United States, the issues are complex and vexing, but the basic choice is simple: construct policies that emphasize and widen the cultural barriers that divide the Middle East from the West, or pursue policies that surmount the barriers.[13]

William Zartman argues that the two currents of political Islam and democracy are not necessarily incompatible. The Qur'an might be interpreted to support different political behaviours. A synthesis might emerge between Islam and democracy where constitutional checks can be employed. He suggests five measures to democratize and make sure that democracy will triumph including, "to practice the forms of democracy whenever scheduled, let the most popular win, and let them learn democracy on the job."[14] Again, in "Democratization and Islam," John Esposito and James Piscatori argue that the process of liberalization and democratization in the Muslim world requires, as happened in the West, a process of reinterpretation of the divine texts. While Islam lends itself to different interpretations, some important fundamentalist thinkers have already started the process of accommodating Islam with democracy and liberalism[15] – itself an inclusionary process.

While the above discussion indicates the existence and emergence of a fundamentalist tendency to include some principles of Western civilization such as liberalism, democratization, as well as a free economic system – which in themselves represent features of an inclusionary mentality of political Islam – it also shows that there is a major and influential tendency among Western politicians and scholars alike to reject the Islamization of democracy and liberalism and, on the other hand, to insist on the 'Westernization' of raw materials and markets under the pretext of national security or the clash of civilizations. The same tendency that stands opposed to the ascendancy of fundamentalism through democracy, because of the assumed fundamentalist authoritarian nature, supports authoritarian regimes for the sake of maintaining a non-existent democracy – an indication of an exclusionary attitude and intolerance directed at Islam under the guise of fundamentalism and a sign of a twisted logical structure.

It seems so far that most international and regional actors have a vested interest in pushing away fundamentalists from any legitimate role in internal, regional or international affairs. The argument against the fundamentalists outlined above has its counterpart in the

Middle East. In "Liberalization and Democracy in the Arab World," Gudrun Kramer shows why Arab regimes are not yet ready for democracy. However, democracy is now one of the common themes among political movements and differs in nature and extent from one movement to another, ranging from the adoption of a liberal pluralistic Western model to "an Islamic model of participation qua consultation." However, the two movements "converge on the issues of human rights and political participation." And although some regimes have adopted certain classic mechanisms to liberalize and democratize such as the *infitah* (open-door policy) and the multi-party system in Egypt, the limitations are nevertheless classic as well. As Kramer says, "Formal constraints also limit the scope of legitimate political expression and action, usually a party law restricting the bases of party formation and a national charter defining the common and inviolable intellectual and political ground." Thus, for instance, the moderate Muslim Brethren in Egypt are not legally allowed to form a party, but nevertheless are allowed to participate informally by the regime. Kramer goes on to say that "even an Islamic political order may be able to incorporate Western notions of political participation and human rights." Furthermore, "liberalization," she adds,

> will inevitably give more room for maneuver to political actors critical of the West and openly hostile towards Israel. While the public demands a greater distance from the West and a tough stand *vis-à-vis* Israel, the socio-economic crisis intensifies dependence on Western governments and international agencies.[16]

The regimes are no longer capable of relying on repression. What supports this argument is that the Egyptian government has decided to intellectually counterattack the current tide of political Islam by having the General Egyptian Institute for Books publish a series of books under the general title "Confrontation" or *al-Muwajaha*. The series focuses on republishing books of scholars and intellectuals that have in common the goal of refuting the doctrines of radical groups by using the moderate religious and political thought prevalent in Egypt in the late nineteenth and early twentieth centuries such as that of Jamal al-Din al-'Afghani, Muhammad 'Abduh, 'Ali 'Abd al-Raziq, Taha Hussein, 'Abbas al-'Aqqad and others. The specific objectives are outlined in the following points:

- to circulate the opinions of the pioneers of "enlightenment" (*al-tanwir*)

- to positively focus on the moderate views of Islam
- to refute the radical ideas in relation to Islam's view of government and state and the application of the *shari'a*.[17]

However, this "intellectual" governmental activity is only a belated and subsidiary supplement to the doctrine of confronting the fundamentalists, i.e., the "security confrontation" doctrine that has been officially adopted by the Arab and Foreign Affairs Committee of *Majlis al-Shura*, the highest judiciary council in Egypt. The solution, to be developed through the consolidation of security apparatuses, comes first and foremost, followed, secondly, by a religious confrontation that should be launched by the religious officialdom, and, thirdly and most surprisingly, the legislature which must produce a state-of-the-art law against terrorism. But no substantial mention is made of rectifying the severe economic conditions of poverty, loosening political manipulations through liberalization and demo-cratization or respecting human rights. When the report of the Committee suggests paying greater attention to the social develop-ment of poor rural and isolated areas with special focus on the youth, the objective is to control the hotbed of fundamentalists. The committee also proposes a further supplement to the law, already passed by the Egyptian Parliament, restricting the multiplicity of professional unions and the communication of local parties with foreign parties without an official permission.[18]

The "religious confrontation," led by Shaykh al-Azhar, seems to give credit to the measures taken by the government and also to provide indirect legitimacy to political Islam in addition to weakening the modernist and secular tendencies in Egypt. In a long interview, Shaykh Jad al-Haq categorically rejects the separation of the state from Islam. He argues that Islam is made up of both *din wa dunya* or, loosely translated, a religion and a way of life – basically identical to fundamentalist interpretation. The Prophet Muhammad did not differentiate between the political and the religious. Again, the ruler should be appointed by *shura* (consultation) that may be conducted through different methods and technologies. After accepting the ideology of the Muslim Brotherhood as being Islamic, he only objects to the use of violence by some radical groups. However, the Azhar considers the Egyptian government's policies as Islamic and defends its actions against criticisms by radical and moderate fundamentalist groups.

Shaykh Jad al-Haq convened in 1994 the First General Conference for those shaykhs in charge of the official mosques for the specific objective of counterbalancing the activities of the radical groups. The conference was attended by 1,500 shaykhs who participated in its sessions along with, very interestingly, the Ministers of Foreign Affairs, Interior, Religious Endowments, Information, Housing and Agriculture. The Interior Minister emphasized the organic link between the security confrontation and the religious one through the collaboration between the mosques and the media to curb terrorism. The Information Minister affirmed that the media had plans to uncover terrorism, but that depended on the 'true' explanation of Islam. While refusing to lift media censorship and to license private TV stations, he affirmed the role of the Azhar as an "information authority" to confront "foreign fundamentalist" dangers. For an information revolution has been going on, especially now since fundamentalists outside Egypt correspond with those in Egypt by fax.[19]

The Azhar plays – with the tacit approval of the government – the role of a modern "Court of Inquisition." Naguib Mahfouz, a Nobel Prize winner, has announced his readiness to rescind his book, *Awlad Haritna* (The Children of our Neighborhood) if the Azhar convinces him that it contains any blasphemous remark against Islam. Although Ri'aft al-Sa'id, a secular leftist intellectual, condemns the fundamentalists for banning the book – in fact it was banned thirty-four years ago by the Azhar under Nasir's presidency – he asks the government to face "the terrorists" not only by security measures but also by curbing their media. As one of the "enlightened thinkers" – a term used by Sa'id to describe himself and his intellectual colleagues – he calls for the suppression of whatever media freedom is left to Islamic thinkers because radicalism starts initially as an idea;[20] forgetting that inclusion, tolerance, pluralism and democracy started as ideas as well.

Again, the case of associate professor at Cairo University, Nasr Hamid 'Abu Zayd, who was not promoted to the rank of Professor but was brought to a "secular" – and not a fundamentalist – court in Egypt because of his heterodox views, shows how the government fights not only intellectual "terrors" of fundamentalism but also those of modernism. Because he has been convicted of the charge brought against him, he is considered an apostate that should be separated from his wife. The charge focused around his books which showed "animosity to the texts of the Qur'an and the *sunna*," "non-belief" and "recanting Islam."[21]

While the government uses its legal apparatus to exclude major modernist figures and trends, it uses it as well to exclude moderate fundamentalism. An Egyptian newspaper, *al-Shaʿb*, published an article on capital punishment stating that the Egyptian government had moved from civil and penal law to emergency laws. This allowed the employment of the "iron fist" policy for the containment of fundamentalists. During Mubarak's presidency, from 1981 until 1993, the policy had resulted in the political execution of forty-eight individuals, almost double the number (twenty-seven) of those who were executed for similar political reasons during a whole century in Egypt, extending from 1882 until 1981, including the presidencies of both Nasir and Sadat. In 1995, the number has risen to 58.[22]

A member of the Parliament stated in a parliamentary session that Egypt lives on the margin of democracy, for democracy means the peaceful and voluntary hand-over of power, a feature that does not exist today. The President of *Majlis al-Shaʿb*, Hilmi, responded very unconvincingly that President Mubarak does not say that Egyptians have reached democracy but rather that democracy should be deepened – as if Mubarak's remark makes the absence of democracy any easier. Hilmi goes on to say that democracy is represented by the existence of thirteen political parties that are free and secure to associate and publish. The State Minister for Parliamentary Affairs adds that it is unbelievable that the parliamentarians should talk about the succession of power because it is elections and not governmental decrees that bring about political authority – and of course the minister insulted by this remark the intelligence of the parliamentarians. The party that receives the highest votes becomes the ruling party, he adds. It is well known, however, that the truth is otherwise: the ruling party gets the highest votes. This notwithstanding, both officials forget, for instance, that one of the most popular movements, the Muslim Brotherhood, is excluded from official representation in government, parliament or party systems, though at times tolerated when running under the labels of other parties.[23]

Again, when the Egyptian government wanted to conduct a national dialogue, it basically launched it with itself. Thus, twenty-six of the forty individuals who were "appointed" by President Mubarak as a preparatory committee to set the agenda for the conference on political dialogue were from the ruling party, *al-Hizb al-watani*. Worse than this, 237 out of the 279 conferees were from the ruling party; major political blocs were excluded. Though one might understand the exclusion of the radical groups that rejected "inclusionary" policies, one cannot really understand the government's exclusionary policies towards the Muslim Brotherhood, which has exhibited both intellectually and politically inclusionary tendencies through its acceptance of pluralism and democracy as well as the legitimacy of the regime. So who is dialoguing with whom? The Muslim Brotherhood sought to be included in the much publicized national dialogue during 1994. While the government refused the official representation of the Muslim Brotherhood in that dialogue, nevertheless the Brotherhood tried to be included through its unofficial representatives in professional unions such as lawyers, medical doctors, and engineers. The Muslim Brotherhood's view on the dialogue can be represented by what Ahmad Sayf al-Islam Hasan al-Banna, the general secretary of the Lawyers' Union and the son of Hasan al-Banna, said about the organization's willingness to participate in the political dialogue if the government were to include them. Later on, the government rejected their participation and pressured political parties to disassociate themselves from the Brotherhood. The Brotherhood's view was that though excluded as a political party, it could still be included as a representative of civil society. Instead, the government resorted to the repression of the Brotherhood in sweeping security measures that resulted in the death of a pro-Ikhwan lawyer while under arrest, an act that produced a strike by the Lawyers' Union and direct confrontation with security forces in 1994.[24]

Ma'mun al-Hudaybi, the spokesman for the Egyptian Muslim Brotherhood, said in an interview, that the exclusion of the Muslim Brotherhood from the dialogue, along with independent fundamentalist thinkers such as Muhammad al-Ghazali, was an example of the exclusion of those who did not adopt or conform to governmental views. While the government does permit some thinkers to attack religion, it does not allow any open criticism to be directed at slanderers. He characterized the cause for violence in Egypt as being the result of governmental policies; for when the individual "finds no door open, he will destroy the wall [to get out of prison]. The one who thinks of destroying the wall is the prisoner. But those who find the door open but try to break the wall are very rare." In other words, being excluded from peaceful participation in political and public affairs, some groups were bound to be turned into radicals, because of the "closed-door policy." He expressed the Brethren's opinion that they were oppressed because of governmental prohibition on holding public meetings, an act considered by the government as a mutiny against the state.[25]

Following the same line of thinking, Muhammad Salim al-'Awwa, a moderate fundamentalist thinker, lawyer and university professor, puts the problem of exclusion in the following way: the government imposed novel kinds of laws such as the law against terrorism, emergency laws, the law of Shame (*al-'ayb*), and the Values Court (for the violation of social norms) and so on in order to cripple the society from moving ahead. Again, political parties in the Arab world have been of two sorts: governmental parties that were made by and serve the government but did not represent the majority, even when claiming to do so; and other kinds of parties, which may be unlicensed, such as Egypt's Muslim Brotherhood, or recognized by the government such as the Muslim Brotherhood in Jordan. These others had to be encouraged and dealt with. However, this was not the case.

But would the establishment of a recognized fundamentalist party in Egypt resolve the problem of radicalism? 'Adil al-Jawjari argues that the concept of *shura* provides the Islamic movement with the method that allows for peaceful coexistence between the government and an Islamic party. The alternative to radicalism must be a party where fundamentalists can vent out their grievances and participate in the political life of Egypt. The containment policy that is being imposed from above by the government has proved its futility, and the only meaningful and peaceful solution is the establishment of a legal fundamentalist party where the rights of minorities and political pluralism and other essential issues became part of the party's constitution.[26]

Though the Muslim Brotherhood published a manifesto in Islamabad – and not in Cairo because the Brotherhood's name cannot be undersigned publicly in Egypt – condemning violence and terrorism, which has been its proclaimed public policy any way, it seems now that neither dialogue nor political life are developing or leading to any substantive positive changes. The Muslim Brotherhood is being excluded from normal public life further and further, and the horizon for including them in the public political life with the current regime seems untenable. It might be appropriate here to cite a few articles of the manifesto:

- The Brotherhood affirms its stand that it condemns any sort or source of violence and affirms the need to put an end to it. The Qur'an calls on people to use wisdom in the propagation of God's path.
- The Brotherhood condemns the use of revenge and vendetta and calls for the implementation of the shari'a which prohibits

bloodshed and secures honour in addition to the sacred things that people cherish.

- The Brotherhood adds its voice to all those who want to see a real end to violence. The Brotherhood declares that any solution that does not include real popular participation is defective.
- Restrictions on popular participation in politics should be lifted, and freedom of party formation and expression to all political forces should be permitted in order to achieve comprehensive social, economic and political reforms.
- All popular and political forces are required to stand united together in order to extricate themselves from the vicious circle of violence and seek real reforms that fulfil the hopes of the people.[27]

Fundamentalist discourses on pluralism and democracy

Inclusivist discourses

The ideological and political discourse of the Muslim Brotherhood's founder and first supreme guide in Egypt, Hasan al-Banna, lays down the bases of inclusionary views of the theological and political doctrine of God's governance or *hakimiyya*. While it has been used at times, both historically and presently, to exclude whatever is considered un-Islamic and, for some, even non-Islamic, al-Banna transforms it into a source of both legitimacy and compromise – a feature that has been followed more or less by the majority of moderate fundamentalist political movements. Taking into account the circumstances of Egyptian society during the first half of this century, and given the relative freedom that the Egyptians had therein, the question of a forceful seizure of power was not on the agenda of the Brotherhood. Though interested in the Islamization of government, state and society, al-Banna aimed essentially to be included in the then existing political order and competed as well with other political parties.

His call for inclusion was not a fabricated slogan but was indeed applied. Al-Banna himself ran twice for elections along with his party, the Brotherhood. Some of the Brotherhood's founding members were simultaneously members of other political parties; and the same applies to contemporary Brethren. The peaceful involvement of the Muslim Brotherhood in Egypt's political life is well documented. It was involved in the struggle of the Azhar during the 1920s and 1930s and sided as well with the King against the government. During that period, al-

Banna co-operated at times with Isma'il Sidqi, the on and off prime minister, and engaged himself in teaching and lecturing. The Brotherhood built its headquarters from voluntary donations, after which it built a mosque and schools for boys and girls. In 1946, the government provided financial aid, free books and stationery to the Brotherhood schools, with the Ministry of Education having paid all their educational and administrative expenses. Al-Banna also established as well holding companies for schools, and this became a success since most of the Brotherhood's membership was composed of middle-class professionals and businessmen. Only a year after the establishment of the Brotherhood in Cairo, it had fifty branches all over Egypt. Worried about the spread of Christian missionary schools in Egypt, the Brotherhood called on King Faruq to subject this activity to governmental supervision. But after a meeting with a father in one of the churches, al-Banna wrote on the necessity that men of religion should unite against atheism. During the same year, the Brotherhood decided to set up a press and publish a weekly, *al-Ikhwan al-Muslimun*.[28]

Al-Banna also included boy scouts in his organization. The scouts' pledge was essentially of a moral tone, centred around faith, virtue, work, and the family and not political or revolutionary. Al-Banna never denied that the Brotherhood was a movement that sought the revival of religion and had its own political and educational and economic aspirations. This did not mean, however, that the Brotherhood would isolate itself from society. In 1936, the Brotherhood participated, for instance, in the coronation of King Faruq. During 1948, the membership of its scouts exceeded 40,000 and had, by then, spread all over Egypt, working to eliminate illiteracy and cholera and malaria epidemics. By 1948, the Brotherhood had set up 500 branches for social services and established medical clinics and hospitals for the treatment of approximately 51,000 patients. Al-Banna also set up a women's organization in the 1940s whose membership in 1948 reached 5,000 – a high number according to the standards of the time. It played a central role during what is referred to as *al-mihna al-'ula* (first ordeal) in 1948–50, when it catered to the families of the thousands of Brethren who were jailed. The active membership of the Brotherhood was around half a million, and the supporters, another half, had by the time of its dissolution, one thousand branches in Egypt.[29]

In politics, the Brotherhood did not originally resort to violence but rather played the game as long as it was allowed to do so, then playing with violence when it became the name of the game. It was not only the Brotherhood that established secret apparatuses, but these apparatuses were a common denominator with other parties as well as the state which, used political assassination to resolve many problems. This violence manifested itself against the Brethren in the assassination of al-Banna, the jailing of thousands of them, and the dissolution of the organization and liquidation of its assets.

Before then, the Brotherhood had played by the rules. More importantly, the Brotherhood had always accepted the legitimacy of the existing regime, and al-Banna described King Faruq as the legitimate ruler. Al-Banna developed his organization into a political party with a specific political agenda in order to compete with other parties that were, in his opinion, corrupt. In 1942, al-Banna along with other Brethren ran for elections, but the then prime minister persuaded him to withdraw. In exchange, he was supposed to receive more freedom for his organization and a promise from the government to shut down liquor stores and prohibit prostitution. Later that year, Premier al-Nahhas closed down all of the Brotherhood branches except its headquarters. Again in 1945, al-Banna and five other Brothers ran for elections but lost. The Brotherhood competed with the *Wafd*, the communists, and others. Al-Banna became a powerful player e.g., he was called to the Palace in 1946 for consultation regarding the appointment of a new prime minister. At the time, the Brotherhood was especially encouraged in order to stand against the communists and the *Wafd*.[30] Again, his condemnation of Egyptian parties was based not on their neglect of religion, but on their widespread corruption and collaboration with the British. His denunciation of Egyptian pre-Nasir parliamentary experience was therefore a rejection of Egyptian party life, and not of the principle of constitutional life or multi-party politics. He expressed his belief that Egypt's constitutional life had failed and was in need of reorientation.[31]

During the seventies, the Brethren were used by Sadat in order to boost the legitimacy of his government, though they were still not allowed to form their own political party. They broke with him over his trip to Jerusalem, in 1977, and the Camp David agreement and its aftermath.[32] Their protest led to the imprisonment of hundreds of Brethren in addition to members of other radical groups (discussed below). But the Muslim Brethren have not officially sanctioned or used violence to achieve any political or religious objective. Since 1984, the Brotherhood in Egypt and similar movements like those of al-Nahdah in Tunisia and the Islamic Salvation Front in Algeria, have sought to be included in the political process and have been involved in setting up civil institutions. In Jordan, the Brotherhood has functioned since the 1950s as a political party, so some of its members became well placed in the government and the parliament.

Inclusion and recognition in the state's hierarchy, as well as the Brotherhood's attempts to become part of state administration, made the *hakimiyya* basically a doctrinal organizing principle of government and a symbol of political Islam allowing inclusionary and pluralistic interpretative policies. Al-Banna's emphasis on the proper grounding of political ideology does not exclude individual and collective social and political reformulations of the Islamic political doctrines, and stand in accordance with modern society's needs, aspirations, and beliefs.[33]

While Islam contains basic legal substance, for al-Banna, its denotations and connotations can not be restricted to or derived from past historical conditions only. More importantly, he attempts to show that Islamic thought must account for, and deal with, modernity as a worldview, not only as a law. Both the law and the worldview must deal with the real world not in abstract terms, but in practical terms. They must therefore take into account and include other interpretations, political ideologies and philosophies. Because Islam is both a religion and a society and a mosque and a state, it must deal effectively with religion and the world. This means the inclusion of diverse substantive and methodological pluralistic interpretations, while maintaining the basic doctrines of religion.[34]

Because the *shari'a* is viewed as a social norm, al-Banna frees its application from past specific methods and links its good practice to the maintenance of freedom and popular authority over the government and the delineation of the authorities of the executive, the legislative and the judiciary. Western constitutional forms of government do not contradict Islam if grounded in both the constitutionality of Islamic law and objectivity. Constitutional rule is transformed by al-Banna into *shura*, or consultation, by a subtle reinterpretation in light of modernity and in a spirit not contradictory to the Qur'an. *Shura*, as the basic principle of government and the exercise of power by society, becomes inclusionary by definition and employed to empower the people to set the course of its political action and ideology. For al-Banna, because the ultimate source of the legitimacy of *shura* is the people, its representation cannot be restricted to one party which usually represents only a fraction of the people. A continuous ratification by the community is required because governance is a contract between the ruled and the ruler.[35] Al-

Banna's theoretical acceptance of political pluralistic, democratic and inclusionary interpretations implants the future seeds for its further acceptance by the Muslim Brotherhood – notwithstanding its link to *tawhid* and its political connotation, unity. This acceptance does not exclude even the existence of many states. Party politics and political systems do not preclude for al-Banna the acceptance of substantial differences in ideologies, policies and programs. An Islamic state, however, does exclude parties that contradict the oneness of God.[36] The illegitimacy of atheistic parties is not in al-Banna's view an infringement on the freedom of expression and association. This is so insofar as the majority and the minority accept religion as the truth. Such parties would be outside the consensus of society and therefore, threaten its unity. If Islam is chosen as the basis of government and society, then its opposition becomes a matter of anarchy and opposition to society, not freedom. Still, this is not a negation of pluralism in Islam since foreign ideas and systems of thought can be incorporated.[37] The state must reflect the social agreement and provide a framework for peacefully resolving conflicts.[38]

Furthermore, al-Banna's system includes different social and religious groups such as Christians and Jews, who along with Muslims, are united by interest, human good, and the belief in God and the holy books. Where religion is acknowledged as an essential component of the state, political conflicts ought not to be turned into religious wars and must be resolved by dialogue. In al-Banna's view, individuals enjoy civil as well religious, political, social, and economic equal rights and duties. The principle of individual involvement, to enjoin the good and forbid evil, is the origin of pluralism, and thus leads to the formation of political parties and social organizations or, simply, the democratization of social and political processes.[39]

Another important thinker, Taqiy al-Din al-Nabahani, the founder of *Hizb al-Tahrir* in Jordan and Palestine, follows in al-Banna's footsteps. While accepting into his *Al-Takatul al-Hizbi* multi-party politics a contemporary synonym to the duty of "enjoining the good and forbidding the evil," he laments the loss of political movements for many opportunities. This is due to the lack of proper awareness of the role of parties in communal renaissance. For al-Nabahani, a good party life must be based on a set of principles that commits the community to act. Only in this manner can a real party rise, represent the people, and push forward major positive developments. Without popular support, civil actors cannot work properly.[40]

Al-Nabahani imagines a gradual process of development that

centres around a three-fold program: first, propagating the party's platform to acquaint people with its principles; second, social interactions to sharpen the awareness of the people on essential issues; and third, the quest for power in order to rule in the peoples' name. The party must always play the role of a watchdog and must not dissolve itself into state apparatuses. Its independence from the government is essential for its credibility. While the government's role is executive and must represent the people, the party's role is ideological. In this sense, the party must always watch over the government. The government should not isolate itself from the society, but rather it must be responsive to it. Even when represented in government, the party must stay as a social force that supervises state actions. Put differently, for al-Nabahani, the civil institutions of a society are above the government, which must ultimately yield to public demands and interests. Nevertheless, this situation must not be in contradiction to any Islamic principle.[41]

Al-Nabahani views the institutions of the community at large as the legal source of authority; the government therefore must respect the wishes of the community and enact its will. The people are free to give or withdraw authority, especially since a consultative council or *majlis al-shura* must decide the outcome of elections, and not appointment. Al-Nabahani downplays the importance of executive power and highlights the pivotal functions of elected bodies. They are simply there to represent the people and protect of their "natural rights," including the right to form parties.[42]

But as a matter of fact, *Hizb al-Tahrir* has not been able or enabled, since the fifties, either in the East or West Banks, to act according to its program and play its imagined role. In 1976, the Jordanian government banned the party because its actions were perceived as threatening to the stability of the monarchy, especially because of its emphasis on the necessity of elections for the legitimacy of government. As a result of persecution, al-Nabahani went to Damascus and then to Beirut. His party did not get a license because the Jordanian government viewed the party as aiming at the ending the monarchy.[43]

Another fundamentalist thinker previously linked to *Hizb al-Tahrir*, Munir Shafiq, argues that the relationship between governments and their societies face major obstacles, foremost among which is the lack of social justice, human dignity and *shura*. These issues transcend the Western ideas of human rights, and the sovereignty of law and democracy, and form the base for a proper relationship between the ruler and the ruled. He does not accept any justification for the conditions that beset the Muslim life, such as the absence of political freedom in the interest of the ruling elite and the existence of widespread economic injustice that ruins the people. Thus, any modern resurgence must address these issues by spreading social justice, uplifting human dignity, maintaining man's basic rights and the sovereignty of law and extending the meaning of *shura* and popular political participation through the development of representative institutions.[44]

Similarly, Sa'id Hawwa, the Syrian Muslim Brotherhood's leader and thinker, argues that in an Islamic state, all citizens are equal and protected from despotism and arbitrariness. The distinction between one individual and another should not center around race or belief. As to the exercise of power, it should be based on *shura* and the freedom of association – specifically political parties, unions, minority associations and civil institutions. The one-party system is unworkable in an Islamic state. Furthermore, he adds that the rule of law must reign supreme, and that people should have access to courts to redress their grievances. More importantly, the state must guarantee the freedom of expression, whether on a personal or the public level.[45]

In particular, Hawwa shows sensitivity to the importance of arguing for equal rights for Syrian minorities with the majority. While ultimate authority should be within the confines of Islamic teachings, and while individuals from minorities can be members of cabinets or parliaments, political representation (for him) must be proportionate. However, the administration of the minorities' internal affairs, such as the building of educational institutions and maintaining, religious courts are the domain of minorities themselves and must not be subjected to others.[46]

Other thinkers, like Muhammad S. al-'Awwa, a distinguished Egyptian member of the Brotherhood, go beyond these general statements and directly address the standing issues of democracy and rights. Starting from al-Banna's discourse, al-'Awwa elaborates further on the absolute necessity of both pluralism and democracy. Islam, to al-'Awwa, is falsely accused of being opposed to pluralistic societies. For him, a society is civil when institutions aimed at effecting political life, are free to function and to develop without interference from the state; the existence of particular forms of association is in itself not a guarantee of the existence of a civil society. Because the institutions of society change from one time to another, al-'Awwa does not specify the kinds of institutions that make a Muslim society civil or pluralistic. He links this to the function of institutions: in the West – unions, clubs, and parties function as such; in the Muslim world – mosques, churches, religious endowments, teaching circles, professions, craft organizations and the neighbourhood function similarly. However, all these institutions are important in themselves as instruments of representation. Muslims ought to develop what is conducive to a pluralistic life; their institutions do not have to be imitations of Western institutions in order to be civil.[47]

That despotism was the general practice of the historical Arab-Islamic state is accepted by al-'Awwa as a general description, but this does not mean that Islam, by its very nature, is opposed to pluralism and democracy. Again, he uses historical examples – like the first state in Islam founded by the Prophet – to show that despotism, though tolerated by the general populace, as a political concept, had not enjoyed any credibility. The historical state is not the sole representative of legitimacy and therefore its model must not be imposed on the people. For al-'Awwa, the first step to major changes is the reorganization of society in a way that allows civil institutions to develop freely, without any state control. Current conditions hinder the development of pluralistic societies where real civil institutions serve the interests of groups. Islamic states have created their institutions in order to preclude rather than include, the real representative institutions, and consequently, force them to go underground. Thus, al-'Awwa calls for the revitalization of civil society as a means toward freeing society from the grip of the state and its unrepresentative institutions.[48]

Pluralism, for al-'Awwa, is the tolerance of diversity, political, economic, religious, linguistic and otherwise. This diversity is a natural human tendency and an inalienable right, especially when considering that even the Qur'an allows differences in identity and belonging.[49] Al-'Awwa identifies six doctrines that make Islam tolerant and pluralistic: Islam does not specify a particular social and political system but provides general ideas; the ruler must be elected by the people through *shura*; if Islam permits religious freedom then all other kinds of freedom are legitimate; all people are equal in terms of both rights and duties; God's command to enjoin the good, and to forbid the evil, is a communal religious duty; and, finally, rulers are accountable to their communities.[50] However, the legitimacy of pluralism hinges for al-'Awwa on two conditions: first, it should not contradict the basics of Islam and, secondly, it should be made in the interest of the people. In all other respects, individuals and groups may associate with each other in any manner deemed necessary, especially as political parties, which act as a safety valve against limiting freedom and a means for limitting despotism.[51]

Hasan al-Turabi, a constitutional lawyer, and a leading and powerful fundamentalist thinker of contemporary Islamic movements, who was also the former general guide of the Muslim Brotherhood and head of *al-Jabha al-Qawmiyya al-Islamiyya*, and who now heads the Islamic and Nationalist Congress in the Sudan and is the supposed broker of power behind al-Bashir's regime, theoretically breaks many taboos relating to the state. He drops many conditions about the nature of institutions that may be allowed by an Islamic constitution and in an Islamic state. More than al-Banna, he imposes more "Islamic" limitations on the power of the state and equates them with those of liberalism and Marxism. The state must not go beyond putting down general rules enabling a society to organize its affairs. Accepting the idea that the *shari'a* limits the powers of the state and frees society, he grounds it in the religious command "to enjoin the good and to forbid the evil."[52]

This command for al-Turabi becomes parallel to pluralism because its performance is obviously of a communal nature. Because the powers to exercise *shura* and *ijma'* are the prerogatives of the people, this requires primarily the existence of many opinions or *ijtihadat* so that the community could choose one of these opinions. This task is more urgent today since Muslims are beset by dire conditions and unprecedented challenges. The situation demands a new understanding of religion, one that transcends mere addition and subtraction of particulars here and there, to the need for providing new organizing principles appropriate for modernity.[53]

Al-Turabi theoretically justifies such a need by arguing that both the specifics and organizing principles of religion are historically developed and, consequently, subject to change according to the community's needs. The historical nature of these principles means that no normative standing is attributed to them, and that their replacement, with new specifics and principles, is not a violation of religion. While this replacement, does involve the Qur'an and the *sunna*, the new *'usul* or organizing principles must be the outcome of a new *ijma'*, itself the consequence of a popular choice in the form of contemporary *shura*.[54]

For al-Turabi, if *shura* and democracy are viewed outside their historical conditions, then they might be used synonymously to indicate the same idea. While it is true that ultimate sovereignty in

Islam belongs to God, practical and political sovereignty is the people's. *Shura*, for al-Turabi, does not therefore take away communal freedom to select an appropriate course of action and set of rules or even representative bodies. Al-Turabi, however, cautions against breaking any fundamental Qur'anic principle.[55]

Thus, ultimate political authority is reserved by al-Turabi to the community, which draws a contract with an individual to lead the community and organize its affairs. This is done only through delegation of power for the well-being of the community. Al-Turabi accepts any state order that is bound by, and is based on, contractual mutuality, where the ruler never transgresses against the individual and communal freedom provided for by the Qur'an. For the main Qur'anic discourse is directed primarily not to the state, but to people, and more specifically, to the individual. A proper Islamic constitution must guarantee all sorts of individual and communal freedoms. Proper representative bodies must then be set up to counter the possibility of despotic rule by the government.[56]

Al-Turabi looks at the freedom to organize political institutions as the absolute necessity for an Islamic revival. A reformation that lacks a true philosophic and political reformulation of Islam will not propel the sought-after cultural revolution. Again, mere religiosity along traditional lines would not be conducive to revolution. The revolution, however, must be based on religion, and supersede temporary interests and be underpinned by a social consensus. For consensus must be the source of communal interests; and the social setting is the environment that enables the individual to enjoy freedom.[57]

While the *shar'ia* is pivotal to al-Turabi, it does not exclude non-Islamic doctrines and institutions, especially if an Islamic society needs them. Al-Turabi exhorts Muslims to keep in mind the objectives of religion. Justice, for instance, does not mean one thing throughout history. Individual interpretations of it must change from one time to another. But there must be no opposition to a Qur'anic text.[58] As an example, al-Turabi explains the "true" Islamic position on woman by arguing that Islam has provided her with complete independence. The Qur'anic discourse speaks to her without a male mediator; her belief, like the male's, could not be meaningful without her sincere conviction. If the Qur'an postulates her complete religious freedom, it stands to reason that she is free, as well, in other aspects of her life; in society and state, in economics and politics. She has equal rights in public life. While al-Turabi acknowledges the historical lower status and mishandling of women, he attributes all of this to misinterpretations of Qur'anic verses on women, in addition to the social environment. However, these two problems must be solved both theoretically, by a re-reading of the text, and practically, by giving women their proper place in society.[59]

This kind of change cannot take place through minor adjustments but requires, for al-Turabi, comprehensive adjustments of the mental and social restructuring of the community's experiences within a modern program. This program does not lead only to redressing the peculiar grievances of woman, but also all other contemporary problems. The starting point, however, relates to freeing individuals and groups to pursue what they consider as new means toward development, for the historical experience of the Muslims is now defunct and can not be of major use. They are experiencing what is not developed by them; simply, it is a new world that requires new thinking.[60]

This leads al-Turabi to call for the founding of a modern jurisprudence that is not based on past history, but rather on modern experience. A modern Islamic jurisprudence that is based on freedom of research without the past restrictions imposed by the jurists and the states interference, seems to al-Turabi, capable of providing Muslims with the necessary instruments for the onset of revival. In this process, the state's role should be a formal one, there to conduct *shura* and therefore, to codify communal opinions. It must refrain from forcing its views on the public and allow a new breed of *'ulama'* to develop and restructure Islamic thinking. Official institutions have no right to seize the communal rights of legislating and thinking.[61]

Al-Turabi postulates further on comprehensive freedom as a fundamental right and formative principle in the lives of people. More specifically, he denies the government any right to impose recognized legal views on the community. For such an action, he believes, constitutes an uncalled for interference by the state in the life of the community and is a breach of *shura*. Again, "enjoining the good and forbidding the evil is the source of the legitimacy of the superiority of the people over the state".[62]

For al-Turabi this does not mean that the views of the community should be one and the same. On the contrary, he believes that the existence of only one public opinion may constitute an obstacle to progress and inflexibility about change. While public opinion expressed in the media or other means does not constitute an alternative to *shura*, policy-makers should take that into consideration. Again, while the *ijma'* of the jurists on a specific issue is not binding on the community, the state should not dismiss it altogether. However, the community should neither be subjected to jurists nor to outspoken public opinions. A democratic interpretation of Islam requires, in al-Turabi's view, the existence of proper and free relationships between the state, individuals, the community and its institutions.[63]

According to al-Turabi, without freedom, man loses his and the religion's true essence and becomes indistinguishable from animals. The original freedom includes the freedom of expression and of belief. For God convinces and does not force man to believe. Again, if this is the case with religion, so should it be with political matters. Tyranny from an Islamic point of view cannot be justified, and the *shari'a* calls on people to voice their views. Today's powerful rulers, however, force the people to follow certain ideologies and political programs. This act contributes thus, to the marginalization of the people and their aspirations. Al-Turabi stands, in theory then, against the identification of the individual with the state. For the individual's original freedom cannot be given to institutions and to society; and any institutionalization of freedom means its destruction. The only normative individual commitment for al-Turabi is to Islam, which frees the individual from having to accept or yield to imposed principles or ideologies.[64]

Al-Turabi cites a few examples of the powers that Islam has given to both the individual and the society. For instance, the Muslim society has the power to legislate and impose taxation. While the West, according to al-Turabi, has surrendered such powers to the state, Muslim societies have reserved them for themselves, so there is no delegation as such. Strictly speaking, they are social, not political powers. Their surrender to the state negates the possibility of independent social development and subjects the society to the state. As for a modern manifestation of the social power to legislate, al-Turabi offers the example of political parties or legal schools. Whereby a political party expresses the individuals' co-operation and unity and multi-party politics may be the expression of *shura* in a structured system.[65]

Such freedom must not in any way lead to breaking the Muslim society into combatant ideological groups such as happened in the history of Islam, where the community has been split into Shi'ism and Sunnism. While pluralism is recommended by al-Turabi, its good practice revolves around its consensual context, based on a set of principles that is agreed upon. This context will also guarantee the indivisibility of society and provide an equilibrium between freedom and unity.[66] The Mosque is cited by al-Turabi as a typical place where the true spirit of Islamic democracy is exemplified. It is a place formed by ideological bonds and unified by social and political orientations. More importantly, it is a prototype for communal unity, solidarity, unified organization, communication and leadership. Even the democratic aspect of religion is so obvious that prayer leadership is subject to the selection of the people and cannot be legitimately forced on the community. Also, in spite of colour, origin, wealth and languages, equality permeates all aspects of the religious life. This, for al-Turabi, is a good example that ought to be copied into politics.[67]

The leader of *Al-Nahda* in Tunisia, Rashid al-Ghannushi, is not far from the views of al-Turabi. Al-Ghannushi argues for the need of maintaining public and private freedom as well as human rights. Both freedom and rights are called for by Qur'anic teachings and ratified by international covenants. They are not contradictory to Islam and are involved primarily with the freedom of expression and association, political participation and independence and call for the condemnation of violence and the suppression of free opinions. Such principles for al-Ghannushi should become the center of peaceful co-existence and dialogue between society and the state.[68]

Al-Ghannushi ties the political legitimacy of any political system, however, to its provision of freedom for political parties and different elements of society. They should be allowed to peacefully compete over social, political and ideological agendas. This system must permit free elections to representative councils and institutions so that they contribute to the state administration. If this takes place, the Islamic movement lends its popular support to and provides legitimacy for, this system. For the popular authority, grounded in God's governance, is the highest authority in society. Accepting the freedom of association leads him even to accept parties, like the communists, that do not believe in God.[69] For al-Ghannushi, the reason behind this is that some groups may find it in their best interest to form parties and other institutions that might be irreligious. This does not constitute a breach of religion since pluralism, and more specifically, the freedom of belief, is sanctioned by religion. For al-Ghannushi, the sacred text represents a source for, a reference to, and an absorption of the truth, while its human interpretations are grounded in diverse discourses representing different understandings of changing social, economic, political and intellectual complexities. Unfettered possibilities of systematic development should be encouraged.[70]

Openness and dialogue become a must for al-Ghannushi, not only within the Muslim world but within the whole world – the West in particular. He argues that the world is transformed by scientific advancements into a small village that cannot any longer tolerate war. This poses the necessity of serious rethinking about the future of this village, since it has a common fate. This is true if the inhabitants of this village are serious enough to have a common fate, which presupposes, among other things, putting an end to the abstract geographic and cultural division of the world into East and West and to the idea that, while one of them is rational and democratic, the other is perverse and despotic. Such a division is nothing but a recipe for war. Any objective analysis testifies to the fact that the negative and positive values and the forces of goodness exist here and there. The forces of goodness are invited to dialogue and to search for avenues for intercourse.[71]

The views of the fundamentalist trend that legitimize pluralistic civil society and democracy can be aptly derived from the circulated text of a pact (*mithaq*) that has been published and distributed by Muhammad al-Hashim al-Hamidi to other fundamentalists. He states that the success of the Islamic movement, after it grasps government, hinges on its establishment of a just and democratic system in the Arab world. Remains the community from within the tyranny that it has been plunged into necessitates that the Islamic movement instigates limits, and a program for justice, *shura* and human rights. The program must include the rights to life, equality, justice, a fair trial, political participation and the rights of minorities and women, as well as the right to freedom of thought, belief, expression and religion. His suggestions of the basic principles governing the formation of parties and associations include the freedom to form parties and political associations for all citizens – without exception. Moreover, parties do not need to be licensed by the government. Internal party life must also be governed by democracy. The call for dictatorship and totalitarian rule is prohibited under any circumstance, slogan or political propaganda. Furthermore, secular citizens, including the communists, have the right to form parties, to propagate their ideology and to compete for power. Finally, racial, tribal, sectarian or foreign affiliations cannot be the base of any legitimate political propaganda.[72]

Along the same lines, the political program of *Jabhat al-Inqadh* in Algeria calls for adherence to *shura* in order to avoid tyranny and also to eradicate all forms of monopoly, whether political, social or economic. Political pluralism, elections, and other democratic means of political and social life are called for as the means for the salvation of the community.[73]

Exclusivist discourses

More than anything else, the discourse of Sayyid Qutb develops the underpinnings of radical Islamic fundamentalism, the second major trend. The study of Qutb's thought – the founder of radicalism in the Arab world – shows us why many Islamic groups moved to religious radicalism. Qutb, himself, was both its foremost theoretician and victim. He was transformed under 'Abd Al-Nasir's regime from a very liberal writer in Egypt to the most radical fundamentalist thinker in the Arab world. His imprisonment and ferocious torture have been transformed into a radical political theology of violence and isolation. It may be that this was his psychological compensation for the violence and repression inflicted by the regime.

Sayyid Qutb, born into a middle-class family, received, his Bachelor of Arts degree, from Dar al-'Ulum, like al-Banna. Afterwards, he worked as a teacher and columnist and was associated with Taha Hussein, 'Abbas Mahmud al-'Aqqad, and other liberal thinkers. From the time he started to write for journals and magazines, he showed a general tendency to be in opposition to the government and critical of Egypt's state of affairs. He was very daring in his opposition to the government and in his "radical liberalism", manifested in the writing of free-love stories and calls for nudity. His first writings revealed existential, skeptic and liberal bents. Because of his opposition to government, he was first exiled to the countryside, and the two journals of which he was editor-in-chief, *al-'Alam al-'Arabi* and *al-Fikr al-Jadid*, were closed down. Then, in 1948, he was sent by the Ministry of Education to the United States of America to continue his studies on education.[74]

Qubt's first book adopting fundamentalism as a way of life along with a political agenda, *Al-"Adala al-'Ijtima'yya fi al-Islam* (Social Justice in Islam), appeared during his stay in the United States, and was far removed from radicalism, lying closer to al-Banna's discourse. His stay in the United States, from 1948–51, made him review his previous attitude and adoption of Westernization. His dislike of materialism, racism, and the pro-Zionist feelings of the West – which he personally experienced there – seems to be the beginning of his alienation from Western culture and his return to the roots of the culture that he was brought up in. Upon his return to Egypt, after the death of Hasan al-Banna and the first ordeal of the Brotherhood mentioned above, he joined the Brotherhood and became very active in its intellectual and publishing activities and wrote numerous books on "Islam as the solution." However, until then, no radicalism or violence were involved. His priority was to rewrite a modern understanding of Islam and the solutions it provided to the basic political, economic, social and individual problems of Egypt and the Arab and Islamic worlds.[75]

In 1953, Qutb was appointed editor-in-chief of the weekly *Al-Ikhwan al-Muslimun*, which was banned along with the dissolution of the Brotherhood in 1954 after a falling-out between the Brethren and the Free Officers' regime. He was briefly imprisoned. The Brotherhood in general, and Qutb in particular, were instrumental in the Officers' paving the way for the Revolution of 1952. The Brotherhood refused to accept the absolute power of the Officers and called for a referendum to show the kind of constitution that the people wanted. Furthermore, it supported General Najib against Colonel 'Abd al-Nasir. After major disagreements between the Brotherhood and 'Abd al-Nasir, the Muslim Brethren were accused of co-operating with the communists to overthrow the government. Their movement was dissolved again in 1954, and many Brethren were jailed, including Qutb. He was released that same year and then arrested again after the *Manshiyya* incident, where an attempt was made on 'Abd al-Nasir's life. In 1955, Qutb and others were accused of being affiliated with the movement's secret military section, and Qutb was sentenced to fifteen years in prison; there, he and thousands of the Brethren and their supporters were subjected to ferocious torture that have left unhealed wounds. In this context, he shifted to radical fundamentalism and exclusiveness. Once again, isolated from the outside world, and under the daily pressures of witnessing the slaughtering of dozens of the Brethren in a prison hospital, Qutb could not help blame those who were free outside the prison; neither would he defend the unjustly imprisoned and ferociously tortured. These people became for Qutb accomplices in the crimes of the regime and therefore, like the regime, infidels. His most important books or the gospels of radicalism, *Fi Zilal al-Qur'an, Ma'alim fi al-Tariq, Hadha al-Din* and *Al-Mustaqbal li Hadha al-Din* and others, were written because of the torture that he and others tolerated year after year. Qutb was released in 1965, then once again arrested on charges to overthrow the government; he was executed in 1966.[76]

To help him tolerate the pain of torture and the poor prison conditions, Qutb transformed his discourse into an exclusivist discourse so that it was not the state and the society that were excluding him, but rather he, as the leader of the believing vanguard, who was excluding individuals, societies and states from the true salvation. The whole world became a target of his condemnation and isolation. The state's vengeful exclusion and repressive intolerance to any sort of popular opposition was counterbalanced by his own desperate spiritual, moral, social and political exclusion and intolerance. This is a clear contextual and historical example of how the parameters of radical fundamentalism developed. From there on, and from his cell, he starts developing his theoretical exclusivism.

He argues that divine governance, or *hakimiyya*, the essential political component of *tawhid*, must be upheld at all times when forming a virtuous and just society, or when providing personal and social freedom, under all conditions – in the prison or outside of it. Freedom is perceived in a negative way; the people are free insofar as their choice of social and political systems does not violate the divine governance and does not hinder the religious life. He perceives the state to be the moral agent for creating and maintaining morality, both individually and collectively. Because of the divinity of legislation, neither individuals, societies nor states can legitimately develop normative rights and duties, whether related to political freedom, pluralism, political parties or even personal and social freedom. Universal divine laws, as outlined in the Qur'an, are viewed by Qutb as the bases for all sorts of freedom and relationships. In other words, all people – Muslims and non-Muslims alike – must link their views of life with the Islamic worldview, and Muslim and non-Muslim countries must finally submit to the divine laws – without exception. The state and civil institutions, as well as individuals, may only codify legal articles if needs arise.[77]

Though this perspective postulates communal precedence over state control, the legitimacy of both is linked to the application of divine prescriptions. Qutb argues that because obedience to the government is not absolute, people should revolt when the government violates Qur'anic prescriptions because then it loses its legitimacy. Thus, while ultimate sovereignty for Qutb is reserved to God, its human application is a popular right and duty. This leads Qutb to argue that the state authority is not based on any divine text, but must be popularly justified. Only free popular consent makes social, political and intellectual institutions legitimate. Adherence to

Islamic law must be from a popular viewpoint, not an official interpretation. For it is the people who represent the divine will.[78]

Qutb's view of jurisprudence as a practical discipline severs it from its past golden and theoretical pedestal, and links it to contemporary needs. People are then freed to reconstitute modern Islamic political theories and institutions. His rejection of a historical normative compendium of Islamic disciplines leads him to uphold the people's freedom to re-order their systems and lives.[79]

Qutb denies then the unique legitimacy claims of any specific system or form of government, e.g., he would legitimate any form, whether republican or otherwise, insofar as its base is a consensual agreement.[80] However, theocracy cannot be a sound Islamic state because no elite may claim divine representation. A proper Islamic state for Qutb is both communal and constitutional; both the judiciary and the legislature as well as the executive rule only through delegated powers by means of *shura*, the central political, theoretical and practical doctrine of government and politics. Any social agreement that does not contradict *shari'a* is Islamically sound and can be included; elitism, however, is excluded and rejected on principle.[81]

Qutb's discourse so far gives the impression that even radical fundamentalism respects and honours communal choices. While this may be partially true, it still excludes pluralism, free civil society and multi-party systems in particular, or simply, liberal democracy. For the basis of freedom, the command to enjoin the good and forbid evil must be subjected, according to Qutb, to general communal interests like unity – to which political, social or personal interests, such as elitism and monopoly, must be subjected. Personal freedom tuned to communal interests, and united in broad unitary ideological orientations, is the source of social peace. For Qutb, a religiously good society cannot rise on ideologically and religiously conflictual bases, but requires goodwill, solidarity, security, peace, and equality.[82]

As an example, Qutb cites self-interest. Self-interest weakens communal solidarity, while mutual responsibility (*takaful*) strengthens that solidarity, itself a religious duty for the society. Although Qutb argues that this responsibility is social in nature, it may turn into a political responsibility carried out by the state. This responsibility includes the provision of education, health and employment. While the state's interference must theoretically be limited for Qutb, any failure of society to take care of its own affairs leads practically to the state's moral responsibility to dominate society. Again, while state institutions are of a supplementary nature for Qutb, they ultimately replace as well as exclude the institutions of civil society. Interest groups are allowed only if their objectives are broad, such as caring for the poor or the sick. Others, like women«s liberation movements, developed along Western models and are not welcomed or included. For Qutb, women's freedom to pursue their personal interests without regard to the family weakens society. To Qutb, because Western political systems are practically and theoretically false, he excludes them and prohibits group formation along Western models. A good society for Qutb is then composed of religious groups sharing similar interests and perceptions of life as well as unified political orientations.[83]

Qutb excludes not only the legitimacy of multi-party systems, but also of one-party systems, and replaces the two with a religious "vanguard" whose job is salvational in the first place. Thus, any ideological group or system that is not based on Islam, is not allowed to operate. Minorities are included religiously, insofar as they can keep their faith, but are excluded politically, since they are not given any right to form political parties or even a "vanguard." Qutb also links any valid free expression to the parameters of Islamic ideological understanding. All those societies and parties that do not conform to such an understanding are described as *jahili* or paganist.[84] Thus, only an Islamic ideology may be represented in a political party (the vanguard or *tali'ah*). His book, *Ma'alim fi al-Tariq* (Signposts on the Road), is specific about the mission that this vanguard should carry out, maintaining an exclusive and uncompromising attitude with respect toward all other ideologies, societies and ways of life. However, the establishment of an Islamic system permits the involvement of different institutions in political processes so that the public will is known in the context of an Islamic ideology.[85]

The particular issue that Qutb uses to exclude Western models of unions and federations is their selfish and materialistic nature. However, he argues that *al-naqabat* or unions in Islam, which were originally the models for their Western counterparts, are based on brotherhood and solidarity. Thus, Qutb – like Miller and Huntington – sees only a mutual exclusivity between Western philosophies, ideologies and institutions, and those of Islam. The former are *jahili* and, as such, belong to *hizb al-shaytan* (the party of Satan); the others are Islamic and, as such, belong to *hizb Allah* (the party of God).[86]

Once out of prison in 1964, he formed a "party" that adhered to the above-mentioned rationalizations and included the following principles: human societies do not follow Islamic ethics, system and *shari'a* and are in need of an essential Islamic education; those individuals who respond positively to this education should undertake a course of study on Islamic movements in history in order to set a course of action so as to fight Zionism and colonialism; no organization was to be established until a highly ideological training was undertaken.[87] Qutb's implementation of this vanguard program ended with his execution by hanging in 1966.

Most of the radical fundamentalist groups in the Arab world, and specifically in Egypt, have been influenced both directly and indirectly by this Qutbian radical exclusivist discourse, and by his notions of paganism of the "other" at all levels i.e., personal, social and political as well as cultural and philosophical. A few examples may suffice here:

The *Liman Tarah* prison in Egypt played an important role in the Qutbian radical education of himself and of others. Mustafa Shukri, an inmate with Sayyid Qutb, accepted the latter's views and established the exclusivist *Jama'at al-Muslimin* (the Community of the Muslims), notoriously known as *Al-Takfir wa al-Hijra*, as a fulfillment of the Qutbian vanguard. Shukri denies the legitimacy of pluralism and calls on people to adhere to the Qur'an and the *sunna* only. In his trial before a martial court in Egypt, he explains the exclusivity of his group in its rejection of theories and philosophies that are not textually derived; the Qur'an and the *sunna* are the only criteria of legitimacy and truth; therefore, the government is in violation of the divine governance. Furthermore, Shukri brands as unbelievers all other Muslims who do not view Islam in his own manner, and turns migration *(hijra)* from Egyptian society into a religious duty. In this fashion, he alleges that his isolated community is the only true Muslim society.[88]

Salih Sirriyya, originally associated with *Hizb al-Tahrir*, and the leader of *Tanzim al-Fanniyya al-'Askariyya*, yet another radical and militant fundamentalist group, fell under the spell of Qutb as well. His exclusivity can be seen in his categorization of mankind into three groups only: Muslims, infidels and hypocrites. Any neglect of an Islamic duty makes the individual an apostate and subjects him to death. Multi-party systems and diverse legal schools negate unity and lead to substantive conflicts.[89] While Shukri turned his back to the *jahili* society, Sirriyya allows the temporary use of democracy in order to set up an Islamic state. If the activists are persecuted, then it is possible for such activists to secretly infiltrate the political system and even become cabinet ministers. For the struggle to topple un-Islamic governments and any irreligious organization is a religious duty that ends only on the day of judgement. The defence of un-Islamic governments, participation in un-Islamic ideological parties, and adhering to foreign philosophies and ways of life are cited by Sirriyya as obvious instances of unbelief that incurs death. That sovereignty belongs to God is used by him to divide mankind into the inclusive *hizb al-shaytan*, consisting of all individuals and institutions that do not believe in or practice Islam, and the exclusive *hizb al-Allah*, consisting of those who struggle to establish the Islamic state. Out of this logic, Sirriyya attempted a *coup d'état* against Anwar al-Sadat which resulted in the former's execution in 1974 (as happened later to Shukri in 1977).[90]

'Abud al-Zumar, an army intelligence officer, and the military leader of *Tanzim al-Jihad*, as well as the leader and one of the founders of *Jama'at al-Jihad al-Islami*, also follows Sayyid Qutb's rationalization in stressing the importance of active involvement in a total opposition to the state. His program of action focuses on an applicable Islamic vision that contributes in to uniting Islamic movements within one framework, and which leads to forgo individual and public differences. Employing a Qutbian political key term, *ma'alim al-tariq* (signpost of the road), he urges the Islamic movement to concentrate on its basic objective, the Islamic state. This requires an uncompromising and exclusive attitude towards all aspects of the *jahili* systems and societies. The alternative for him is to employ a radical transformation and total Islamization of all facets of life, including the unstinting rejection of secularism, nationalism and parliamentary life. All this change has to start, however, by dethroning current rulers who do not adhere to the *shari'a*. In line with his exclusive radical ideology, al-Zumar tried but failed to kill President Sadat, who was nevertheless, eventually killed later by members of *Tanzim al-Jihad* with al-Zumar's aid.[91]

Al-Jama'a al-Islamiyya al-Jihadiyya, a branch of *Tanzim al-Jihad* in upper Egypt headed by 'Umar Abd al-Rahman (now residing in a US prison), is no less exclusive. 'Abd al-Rahman even divides the Islamic movements into two trends; the first trend, spearheaded by the Muslim Brotherhood, accepts the existing Egyptian regime as legitimate, and therefore adopts pluralism and democracy as legitimate tools of political action to establish an Islamic state; the other trend, spearheaded by *al-Jama'a al-Islamiyya*, denies legitimacy to the regime and publicly follows a course of total confrontation. 'Abd al-Rahman accuses the Brotherhood of complacency toward with the government, for working with Sadat and Mubarak, condemming Sadat's death and violence in general, and for paying visits to the Coptic Pope. He further rejects its inclusive and compromising attitude in allying itself with the *Wafd* party, as well as the *al-'Amal* and *al-'Ahrar*. Instead, he calls for replacing the inclusivity of the Brotherhood with the exclusivity of the *Jama'at* by rejecting integration in democratic institutions and by adopting a course of forceful resolution regarding basic issues of identity, ethics and value system.[92] Also in line with Qutb's argument, he describes any system that adopts foreign principles as belonging to *kufr* and the *jahiliyya* and legalizes its overthrow.

This view leads *al-Jihad* to declare war against the Egyptian Parliament; for the Parliament gave itself (Article 86 of the Constitution) the right to legislate and permitted democracy, a concept that treated the believer and non-believer equally as citizens.[93] "The 'assumed democratic system' in Egypt wants us to enter into party politics in order to equate Islam with other ideologies," 'Abd al-Rahman explains. However, the Islamic movement believes in its distinctive superiority and does not respect the *jahili* positive law. He further rejects any role for representative bodies as avenues for Qur'anic interpretation and adjudication. Qur'anic legitimacy stands on its own. Thus any violation of Qur'anic texts leads a ruler to *kufr* punishable by death. 'Abd al-Rahman himself was viewed as the instigator of Sadat's assassination, especially since he argued that illegitimate rulers deserved death.[94]

Assessment

It is clear from this chapter, that fundamentalism, though perceived as being one exclusive phenomenon in both practice and theory, is in fact otherwise. Fundamentalism, whether Jewish, Christian, Islamic or even Hindu has indeed become a world phenomenon. However, it is only Islam that is identified in an essentialist manner with fundamentalism. Agreements on the superstructure of Islam – which have been treated in the chapter on epistemology and political philosophy – not only might lead to confuse radical fundamentalism with moderate fundamentalism, but even involve Islam as well. If an ordinary practicing or non-practicing Muslim is asked whether the Qur'an postulates God's governance in all aspects of life, the answer is "yes, of course." This belief does not, however, make that Muslim a fundamentalist by necessity. Conversely, it makes almost all Muslims fundamentalists by definition.

The real issue and decisive character for distinguishing a radical view from a moderate one revolves primarily around the conditions and principles of transforming a political agenda into daily life. As we have seen, even fundamentalism employs diverse methodological and practical processes to intellectual and political formulas. One formula is conceptually based on a theoretical and practical exclusivity and *otherness* that permits violent means to fulfill the real "I". Because radical fundamentalism perceived its own real and imagined isolation as a result of social disunity and exploitation, political violence and the illegitimacy of regimes, as well as from impiety and corruption, it has transformed its political discourse into a purified theology of politics. From this point of view, Islam cannot survive in the consciousness of the individual and society, without the political contextualization of Islam.

Shura is not merely a religious doctrine or a mechanism for elections; it reflects for the radicals the public will, and is a superior doctrine to individual freedom or social agreement. More importantly, it represents the divine will; and as such, any deviation from the divine is a religious violation. The individual cannot but submit to this will; in fact, he is only an appendage to it, with his freedom depending on it. While this will may opt for a political contract with a ruler, it cannot, because of what it represents, allow pluralism and basic differences, leading to disunity. The establishment of an Islamic state becomes, for radicalism, the fulfillment of this divine will, and individuals and groups are therefore subordinated to the state.

Processed through the lenses of the *shari'a*, the institutionalization of *shura* and *ijma'* provides the state, which expresses the general will – a normative role in making basic choices in people's life. The formal legitimacy that the state acquires makes it, in fact, unaccountable to anyone but God or obedience to *shari'a* (itself institutionalized in the state). Henceforth, legitimacy becomes an internal state affair and not a social and public issue, though originally it was so. Insofar as the state is not going against the *shari'a*, no one can legitimately overthrow it. In this context, because the state supervises, the public morality and the application of *shari'a*, individual religiosity becomes subjected to the communal public will (itself transformed into state control, both moral and political). Parties, associations and other civil institutions have no intrinsic validity in this hierarchy, operating only in a supplementary manner. An elaboration like this seems to demand, in the end, exclusivity. Indeed, there is no possibility of pluralistic understandings of religion; for the politicization of Islam as the proper Islamic interpretation cannot be represented except by the state. The establishment of inclusive, pluralistic, civil democracies and ways of life seems then, unworkable for theoretical and practical reasons.

The descriptions that Miller, Lewis, Huntington and others attribute to fundamentalism and to all sorts of Islamic movements might be more appropriately restricted to Islamic radicalism. To use the radical groups as representatives of Islamic and Arabic culture is, however, both factually erroneous and culturally biased. Other non-Islamic religious interpretations suffer from very similar phenomena but are never treated in the same manner. One has to keep in mind that the employment of violence by a radical group is not theoretical in origin, but that the theory is historically developed. Put differently, these groups have been committing violent acts not because of their theories but rather, because their theories justifying violence have been derived from the real and imagined violence that they have been subjected to. In fact, practice has been transformed into theory, which has now a life of its own. Both radical groups, and most regimes, are committed to recycling intellectual and practical violence and exclusivity. Violence, whether by secular or by religious groups, has been exercised, most of the time, in reaction to the tyrannies of political regimes. 'Abud al-Zumar, serving a forty-year prison term, attributes, the violence of the radical groups, correctly or not, to the violence of the Egyptian regime. For him, the fundamentalist violence is no more than a reaction to the liquidation of fundamentalists by the regime.[95]

On the other hand, the absence of a pluralistic society with democratic institutions is cited by the moderate trend as the real cause for violence. While this trend has long been excluded from political participation, it still calls for its inclusion into politics and formal institutions. Its involvement in civil society, and its calls for pluralism, are still seen as the road to salvation of the community and individuals. Its inclusionary views do not postulate an eternal or divine enmity between Islam's institutions and systems and the West's institutions and systems. Properly grounded, what is Western becomes Islamic. Here, I think, the moderate fundamentalists may blend the culture of the East with that of the West. For they are providing Islamic arguments for inclusion, not mutual exclusion, as some secular and religious radicals do in the East and West. The conflict between the East and West is viewed as being primarily either political or economic, but not religious or cultural. The two have common monotheistic grounds upon which multi-cultural and religious cooperation and co-existence might be built.

For the moderates, a popular, liberating, democracy grounded in Islamic law, is a political bridge between the East and the West. For authoritarianism and despotism are not specifically cultural or Islamic; they have existed in both the West and the East, but are more prominent now in the Arab world. As opposed to the popular democracy of radical fundamentalism or the authoritarian national-ism of the Arab world, the moderate trend adopts an Islamic interpretation of liberal democracy.

A good example that exposes the real difference between the moderates and the radicals is their view about Islam and the world. Radical fundamentalism proclaims the constitutionality of Islam, even in non-Islamic states, and as such requires no prior popular approval and, thus excluding the possibility of its inclusion in dialogues and cooperation, whether with Arab regimes or the West. On the other hand, moderate fundamentalism seems more amenable and eager to be included in dialogue and compromise within the Islamic world and with the West. It wants to establish itself as a player in internal and international politics, and participate in developing the general discourses about politics, ideology and religion within the context of a civil society. So the question must be asked: If the weakness of fundamentalism, both in its minor radical and, especially, major moderate trends, might lead to free, liberal, pluralistic and democratic societies and inclusive regimes in the Middle East, why has not this happened when Islamic movements were at their lowest ebb, their supporters packed in prison? And why did the liberal West encourage, to a large extent, their re-emergence as Islamic movements (at least in Egypt during Sadat's presidency, and also in Afghanistan during the the Mujahidin Communist regime)?

Yahya Sadowski questions the important issue of the real motivations behind portraying Islamic movements and the essence of Islam in one way or another. He states:

> The irony of this conjuncture needs to be savored. When the consensus of social scientists held that democracy and develop-ment depended upon the actions of strong, assertive social groups, Orientalists held that such associations were absent in Islam. When the consensus evolved and social scientists thought a quiescent, undemanding society was essential to progress, the neo-Orientalists [like Crone, Pipes and Gellner] portrayed Islam

as beaming with pushy, anarchic solidarities. Middle Eastern Muslims, it seems, were doomed to be eternally out of step with intellectual fashion.[96]

Notes

1 On democracy and pluralism in the Arab world, see, *Al-Hayat*, 4 August 1993, p. 19, and 25 September 1993, pp. 14 and 17. The series ran 2–6 August. See also *Qadaya al-Isbu'*, No. 15, 10–17 September 1993, pp. 1–2. For fundamentalists interested in the same issue, see Rashid al-Ghannushi on *Al-Hurriyyat al-'Ama fi al-Islam* (Beirut: Center for the Studies of Arab Unity, 1993) and Fahmi al-Huwaidi, *Al-Islam wa al-Dimocratiyya* (Cairo: Markaz al-'Ahram li al-Tarjama wa al-Nashr, 1993).

2 Will Democracy Survive in Egypt? *Reader's Digest* (Canadian Edition), December 1987, Vol. 131, No. 788, p. 149. "The Arab World where Troubles for the US Never End," *US News and World Report*, February 6, 1984, Vol. 96, p. 24. "The Clash of Civilizations," *Foreign Affairs*, Vol. 72, No. 3, Summer 1993: 22–49.

3 Timothy D. Sisk, *Islam and Democracy.* (Washington, DC: United States Peace Institute Press, 1992), p. vii.

4 *New Perspective Quarterly*, Vol. II, No. 2, Spring 1994, pp. 20–37. The complete titles of the articles are:
   – From Beirut to Sarajevo: Can Tolerance be Born of Cruelty? by Kanan Makiya
   – Laughing at God in North Africa, by Hahar Ben Jelloun
   – When Galileo Meets Allah, by Farida Faouzia Charfi
   – Justice is the Strife, by Tariq Aanuri
   – Against Cultural Terrorism, by Naguib Mahfouz.

5 Ibid., p. 3. The editor is Nathan Gardels.

6 "Media Mongols at the Gate of Baghdad," *New Perspective Quarterly*, Vol. 10, No. 3, Summer 1993: 10.

7 The Islamic-Confucian Connection," ibid., p. 19. See also, "The Clash of Civilizations," *Foreign Affairs*, Vol. 72, No. 3, Summer 1993: 22–49. For similar attitudes, see "Will Democracy Survive in Egypt? *Reader's Digest* (Canadian Edition), Vol. 131, No. 788, December 1987: 149 and "The Arab World where Troubles for the US Never End," *US News and World Report*, Vol. 96, February 6 1984: 24.

8 Ibid., p. 21.

9 Judith Miller, "The Challenge of Radical Islam," *Foreign Affairs*, Vol. 72, No. 2, 1993: 54–55 and see the complete article, pp. 43–55. In the same vein see, Bernard Lewis "Islam and Liberal Democracy," *The Atlantic Monthly*, February 1993: 89–98. This article is used by Miller to support her argument.

10 "One Man, One Vote, One Time," *New Perspective Quarterly*, Vol. 10, No. 3, Summer 1993: 49

11 Ibid.

12 "Inclusion Can Deflate Islamic Populism," Ibid., p. 50.
13 Ibid., p. 51. For studies that deal with similar issues and on the relationships between political elites, Islamists and the West, see Ghassan Salame, "Islam and the West," *Foreign Policy*, No. 90, Spring 1993: 22–37. See also Dale Eickelman, "Changing Interpretations of Islamic Movements," in William Roff, ed. *Islam and the Political Economy of Meaning*. (London: Croom Helm, 1987), pp. 13–30.
14 William Zartman, "Democracy and Islam: The Cultural Dialectic," *ANNALS*, AAPSS, 524, November, 1992, p. 191.
15 John Esposito and James Piscatori, "Democratization and Islam," *Middle East Journal*, Vol. 45, No. 3, Summer 1991: 434. Along the same line of arguments, see Gudrun Kramer, "Islamist Democracy," *Middle East Report*, Number 183, Vol. 23, No. 4, July-August: 2–8.
16 Gudrun Kramer, "Liberalization and Democracy in the Arab World," *Middle East Report*, Number 174, Vol. 22, No. 1, January–February, 1992: 25 and see also pp. 22–24.
17 *Al-Hayat*, 24 April, 1993, p. 19. Some of the books that have been resurrected include *Freedom of Thought* by Salame Musa, *Islam and the Fundamentals of Government* by 'Ali 'Abd al-Razzaq, *the Future of Culture* in Egypt by Taha Hussein, and *The Liberation of Woman* by Qasim Amin, and *The Nature of Tyranny* by 'Abd al-Rahaman al-Kawakibi and many others, including briefs for modernist political thinkers such as 'Abduh and al-'Afghani. See also on the war of ideas and political control, Alexander Flores' article "Secularism, Integralism and Political Islam," *Middle East Report*, No. 183, July–August, 1993: 35–38.
18 *Al-Safir*, 2 April 1993, p. 8.
19 *Al-Hayat*, 3 June 1993, p. 8. See also Flores, "Secularism," pp. 32–33. See also *Al-Diyar*, 22 July 1994, p. 14.
20 For details on this issue see *Al-Safir*, 10 June 1993, p. 1 and *Al-Safir*, 16 June 1993, pp. 1 and 10. On the views of the Mufti of Egypt on violence, see *Al-Wasat*, 11 November, 1993, No. 94, pp. 29–21.
21 *Al-Safir*, 10 July 1993, p. 10. His books include *Al-Imam al-Shafi'i and the Foundation of Moderate Ideology* and *The Concept of Text: A Study in Qur'anic Sciences*.
22 Ibid. On the latest figures, see *Al-Wasat*, 25 July 1994, pp. 4–5. All sentences are not given by the regular courts. 56 of the 58 death sentences are taken by martial courts; the other two by the higher courts of national security (emergency court).
23 *Al-Safir*, 3 April 1993, p. 10. 'Awwa, *Fi al-Nizam al-Siyasi li al-Dawla al-Islamiyya*. (Cairo: Dar al-Shuruq, 1989), pp. 85–113.
24 *Al-Hayat*, 4 February 1994: 7. See also the five long and diversified articles and dialogues that *Al-Hayat* has serialized in 2–5 August under the title "Civil Society in Egypt and the Arab World". On interest in democracy in the Arab world and the resistance of the governments to such a society, see for instance, *Al-Hayat*, 4 August 1993: 19, and 25 September 1993: 14 and 17.
25 *Al-Shu'a*, No. 26, March 1993: 38 and see pp. 39–40.
26 *Al-Hayat*, 3 August 1993: 19. See also, *Al-Hayat*, 3 February 1994: 17. On the democratic changes that have been taking place in the Arab world and North Africa, see Lisa Anderson, "Liberalism in Northern Africa,"

Current History, Vol. 89, No. 546, April 1990: 145–46, 148 and 174–75. See also on the state of democracy in the Arab world, Hilal Khashan, "The Quagmire of Arab Democracy," *ASQ,* Vol. 1, No. 1, Winter 1992: 17–33. Consult also John Esposito, "Political Islam: Beyond the Green Menace," *Current History,* Vol. 93, January 1994: 19–24. Al-Jawjari's views are contained in his book *Al-Hizb al-Islami* (Cairo: The Arabic Center for Journalism and Publications, 1993).

27 *Qira'at Siyasiyya,* Vol. 3, No. 2, Spring 1993: 197–98. *Qadaya Dawliyya* published the Manifesto in its March issue of 1993.

28 Rifa'at al-Sa'id, *Hasan al-Banna, Mu'assis Harakat al-Ikhwan al-Muslimin.* (Beirut: Dar al-Tali'a, 4th edn, 1986), pp. 93–94, 99–100 and 112–16. Al-Sa'id's leftist account is not favorable but still the facts mentioned in it minus the author's analysis serve to show that the Brotherhood has not officially sanctioned or employed violence. On the active involvement of al-Banna and his organization in civil society and their co-operation with other civil segments, see, for instance, Ishaq Musa al-Husseini, *Moslem Brethren* (Beirut: Khayat's College Book, 1956), Richard Mitchell, *The Society of Muslim Brothers.* (London: Oxford University Press, 1964), and Charles Adams, *Islam and Modernism in Egypt.* (NY: Russell and Russell, 1986). See also the views of 'Umar al-Tilmisani in Rif'at Sayyid Ahmad, *Al-Nabiy al-Musallah: Al-Rafidun.* (London: Riad al-Rayyis Books Ltd, 1991), pp. 199–200. On al-Banna's ideology, see Ahmad Moussalli, "Hasan al-Banna's Islamist Discourse on Constitutional Rule and Islamic State," *Journal of Islamic Studies,* Vol. 4, No. 2, 1993: 161–74.

29 Sa'id, *Hasan al-Banna,* pp. 101–07, 112, 117 and 122–24.

30 Ibid., pp. 129, 132–39 and 169–79.

31 Banna, *Majmu'at Rasa'il al-Shahid Hasan al-Banna* (Beirut: Dar al-Qur'an al-Karim, 1984) (hereafter cited as *Rasa'il al-Imam*), pp. 48 & 56–60; Banna, *Majmu'a,* pp. 14, 169, 309, 331–22 and 335–37; Banna, *Kalimat Khalida* (Beirut: n.p., 1972), p. 45.

32 Henry Munson, *Islam and Revolution in the Middle East.* (New Haven: Yale University Press, 1988), pp. 78–79. See also Dilip Hiro, *The Rise of Islamic Fundamentalism.* (New York: Routledge, 1989), pp. 69–72.

33 Hasan al-Banna, *Din wa-Siyasa.* (Beirut: Maktabat Huttin, 1970), pp. 40–45; and Banna, *Majmu'at Rasa'il al-Shahid Hasan al-Banna.* (Beirut: Al-Mu'assasa al-Islamiyya, 4th edn, 1984) (hereafter cited as *Majmu'at Rasa'il*), pp. 161–65. On al-Banna's biography, see, for instance, *Memoirs of Hasan al-Banna Shaheed,* translated by M. N. Shaikh (Karachi: International Islamic Publishers, 1981), and Rif'at al-Sa'id, *Hasan al-Banna, Mu'assis Harakat al-Ikhwan al-Muslimin.*

34 Banna, *Majmu'at Rasa'il,* p. 165, Banna, *Majmu'at Rasa'il al-Imam al-Shahid Hasan al-Banna* (Beirut: Dar al-Qalam, n.d.) (hereafter cited as *Majmu'a*), pp. 304 and 343–47; and Banna, *Din wa-Siyasa,* pp. 57–59.

35 Banna, *Majmu'at Rasa'il,* pp. 160–61 and 317–18; and Banna, *Al-Imam Yatahadath ila Shabab al-'Alam al-Islami* (Beirut: Dar al-Qalam, 1974), p. 99; and, Banna, *Majmu'a,* pp. 99 and 332–37.

36 Al-Banna, *Majmu'at Rasa'il,* pp. 95–96, 165–67, 317, 320–23, 325 and 328–30; al-Banna, *Minbar al-Jum'a.* (Alexandria: Dar al-Da'wa, 1978),

pp. 78–79 and 136; al-Banna, *Al-Da'wa*, No. 7, 1979: 9. On centrality of this demand, the Islamic state, in the fundamentalist thought, see Bruce Larwrence, *Defenders of God: The Revolt against the Modern Age*. (San Francisco: Harper and Row, 1989), pp. 187–226.

37 Al-Banna, *Majmu'at Rasa'il*, pp. 96–97, 161–63 and 167–169; and al-Banna, *Rasa'il al-Imam*, p. 53.

38 Al-Banna, *Nazarat fi Islah al-Nafs wa al-Mujtama'*. (Cairo: Maktabat al-'I'tisam, 1969), p. 194; al-Banna, *Minbar al-Jum'a*, pp. 24–25, 63, 72 and 347; al-Banna, *Majmu'at Rasa'il*, pp. 317; al-Banna, *Majmu'a*, pp. 63, 72, 101, 104 and 317; al-Banna, *Rasa'il al-Imam*, pp. 53–55; and al-Banna, *Al-Imam al-Shahid Yatahadath*, pp. 15–17.

39 Al-Banna, *Al-Salam fi al-Islam*. (Beirut: Manshurat al-'Asr al-Hadith, 1971), pp. 27–29. On his acceptance of pluralism, see 'Abd al-Khabir Mahmud 'Ata, "Al-Haraka al-Islamiyya wa Qadiyat al-Ta'addudiyya," *Al-Majallat al-'Arabiyya li al-'Ulum al-Siyasiyya*, Nos. 5 and 6, April, 1992: 115–16; on al-Banna's own declaration of accepting equal rights and pluralism, see *Al-Islam wa al-Salam*, p. 37 and *passim*. For similar views in Jordan, see Taqiy al-Din al-Nabahani, *Al-Takatul al-Hizbi* (Jerusalem: n.p., 2nd edn, 1953), pp. 23–57 and *Nizam al-Hukm* (Jerusalem: Matba'at al-Thiryan, 1952), pp. 56–59.

40 Taqiy al-Din al-Nabahani, *Al-Takatul al-Hizbi*, pp. 23–25.

41 Ibid., pp. 24–57.

42 Al-Nabahani, *Nizam al-Hukm*, pp. 56–59.

43 Iyad Barghouty, "Al-Islam bayna al-Sultah wa al-Mu'arada," *Qadaya Fikriyya: Al-Islam al-Siyasi, al-'Usus al-Fikriyya wa al-'Ahdaf al-'Amaliyya*. (Cairo: Dar al-Thaqafah al-Jadidah, 1989), pp. 237–38. On an update of the current status of Islamic parties in Jordan, see "'Itijahat al-Harakah al-Islamiyya fi al-'Urdun," *Al-Safir*, 20 August, 1993: 13; and "Tanzimat al-Harakat al-Islamiyya: Harakat al-Ikhwan al-Muslim fi al-'Urdun: Al-Nash'ah wa al-Tatawwur," *Al-Hayat*, Tayyarat Section, 14 August 1993, p. 3. On the importance of justice as a political doctrine in Islamic political thought, see Charles E. Butterworth, *Political Islam*, *ANNALS*, AAPSS, 524, November 1992: 26–37.

44 Munir Shafiq, "Awlawiyyat 'amam al-Ijtihad wa al-Tajdid," *Al-Ijtihad wa Tajdid fi al-Fikr al-Islami al-Mu'asir*. (Malta: Center for the Studies of the Muslim World, 1991), pp. 64–65.

45 Sa'id Hawwa, *Al-Madkhal ila Da'wat al-Ikhwan al-Muslimin bi-Munasabat Khamsin 'Aman 'ala Ta'sisiha* (Amman: Dar al-Arqam, 2nd edn, 1979), pp. 13–18. On the Muslim Brotherhood's participation in elections in Syria, see al-Habib al-Janhani, "Al-Sahwa al-Islamiyya fi Bilad al-Sham: Mithal Suriyya," *Al-Harakat al-Islamiyya al-Mu'asira fi al-Watan al-'Arabi*. (Beirut: Center for the Studies of Arab Unity, 2nd edn, 1989), pp. 105–20.

46 Hawwa, *Al-Madkhal*, p. 282.

47 Muhammad S. al-'Awwa, *Al-Hayat*, 3 August 1993, p. 19. See also 'Awwa, *Al-Ta'adudiyya min Manzur Islami*, *Minbar al-Hiwar*, Vol. 6, No. 20, Winter 1991: 134–36.

48 Ibid., p. 19. On the Islamic movement in Egypt, see Muhammad A. Khalafallah's article in *Al-Haraka al-Islamiyya fi al-Watan al-'Arabi*,

pp. 37 and *passim*. See also Rislan Sharaf al-Din, "Al-Din wa al-Ahzab al-Siyasiyya al-Diniyya," *Al-Din fi al-Mujtama' al-'Arabi*. (Beirut: Center for the Studies of Arab Unity, 1990), p. 180 and *passim*.

49 Al-'Awwa, "Al-Ta'adudiyya al-Siyasiyya min Manzur Islami," pp. 129–32 and *passim*.

50 Ibid., pp. 133–34. For a summary of the historical acceptance of pluralism by the scholars such as Ibn Taymiyya and authoritative exegesis of the Qur'an such as *Tafsir al-Jilalain*, see pp. 136–52. On an independent source for the views of the scholars who accepted the people's choice as the legitimate means of government, see Zuhayrkibi, ed. andintro. *Abu Bakr al-Jassas, Dirash fi Fikratihi: Bab al-Ijtihad*. (Beirut: Dar al-Muntakhab, 1993), pp. 29–41; on those who rejected it such as the generality of Shi'ites, see 75–86. On the relationship between actual politics and the development of religion and *ijtihad*, see Ismail, *Sociolojia*, pp. 139–38.

51 Al-'Awwa, *Fi al-Nizam al-Siyasi*, p. 77; and al-'Awwa, "Al-Ta'adudiyya al-Siyasiyya min Manzur Islami," pp. 136–37 and 152–53.

52 Hasan al-Turabi, "Islam, Democracy, the State and the West: Summary of a Lecture and Roundtable Discussion with Hasan al-Turabi," prepared by Louis Cantouri and Arthur Lowrie, *Middle East Policy*, Vol. 1, No. 3, 1992: 52–54.

53 Hasan al-Turabi, *Tajdid 'Usul al-Fiqh* (Jedah: Al-Dar al-Su'udiyya li al-Nashr wa al-Tawzi', 1984), pp. 10–16; and Turabi, *Qadaya al-Hurriyya wa al-Wahda, al-Shura wa al-Dimocratiyya, al-Din wa al-Fan*. (Jedah: Al-Dar al-Su'udiyya li al-Nashr wa al-Tawzi', 1987), pp. 17–18.

54 Al-Turabi, *Tajdid al-Fikr al-Islami*. (Jedah: Al-Dar al-Su'udiyya li al-Nashr wa al-Tawzi', 2nd edn, 1987), pp. 20, 73 and 132–33; al-Turabi, "Awlawiyyat al-Tayyar al-Islami," *Minbar al-Sharq*, No. 1, March 1992, pp. 21–26, 69–72, 81–82, 136–38, 167–69 and 198–99.

55 Al-Turabi, *Qadaya*, pp. 25–27 and 31–33, al-Turabi, *Tajdid al-Fikr*, pp. 68–80; and al-Turabi, "Awlawiyyat," p. 16. On the differences between *shura* and democracy, see Salih Hasan Sami', *'Azmat al-Hurriyya al-Siyasiyya fi al-Watan al-'Arabi* (Cairo: Al-Zahra' li al-'I'lam al-'Arabi, 1988), pp. 49–61.

56 Al-Turabi, *Qadaya*, pp. 51–57; and al-Turabi, *Tajdid al-Fikr*, pp. 45, 66–68, 75, 93–97 and 162–63.

57 On al-Turabi's definition of religion and the need for revolution, *Tajdid al-Fikr*, pp. 200–03 and 106–19; on the general bonds and the Islamic ones that make the establishment of society worthwhile, see al-Turabi, *Al-Iman wa 'Atharuhu fi Hayat al-Insan* (Jedah: Al-Dar al-Su'udiyya li al-Nashr wa al-Tawzi', 1984), pp. 181–261; on the social connotations and their fulfillment, see pp. 112–21; on the role of science in society, see pp. 269–301; and on the importance of the unity of society for general interests, see pp. 325–29.

58 Al-Turabi, *Usul al-Fiqh*, pp. 27–29.

59 Al-Turabi, *Al-Itijah al-Islami Yuqadim al-Mar'a bayna Ta'alim al-Din wa Taqalid al-Mujtama'* (Jedah: Al-Dar al-Su'udiyya li al-Nashr wa al-Tawzi': 1984), pp. 6–13 and 42–44. On the essential conditions and requirements for the independence of women, see pp. 45–49.

60 Al-Turabi, *Tajdid al-Fikr al-Islami,* pp. 108–09, 164–65, 133–39 and 160–63.

61 Al-Turabi, *Usul al-Fiqh,* pp. 18–25 and 32–35.

62 Ibid., pp. 36–37 and 42–45; al-Turabi, *Tajdid al-Fikr al-Islami,* pp. 26–31, 36–49, 54–63, 76–77, 148–49 and 172–43.

63 Al-Turabi, *Tajdid al-Fikr al-Islami,* pp. 68–71; for a discussion of the forms of *shura,* see al-Turabi, *Qadaya,* pp. 72–77 and 80–81.

64 Turabi, *Qadaya,* pp. 10–19 and 22–28.

65 Ibid., pp. 20–21 and 29–30.

66 Ibid., pp. 34–37 & 44–47.

67 Al-Turabi, *Al-Salat 'Imad al-Din.* (Beirut: Dar al-Qalam, 1971), pp. 124–33, 138–47 and 156–58.

68 Al-Ghannushi, *Bayrut al-Masa',* 15 May 1993: 15; and al-Ghannushi, "Mustaqbal al-Tayyar al-Islami, *Minbar al-Sharq,* Vol. 1, No. 1, March 1992: 3–32. On a genral discussion of al-Ghannushi and *Harakat al-Itijah al-Islami,* see 'Abd al-Khabir Mahmud 'Ata, "Qadiyat al-Ta'addudiyya," pp. 116–17.

69 Al-Ghannushi and al-Turabi, *Al-Harakah al-Islamiyya wa al-Tahdith* (n.d., n.p., 1981), pp. 34–35. See also Muhammad 'Abd al-Baqi al-Hirmasi, "al-Islam al-Ihtijaji fi Tunis," *Al-Harakat al-Islamiyya al-Mu'asira,* pp. 273–86.

70 Al-Ghannushi, "Hiwar," *Qira'at Siyasiyya,* Vol. 1, No. 4. Fall 1991: 14–15 and 35–37; and, al-Ghannushi, "Al-Islam wa al-Gharb," *Al-Ghadir,* Nos. 10 and 11, 1990, pp. 36–37. On his and other fundamentalists' acceptance of democracy, see also John Esposito and James Piscatori, "Democratization and Islam," *Middle East Journal,* Vol. 45, No. 3, Summer 1991: 426–34 and 437–38. On his political life see al-Ghannushi, "Hiwar," p. 5, and 'Abd al-Qadir al-Zugul, "Al-Istratijia al-Jadida li Harakat al-Itija al-Islami," in *Al-Din fi al-Mujtama',* pp. 346–48. See also on the possibilities of liberalization, Gudrun Kramer, "Liberalization and democracy in the Arab World," *Middle East Report,* January–February 1992: 22–25.

71 Rashid al-Ghannushi, "Al-Islam wa al-Gharb," *Al-Ghadir,* Nos. 10–11, December, 1990: 37.

72 Muhammad al-Hashimi al-Hamidi, "Awlawiyyat Muhimma fi Daftar al-Harakat al-Islamiyya: Nahwa Mithaq Islami li al-'Adl wa al-Shura wa Huquq al-Insan," *Al-Mustaqbal al-Islami,* No. 2, November 1991: 19–21; the quotation is from pp. 14–15.

73 See the Program of the Islamic Salvation Front (Al-Barnamaj al-Siyasi li Jabhat al-Inqadh al-Islamiyya), *Minbar al-Sharq,* No. 1, March. On the Front and democracy, see Esposito and Piscatori, "Democratization," pp. 437–38. Aslo see on the possibilities of civil society in Islam, "Bahth 'an Mujtama' Madani Manshud," *Mustaqbal al-'Alam al-Islami,* Vol. 1, No. 4, Fall, 1991: 225–37.

74 Ahmad Moussalli, *Radical Islamic Fundamentalism: The Ideological and Political Discourse of Sayyid Qutb* (Beirut: American University of Beirut, 1992), pp. 19–24 and *passim.*

75 Ibid., pp. 24–30. See also Sayyid Qutb, *Nahwa Mujtama' Islami* (Beirut: Dar al-Shuruq, 5th edn, 1982), pp. 11–12, *Al-Mustaqbal li Hadha al-Din*

(Cairo: Maktabat Wahba, 1965), pp. 71–90, *Al-Islam wa Mushkilat al-Hadara* (Beirut: Dar al-Shuruq, 8th edn, 1983), pp. 77–78 and 83–87.

76 Moussalli, *Radical Islamic Fundamentalism*, pp. 31–39. See Mitchell, *The Society of Muslim Brothers*, pp. 103 & 187–189. Badrul Hasan, *Milestones*. (Karachi: International Islamic Publishers, 1981), pp. 7–13 and 30–31; Asaf Hussain, *Islamic Movements in Egypt, Pakistan, and Iran*. (London: Mansell Publishing, 1983), pp. 7–11 and 91.

77 Qutb, *Hadha al-Din* (Cairo: Maktabat Wahbah, 4th edn, n.d.), pp. 32 and 123; and Qutb, *Ma'rakat al-Islam wa al-Ra'simaliyyah*. (Beirut: Dar al-Shuruq, 4th edn, 1980), pp. 49 and 60.

78 On the necessity of the choice of people, see *Ma'alim fi al-Tariq*. (Beirut: Dar al-Shuruq, 7th edn, 1980), pp. 50 and 71–77; and Qutb *Al-'Adala al-Ijtima'iyya fi al-Islam*. (Cairo: Dar al-Shuruq, 7th edn, 1980), pp. 73 and 107–08, 206–07; Qutb, *Ma'rakat al-Islam wa al-Ra'simaliyya*, pp. 67, 85 and 75; Qutb, *Fiqh al-Da'wa* (Beirut: Mu'assasat al-Risala, 1970), p. 61.

79 Qutb, *Al-'Adala*, pp. 102–05 and 167; Qutb, *Fiqh*, p. 84; *Ra'simaliyya*, p. 60.

80 Qutb, *Nahwa Mujtama' Islami* (Beirut: Dar al-Shuruq, 6th edn, 1983), pp. 46–52.

81 Qutb, *Al-'Adala*, pp. 37, 107–08, 111 and 157–69; Qutb, *Fi Zilal*, Vol. 1, Part 3, p. 329; Qutb, *Ma'alim*, pp. 58–96, 72 and 132; Qutb, *Ra'simaliyya*, pp. 66–70; Qutb, *Tafsir 'Ayat al-Riba* (Beirut: Dar al-Shuruq, 1970), p. 84; and Qutb *Nahwa Mujtama'*, pp. 46–69.

82 Qutb, *Al-'Adala*, pp. 66–68 and 111; and Qutb, *Al-Salam al-'Alami wa al-Islam*. (Beirut: Dar al-Shuruq, 7th edn, 1983), pp. 102–18.

83 Qutb, *Fi al-Tarikh, Fikra wa Minhaj*. (Cairo: Dar al-Shuruq, 1974), pp. 23–36 and 76; Qutb, *Al-'Adala*, pp. 35, 59, 73–80, 86, 113 and 119; and, Qutb, *Fi Zilal*, Vol. 2, p. 689. On his view on women and family structure, see Qutb, *Fi Zilal*, Vol. 1, Part 1, p. 235, Part 2, p. 234, Part 4, p. 587; Qutb, *Al-'Adala*, pp. 60–65.

84 Qutb, *Hadha al-Din*, pp. 11 and 91; Qutb, *Ma'alim*, pp. 64–67 and 162–63; Qutb, *Al-'Adala*, pp. 107, 198; Qutb, *Nahwa Mujtama'*, pp. 62, 92–99, 102–20, 123 and 134, and Qutb, *Al-Salam*, pp. 161–65.

85 Qutb, *Ma'alim*, pp. 11–15 and 22; Qutb, *Al-'Adalah*, pp. 197; Qutb, *Hadha al-Din*, pp. 11, 29–30 and 65–57; Qutb, *Fiqh*, pp. 15–32 and 88–89. See also, Qutb, *Al-Salam*, pp. 118–20; and Qutb, *Nahwa Mujtama'*, pp. 137–43; and Qutb, *Al-Islam wa Mushkilat al-Hadara*, pp. 189–93. On the proper political system according to Qutb, see *Al-Salam*, pp. 122–43.

86 Qutb, *Al-Islam wa Mushkilat al-Hadara*, pp. 96–107, and Qutb, *Nahwa Mujtama'*, pp. 150–52 and *passim*. On the characteristics of the two parties and the West, see Qutb, *Hadha al-Din*, pp. 84–87; Qutb, *Al-Islam wa Mushkilat al-Hadara*, pp. 7–9; Qutb, *Al-Ra'simaliyya*, pp. 58; and Qutb, *Ma'alim*, pp. 59 and 89.

87 On these issues and his life, see Muhammad T. Barakat, *Sayyid Qutb: Khulasat Hayatih, Minhajuhuh fi al-Haraka wa al-Naqd al-Muwajah ilayh* (Beirut: Dar al-Da'wa, 197?), p. 19; Salah A. Khalidi, *Sayyid Qutb, al-Shahid al-Hay*. (Amman: Dar al-Firqan, 1983), pp. 147–49; Qutb, "Limadha 'A'damuni?" *Al-Muslimun*, March, No. 4, pp. 6–9; Moussalli, *Radical Islamic Fundamentalism*, Chapter One.

88 On the prison experience see Rif'at al-Sa'id's article in *Qadaya Fikriyya: al-Islam al-Siyasi: Al-'Usus al-Fikriyya wa al-'Ahdaf*, p. 15 and *passim*. See also, Moussalli, *Radical Islamic Fundamentalism*, pp. 34–36. On a first-hand and sympathetic account of the torture that Shukri, Qutb and others were subjected to as well as the movement itself see, Muhammad Mahfuz, *Alladhina Zulimu*. (London: Riad al-Rayyis Books Ltd, 1988), pp. 7–141. On Shukri's thought as put forward in his trial, see Rif'at Sayyid Ahmad, Second Document in *Al-Nabiy al-Musallah: Al-Rafidun*, pp. 53–57.

89 Salih Sirriyya, Second Document (1973), "Risalat al-Iman," *Al-Rafidun*, pp. 31–32.

90 Ibid., pp. 42–44 and 48; and, Mahfuz, *Alladhina Zulimu*, pp. 83, 120–23, 222, 233 and 242.

91 'Abud al-Zumar, Third Document, in *Al-Rafidun*, pp. 113–21; and Mahfuz, *Alladhina Zulimu*, pp. 226, 254, 267–68, 271 and 273.

92 Fifth Document, *Al-Rafidun*, pp. 150 and 160–64; and 'Abd al-Khabir, "Qadiyyat al-Ta'aduddiya," pp. 118–20. See also Sa'id, *Qadaya Fikkriyya*, pp. 30–31. Sixth Document, *Al-Rafidun*, pp. 165, 169 and 173–74. On the organization itself, see Rif'at Sayyid Ahmad, *Al-Nabiy al-Musallah: Al-Tha'irun*. (London: Riad al-Rayyis Books Ltd, 1991), pp. 185–86.

93 "Wathiqat 'I'lan al-Harb 'ala Majlis al-Sha'b," *Al-Tha'irun*, pp. 187–89. For a description of how this organization views each political party and the political system in Egypt, see pp. 193–97.

94 "Wathiqat Muhakamat al-Nizam al-Misri," *Al-Tha'irun*, pp. 273–75 and see pp. 290–91 where the diverse kinds of rulers are specified. On similar views see "Wathiqat al-'Ihya' al-Islami" from *Jama'at al-Jihad al-Islami* written by Kamal al-Sa'id Habib, pp. 199–229. On *Tanzim al-Jihad* and its splits and offshoots, which are many and numerous, see Mahfuz, *'Alladhina Zulimu*, pp. 213–83.

95 *Al-Safir*, 25 September 1993, p. 10 and *Al-Diyar*, 25 September 1993, p. 14.

96 Yahya Sadowski, "The New Orientalism and the Democracy Debate," *Middle East Report*, July–August, 1993: 19.

Chapter 5

The ideologization of Islam: meaning, manifestations and causes

Mir Zohair Husain

Introduction

The "ideologization of Islam" is the reaffirmation of Islam as a political idiom in which Islamic symbols, ideas, and ideals are cultivated by practitioners – Islamic revivalists or Islamists – both enlightened and misguided, reactionary and revolutionary, pacifist and violent, rulers and opposition groups. The ideologization of Islam, whereby Islam becomes a comprehensive political ideology, has been referred to in the scholarly literature and in the popular mass media as Islamic revivalism, Islamic reassertion, Islamic resurgence, political Islam, Islamic fundamentalism, Islamism, and in a myriad other ways.

The ideologization of Islam that we are witnessing today encompasses at least five prominent features. First, the spread of Islam from homes, *masjids*, and *madrassahs*, into the mainstream of not only the sociocultural life of Muslim societies, but the legal, economic and political spheres of the modern-day Muslim states as well. There is an increase in the attendance of Muslims of all walks of life at *Jum'ah* (Friday) prayer services and during the annual *haj* to Mecca in the twelfth Islamic calendar month of *Dhul-Hijj*. There is an increase in *zakat* contributions and the veiling of women. Islamic organizations have increased their lobbying activity to ban alcohol, gambling, night clubs, prostitution, pornography and a number of other corrupting influences. Islamists are also pressuring their respective governments to formulate an Islamic constitution and implement the *shariah* which includes severe penalties for a broad spectrum of crimes. In response to the Islamists, Muslim governments, even those run by securalists, are displaying their Islamic credentials by stepping up *masjid* construction and increasing their funding of *masjids* and *madrassahs*.

91

Second, the ideologization of Islam is contributing to the wide-spread debate of Islamic issues in the mass media and resulting in the proliferation of numerous scholarly books and enlightening articles on Islamic subjects. More importantly, this reassertion of political Islam produces efforts at the reformulation and revision of Islamic theory and practice in light of contemporary times.

Third, coming at a time of great disparity of wealth between wealthy elite and the impoverished masses, as well as the socio-political injustice in most Muslim societies, Islam's emphasis on socioeconomic equality and justice has significant populist appeal. In fact, this appeal is one of the most important features in the current reassertion of political Islam.

Fourth, the ideologization of Islam reasserts the relevance of the Islamic approach to solving contemporary problems, while at the same time presenting a critique of the dominant materialist values imported from the West or the Socialist-Communist world. For instance, secularization is especially denounced by Muslim Funda-mentalists and Traditionalists as "un-Islamic" because it implies that, *Almighty Allah* and His Guidance, are relegated to the personal domain of an individual's life, and that the larger political, economic and sociocultural areas should be independent of His influence. Most contemporary Islamic revivalists are eager to accept modern scientific methods and technology from anywhere in the world. However, they are adamantly opposed to, and totally reject, whatever they perceive as "un-Islamic" and harmful to the *umma*.

Lastly, Islamic revivalist movements have strong anti-imperialist and anticolonialist undercurrents. The Islamic revivalists call for an end to international dependence on Western and/or Communist powers. Instead, they desire the development of a united Islamic bloc of fraternal Muslim nations, which in turn could become an influential force in international relation for the good of the *umma*.

There are three prominent manifestations of the ideologization of Islam. The most dramatic and revolutionary manifestation is a groundswell resurgence – involving a broad public spectrum of the Muslim society for an Islamic political system. This has been referred to in the scholarly and popular literature as an "Islamic resurgence" and as "populist Islam." The world has witnessed an Islamic resurgence in Iran and Afghanistan since the late 1970s, and in Algeria, Tajikistan, and the Indian state of Kashmir since the early 1990s. The second major way in which the ideologization of Islam manifests itself is in the ceaseless effort of Islamic movements, parties, and interest groups to establish an Islamic political system. Examples of Islamic organizations striving to establish Islamic systems include the *Ikhwan al-Muslimin* (Muslim Brotherhood), Islamic Liberation Organization, *Jama'at al-Jihad* (Holy War Society), *Takfir wal-Hijra* (Repentence and Flight), *Jund Allah* (Army of God), and *al-Gamaa al-Islamiya* (the Islamic Group) in Egypt; *Jamaat-e-Islami* (the Islamic Association) in Pakistan; *Hizbullah* (the Party of God), *Amal* (Hope), and Islamic *Amal* in Lebanon; *Harkat al-Muqawama al-Islamiya* (Islamic Resistance Movement or HAMAS/Zeal) and Islamic *Jihad* in the Gaza Strip and the West Bank; the Islamic Salvation Front (FIS) in Algeria; the Islamic Tendency Movement (MTI) and *Ennahda* (the Renaissance Party) in Tunisia. The third principal way in which the ideologization of Islam is manifesting itself in the Muslim world is from above, in the form of government-sponsored Islamic policies and programs. The most prominent examples of political Islam being imposed from above are the theocratic regime of Iran, the House of Saud in Saudi Arabia, Colonel Mu'ammar Qaddafi's regime in Libya, Burhanuddin Rabbani's Islamic regime in Afghanistan, General Omar Hassan al-Bashir's National Democratic Alliance in Sudan, and General Muhammad Zia-ul-Haq's military regime in Pakistan (1977–88). The ideologization of Islam is also employed by regimes in Muslim countries to appease influential domestic movements, parties and interest groups; enhance governmental legitimacy; assist in the integration of a fragmented society; and/or acquire funds from rich Muslim countries. The most vivid examples of the latter were the regimes of Muhammad Ja'far al-Numayri in Sudan (1969–85), Prime Minister Zulfikar Ali Bhutto (1971–77), and President Muhammad Anwar al-Sadat (1970–81).

Historically, the ideologization of Islam has occurred in cycles followed by periods of relative dormancy. The current phase of the ideologization may well have started with the humiliating defeat of the Arabs in the 1967 Arab-Israeli war. It gathered much momentum during and after the 1973 Arab-Israeli war and OPEC's oil-price increases. The ideologization of Islam fueled Iran's 1978–79 Islamic Revolution and the concurrent "Islamization" campaigns in Pakistan and Sudan. It was responsible for the 444–day long "hostage crisis" in the US Embassy in Tehran, the assassination of Egypt's President Anwar al-Sadat, and contributed to turmoil in Lebanon. It chased the well-equipped Soviet imperialists from Afghanistan and is an important element in the civil strife in many countries around the world, including Algeria, India, Russia, Tajikistan, Egypt, Tunisia, Sudan, and the Israeli-controlled West Bank to mention but a few.

However, the ideologization of Islam today, differs markedly from the politicization of Islam in the past in several respects. First, the current reassertion of political Islam is not merely a localized or even regional phenomenon, but global in scope. This universality of the ideologization of Islam has been a significant development in international relations and can be explained by the links that bind the world together in ways often unknown in the past. The revolutions in communications, transportation, and computerization have drastically shrunk the world in both time and space. Significant occurrences anywhere in the world may be communicated through CNN almost instantaneously. Furthermore, the establishment of non-governmental and transnational Islamic organizations, like the Organization of the Islamic Conference (OIC) or the *Ikhwan al-Muslimin*, have spread Islam's populist message to Muslims the world over.

Ironically, while our interconnected and interdependent world heightens the probability of Islam's politicization in many parts of the world through the international demonstration effect, it also insures that the contemporary ideologization of Islam is neither monolithic nor homogeneous, but polycentric, pluralistic, heterogeneous, and multifaceted with as many aspects as there are Islamic groups. For instance, the current ideologization of Islam, unlike the past, is a product of the action, reaction, and interaction of at least four categories of Muslim groups, namely: the Muslim Fundamentalists, Traditionalists, Modernists, and Pragmatists (non-practicing Muslims who use Islamic rhetoric and symbolism). In this respect, the reassertion of political Islam is hardly conducive to the creation of a unified Muslim *umma* (brotherhood of Muslims) or united Islamic bloc. Nevertheless, the ideologization of Islam progresses each day with greater vigor and vitality than the day before. The many faces of political Islam have prevented the Islamic reassertion from being discredited as a whole. Thus, the ideologization of Islam has remained a popular idiom of political activity among Muslims, and is perpetuating itself into an uncertain future. Any action taken by secular and corrupt Muslim despots (or non-Muslims) to contain or suppress the revival of political Islam, will only serve to continually strengthen the ideologization of Islam in the eyes of frustrated and angry Muslims the world over.

There is no question that a closer examination of the ideologization of Islam is warranted. The size and potential power of the Muslim world, although currently a "house divided," is demonstrably important for any student of international relations. Muslims number

1 billion people, a little less than one-fifth of humanity. They constitute a majority in over fifty countries, a substantial minority in another seven countries, and a sizeable minority in at least nine others. While present throughout the world, exhibiting numerous cultures, and speaking as many different languages, Muslims are most heavily concentrated in Asia, where they constitute 68.3 per cent of the population. Africa comprises the second greatest concentration of Muslims, where they constitute 27.4 per cent of the population. Muslims countries are active participants in a number of international organizations, such as the Organization of Arab Petroleum Exporting Countries (OAPEC), the Organization of Petroleum Exporting Countries (OPEC), the Arab League, the Organization of African Unity (OAU), the Association of Southeast Asian Nations (ASEAN), the Group of 77, the Organization of the Islamic Conference (OIC), Non-Aligned Movement (NAM), and the United Nations to mention the most prominent.

A better examination of the ideologization of Islam is further merited by the proximity of the Muslim world to seven strategically important sea routes, namely, the Mediterranean Sea, the Bosphorus, the Black Sea, the Suez Canal, the Red Sea, the Persian Gulf, and the Straits of Malacca. This region contains innumerable raw materials, produces nearly half the oil consumed in the West, and controls two-thirds of the world's known oil reserves. Owning an exhaustible and vital international commodity – for which there are countless uses and no immediate substitutes – has greatly empowered the ten predomi-nantly Muslim nations in the twelve-member Organization of Petroleum Exporting Countries (OPEC). Moreover, the Muslim world also possesses a substantial pool of inexpensive labor, and is a lucrative market for goods and services. Consequently, significant political changes in this world interest and concern the interdependent international community. Sadly, the West thus far has discouraged any political change which might threaten a "satisfactory" status quo in an area of such vital importance. The ideologization of Islam represents just such a destabilizing change.

Reasons for the ideologization of Islam

Some hallmarks of Islam make it an ideal political ideology

Islam is a vehicle for political change in the Muslim world because it is a "historical religion," an "organic religion," a religion that emphasizes socioeconomic equity and justice, and a faith that stresses *jihad* (holy struggle). As a "historical religion," Muslims consider history as divinely ordained and believe that Islam explains the beginning and end of human history and the direction it will take. Moreover, Islamists interpret success and failure as indicative of divine grace or anger, respectively. Furthermore, Islamists have also always tried to build a political and socioeconomic order based on principles laid down not only in Islamic theology, jurisprudence, and the *Shariah* (Islamic law), but in specific historical precedents set by Prophet Muhammad and his first four "rightly-guided caliphs."

Islam is an "organic religion" possessing a comprehensive belief system because the divine and immutable *Shariah* incorporates the temporal within the all-encompassing spiritual realm and has something to say about every aspect of a Muslim's life. Islam is a holistic religion in which no distinctions exist between the world of individual worship and community government, between the realm of religion and the realm of politics. The Quran enjoins Muslims to get involved in politics because politics determines the shape of society. Moreover, Islamists believe that only politics based on robust Islamic foundations can be honest, just, and beneficial to all. Islam sets forth universal principles of human behavior in all its aspects. These principles are binding on Muslims and provide for them an answer in all areas of human endeavor. When secular ideologies and systems cannot answer the significant and urgent political, economic, social, and cultural grievances of Muslims, there is always recourse to the ideologization of Islam.

Socioeconomic equity and justice enjoy paramount importance in Islam. There are frequent references in the Quran to justice, fairness, truth, piety, as well as economic and social equality. The Prophet Muhammad repeatedly emphasized the importance of justice and frequently stated that all are equal before Allah and His divine laws on earth, whatever their race, color, sex, creed, and social, economic, or political status. This emphasis is in marked contrast to secular political ideologies that in the Muslim world have led to the increasing misery of the population and the growing gulf between the elite (that keeps growing richer) and the (masses that keep getting poorer). In Islam, all are equal in the eyes of God and none goes unpunished for a crime. Furthermore, Islam provides for specific measures in which socioeconomic equity and justice are to be ensured and safeguarded. This emphasis on equity and justice has greatly enhanced the attraction of political Islam in a Muslim world where equity and justice are notably absent.

Central to an understanding of the ideologization of Islam is the pivotal importance of *jihad*, which literally means "to exert oneself to the utmost" or "to struggle in the way of God." Indeed, the achievement of justice is possible in Islam through the application of *jihad*, a term much maligned and misunderstood. Three categories of *jihad* exist in Islamic theology: personal, *ummaic*, and martial. Personal *jihad* is a non-violent struggle waged by Muslims to purge themselves of their base desires and evil impulses. *Ummaic jihad* is a non-violent struggle for freedom, human rights, socioeconomic justice and equity within the *dar al-Islam* (realm of Islam/Muslim community). Martial *jihad*, the least favored in the eyes of God, and the last resort of Muslims according to the Quran, is an armed struggle fought to protect, defend, and promote the integrity of Islam and the *umma* against hostile unbelievers, whether they are invading armies or "un-Islamic" internal despots. However, what *jihad* represents to most Muslims, particularly *ummaic jihad*, is the peaceful means for realizing socioeconomic justice and equity in the Muslim world. Nevertheless, martial *jihad* gains proponents in proportion to the oppression of political Islam in the Muslim world and to the increasing impossibility of non-violent *ummaic jihad* in the face of such oppression. *Jihad* is popular among Muslims because of the Quranic promise that a *mujahid* (the devout Muslim who fights in a *jihad*) who dies while fighting a *jihad*, will earn the title of *shaheed* (martyr) and be rewarded with *al-Jannah* (Paradise). Unfortunately, the misapplication of martial *jihad* has given the term, as well as Islam itself (where *jihad* plays so pivotal a role) a bad name.

It is the aforementioned hallmarks of Islam that are the keys to understanding why Islam lends itself to politicization. No wonder, in every Muslim community there exists, always has existed, and will always exist, an individual or a group of Muslims who will ideologize Islam. Those in power will make Islam an instrument to enhance their interests and those in the opposition will make Islam an idiom of dissent against shared injustice and inequity. Political Islam, however, need not be violent or revolutionary. It has operated sufficiently well within a democratic context for example, and many Islamists have worked and continue to work within that context with mixed results. In many cases, however, it is the war waged by secular Muslim regimes and non-Muslim governments, against Islamists, that has tended to radicalize Islamists, Islamic organizations, and political Islam.

Four categories of Islamic revivalists

The ideologization of Islam is not merely the work of Muslim Fundamentalists, as the mass media and scholarly preoccupation with Islamic fundamentalism suggests, but the compound effect of the dynamic action, reaction, interaction, and synthesis of the ideas and ideals of four "pure types" or "ideal-typical" categories of Muslim individuals and groups: the Muslim Fundamentalists, Traditionalists, Modernists and Pragmatists. All four types of Islamic revivalists propagate their perception of the "true" Islam and attempt to win over the hearts and minds of the Muslim masses. The combination of all four strands of the Islamic message contribute to the revitalization and reassertion of political Islam. The first three types of individuals and groups can be called "Islamists" because they are devout Muslims and frequently, but not necessarily, promote the creation of an "Islamic state" by teaching, preaching, and/or writing, and on rare occasions even by the force of arms. The fourth category of "Islamic revivalists," namely, the Pragmatists, are not sincere in their practice of Islam, but merely exploit it to further their interests.

Fundamentalists

Muslim Fundamentalists constitute the largest and most conspicuous category of Islamic revivalists or Islamists. They are referred to as "scripturalists," "legalists," and "literalists" because they advocate rigid adherence to the fundamentals of Islam, as literally interpreted from the Quran and the *Sunna* (Prophet Muhammad's sayings and deeds). They often strive to establish an Islamic state based on the rigorous implementation of the *Shariah* and insist that the five *faraidh* (duties) be scrupulously adhered to by all their co-religionists.

Some scholars have called Muslim Fundamentalists the "Puritans" of Islam because many of them would like to purify their religion of all the "unholy," "impure," and "permissive" values, customs, traditions, and institutions that have become part of the faith since Islam's classical period (the era of Prophet Muhammad and his close companions). For instance, Fundamentalists zealously crusade against *taqlid* (unquestioning conformity to legal rulings that developed during the middle ages), secularism and secularization. Sunni Fundamentalists, especially adherents of the Hanbali *madhab* (sect), are so rigorous in their narrow interpretation of *tawhid* (Allah's Oneness) that they regard the veneration of saints, holy men, and even the glorification of Prophet Muhammad and his extended family as *shirk* (polytheism). Indeed, this is why the radical Sunni Fundamentalist Wahhabis of the Hanbali school invaded Shi'ah Islam's holiest cities of Najf and Karbala in 1802 and demolished a number of tombs, mausoleums, and shrines built in the memory of Islam's heroes.

Muslim Fundamentalists have also been called "restorationists" and "restitutionists" because they constantly strive to recreate an Islamic state founded on the same fundamental principles as the first Islamic state which was established in 622 AD by Prophet Muhammad in Madina (and then continued by the *Khulafah-i-Rashidin*: the first four rightly-guided caliphs-Abu Bakr, Umar, Uthman, and Ali). In fact, they try their very best to closely emulate Prophet Muhammad and the pious *aslaf* (Prophet Muhammad's companions).

Moderate Fundamentalists in the late twentieth-century (such as Iran's President Ali Akbar Hashemi Rafsanjani), unlike radical Fundamentalists (such as Muhammad Ahmad Abdallah al-Mahdi or the Mahdi of Sudan in the 1880s), are willing to embrace what they perceive as beneficial modern values that conform to the basic tenets of Islam. For example, although they wish to follow the revered body of *Shariah*, they are willing to interpret the letter of the law more broadly than in the past. Many, though certainly not all Fundamentalists in the modern period, have come to accept the Western notions of democracy: periodic elections on the basis of one vote for every adult person, a multiparty political system, secret balloting, a national assembly or parliament to pass laws for the entire nation, and good relations with non-Western countries, provided those relations are based on mutual respect and the non-interference in each other's internal affairs.

Some of the most prominent Muslim Fundamentalists in Islamic history are Muhammad ibn Abd al-Wahhab who, together with Muhammad ibn Saud, launched the Wahhabi movement in the Arabian peninsula in the late eighteenth century; Sudan's Muhammad Ahmad Abdallah al-Mahdi, who established an Islamic state in Sudan in 1885; Egypt's Hassan al-Banna, who established one of the first populist, urban-oriented, and transnational religiopolitical organizations in the Muslim world in 1928; and Ayatollah Ruhollah Khomeini, who contributed to Iran's Islamic Revolution (1978–79) and established the first Islamic state in modern times.

Traditionalists

Muslim Traditionalists constitute the second category of Islamic revivalists or Islamists. The products of traditional *madrassah* (Islamic schools) education, Traditionalists are often drawn from the ranks of the devout and learned *ulama* (Islamic scholars), and are just as opposed to secularism (the religious neutrality of the state) and the increasing secularization of society (the institutional separation of Islam from politics and the governmental system), as the Fundamentalists. In the educational sphere, the Traditionalists, like the Fundamentalists, demand the generous funding of *madrassah*s; advocate syllabi that contain mainly Islamic disciplines; and promote the segregation of the sexes and extreme modesty in dress in educational institutions. In the legal sphere, both Traditionalists and Fundamentalists demand an Islamic constitution drawing heavily upon the Quran, the *Sunna*, and the *Shariah*, and the establishment of Islamic law courts presided over by *qadhi*s (Islamic judges) and based on the *Shariah*. In the social realm, the Traditionalists, like the Fundamentalists, encourage monogamy while at the same time allowing Muslims who meet certain criteria to have up to four wives; and enjoin women to adopt *purdah* (veiling, segregation and seclusion). In the economic sphere, both advocate the institution of the *zakat* and *ushr* taxes, as well as the prohibition of *riba* (usury).

However, Traditionalists and Fundamentalists also have major differences. While Muslim Fundamentalists ceaselessly crusade for these beliefs and are often in the vanguard of the ideologization of Islam, Muslim Traditionalists disdain political activism and are generally detached, non-violent, apolitical Islamic scholars, teachers, and preachers. No wonder Traditionalists are often perceived by many Muslims as having been co-opted by Muslim regimes to support the status quo. But when Islam or the *umma* – whether at local, regional, or global levels – appear to be in imminent danger, Muslim Traditionalists have temporarily abandoned their passivity and vigorously asserted themselves in the political arena.

Furthermore, unlike the Fundamentalists, the Traditionalists conserve and preserve not only the Islamic beliefs, customs, and traditions practiced in the classical period of Islam, but also those of subsequent Islamic periods. They are tolerant of sufism and numerous local and regional customs and traditions commonly referred to in the aggregate as "folk Islam" or "popular Islam." Traditionalists believe that Islam is not merely a set of abstract and utopian principles, but a comprehensive and living belief system that interacts with the historical and cultural traditions of devout Muslims. To suppress these traditions, therefore, would be to weaken the popular form of devotion of the Muslim majority. The Fundamentalists, in contrast, are often opposed to "folk Islam" and discourage its practice as essentially un-Islamic.

Most Sunni Traditionalists are staunch opponents of *ijtihad* (which encourages independent thought in legal matters) and committed proponents of the dogma of *taqlid*. For the Traditionalist *ijtihad* represents an attack on traditional values and practices and therefore, undermines Islam.

While Muslim Traditionalists are respectable Islamic scholars, they are often naive, if not ignorant, of modern natural and social sciences. If they read modern scientific theories at all, they either accept or reject these themes according to the Quran and the *Sunna*. Muslim Traditionalists are generally oblivious to the complexities, institutions, and processes of modern governments and international relations in an interdependent world (although they do not perceive this ignorance as a shortcoming). They are convinced that the perfect religion of Islam, in which they are well versed, reveals all truths and can help to resolve all internal crises and external threats facing Muslim societies around the world. For Muslim Traditionalists, Islam has not, cannot, and should never change, for it is founded on God's immutable words and laws. Consequently, they argue that immutability is not the cause of the Muslim world's decline, but rather, that the problem arises from the Muslim world's inherent imperfections, and because Muslims have not steadfastly followed the letter and spirit of the religion.

One of the most prominent Muslim Traditionalists was Iran's Ayatollah Sayyid Kazem Shariatmadari (d. 1986). Other prominent Traditionalists were the Farangi Mahallis, Barelvis, and Deobandis on the Indian subcontinent. Many of the *mufti*s (Islamic theologian-jurists who issue *fatwa*s or authoritative decrees) and *shaykh*s (Islamic scholars) of Al-Azhar in Cairo could also fall into this category. For example, Shaykh Ali Gadd el-Haqq, the seventy-nine year old Traditionalist *alim* of Al-Azhar, who died in Cairo on 15 March 1996, was a supporter of government policies.

Modernists

The third category of Islamic revivalists or Islamists are the Muslim Modernists, also known as "adaptationists," "apologists," "syncretists," and "revisionists." The Modernists are devout and knowledge-able Muslims whose mission is to redefine and reinterpret Islam in a rational and liberal manner; emphasize the basic ideals of Islamic brotherhood, tolerance, socioeconomic equity, and political justice; and to interpret the teaching of Islam in such a way as to bring out its dynamic character in the context of the intellectual and scientific progress of the modern world.

Modernists, like Fundamentalists, feel the primary causes in the decline of Islamic culture and power are the inhibition of independent, creative, and critical thought, and the lack of vigorous discussion about Islamic laws and issues. Convinced that Islam is a progressive, dynamic, and rational religion, the Muslim Modernists denounce the inhibiting dogma of *taqlid* and advocate utilizing *ijtihad* to reinterpret and reformulate Islamic laws in the contemporary light of modern thought. Indeed, they feel dynamic change in Islam is not only possible, but desirable. Therefore, according to most Modernists, Islamic laws must be carefully revised to be flexible and adaptable enough to incorporate modern political, economic, social, cultural, and legal conditions.

In addition to being devout Muslims who are enlightened about Islam, Modernists are also knowledgeable about modern non-Islamic (especially Western) ideas, to which they are exposed in their formal and/or informal education, either in their homeland or abroad. Consequently, unlike the radical Fundamentalists and conservative Traditionalists, Modernists do not fear or dislike non-Islamic ideas and practices, but welcome them if they are able to help Muslim societies. No wonder Modernists are constantly endeavoring to reconcile differences between traditional religious doctrine and secular scientific rationalism, between unquestioning faith and reasoned logic, and between the continuity of Islamic tradition and modernity. Their imaginative synthesis of Islamic and Western ideas tends to produce a reasonable and relevant reinterpretation of Islamic thought with enlightened cosmopolitan, liberal, and realistic perspec-tives. For instance, Modernists are profoundly concerned about the divisions and frictions between the various *madhab*s (sects) and therefore tend to spend considerable time and effort advocating Muslim reconciliation and unity. Their tolerance for diversity and their willingness to adjust rapidly to a changing environment contributes to the emancipation of the individual Muslim and to the progress of Muslim societies.

Some of the most prominent Muslim Modernists are Jamal ad-Din al-Afghani (1838–97) of Persia/Iran; pre-partition India's Sir Sayyid Ahmad Khan (1817–98); Egypt's Muhammad Abduh (1849–1905), who became the grand *mufti* of al-Azhar's; pre-partition India's Muhammad Iqbal who conceived of Pakistan and encouraged the Muslim League leadership to pursue the establishment of such a homeland; Iran's Ali Shariati (1933–77), the intellectual father of modern revolutionary Shi'ism, who contributed significantly to Iran's Islamic revolution (1978–79); Mahdi Bazargan (b. 1905), the first interim president of Iran under Ayatollah Khomeini; and Abulhassan Banisadr (b. 1933), the first popularly elected president in Ayatollah Khomeini's Islamic Republic of Iran.

Pragmatists

Comprising the fourth and least religious of Muslim groups that tend to engage in the ideologization of Islam are the Muslim Pragmatists. Generally Muslims by name and birth, the Pragmatists are nominal Muslims with a veneer of a liberal and eclectic version of Islam. They are influenced by their formal and informal secular Western education and experiences at home and/or in the West, and consequently are more knowledgeable about Western intellectual thought than Islamic thought. This background makes them view Islamic doctrines and practices as anachronistic and impractical for contemporary purposes. They concern themselves with the dynamic modernization of their societies, adopt concepts and ideologies from both capitalist and socialist countries, and display an interest in addressing realities in a non-religious and pragmatic manner. Though at times pressured by the Islamists to promote and defend the faith, they often prefer a state whose guiding principle is secularism, and believe that the secularization process is part of modernization and therefore, not only inevitable, but desirable.

Though a minority in all Muslim societies, the Muslim Pragmatists wield a disproportionate degree of wealth and power. They are in the upper echelons of their governments' civil service and armed forces. They are heavily represented in the mass media, educational institutions, business community, among the landlords and throughout a broad spectrum of other professions. They are aware of events in their country and in the world at large, and comprise the most assertive and vocal segment of their societies.

While Muslim Pragmatists comprise the privileged class, they shrewdly and hypocritically point to Islam's emphasis on equality, and its aversion to the formation of any privileged class (including a priestly one) which fosters elitism and encourages differentiation between men. According to the Pragmatists, the *ulama* are experts in the Islamic religion only, and are therefore fully entitled to impart their invaluable religious guidance in the affairs of the state. However, in economic, political, technical, international, and non-Islamic legal matters, the *ulama* cannot claim the right to impose their viewpoint on the nation. Muslim Pragmatists are pleased that Islam does not give a privileged status to the *ulama* in the governance of Muslim societies and iterate the view that there is no institutionalized clergy in Islam, but that all Muslims are responsible to God for their thoughts and deeds.

Ironically, Muslim Pragmatists often find it expedient to use Islamic rhetoric and symbolism to capture the support of the Muslim masses despite their essentially secular worldview and their firm conviction that religion is a personal affair between man and God. In the short run, their use of Islamic rhetoric and symbolism allows them to gain or enhance their legitimacy, integrate and unite their fragmented Muslim societies, and inspire and mobilize the Muslim masses. But in the medium to long run, the politics of Islam in which they so astutely engage to win over the masses and consolidate their power, leaves them exposed and vulnerable to the whirlwind of the mass-based Islamic movement.

The five most prominent Muslim Pragmatists who contributed to Islamic revivals were Pakistan's founding father, Muhammad Ali Jinnah, in the 1940s; Sudan's President Jafar al-Numeiri in the first half of the 1980s; Pakistan's Prime Minister Zulfikar Ali Bhutto during the 1970s; Egyptian President Muhammad Anwar al-Sadat during the decade of the 1970s; and Iraqi President Saddam Hussein during Operations Desert Shield and Desert Storm (August 1990–March 1991).

Failure of secular ideologies espoused by secularists and pragmatists

Following the independence of Muslim societies from colonial rule, Muslim secularists (those who adhere to secular territorial national-ism, secularism, and secularization), and Muslim Pragmatists (those who have the same worldview as the secularists, but merely use Islamic rhetoric and symbolism), were the first to fill the power vacuum left by the departing colonial administrators. The euphoria of independence from the West initially endeared the Muslim secularists and Pragmatists to the masses, and they were enthusiastically swept into power on the basis of unrealistic promises. However, the incompatibility of poorly implemented government modernization programs, with traditional Islam, has deeply alienated the masses over time. After imposing secular socialism, secular capitalism, or a mixture of both, the Muslim secularists have failed to deliver on their promises of economic, social and political development.[1] Even the rapid economic growth registered in some Muslim countries has mainly gone to a privileged elite, not significantly benefiting the disappointed and impoverished masses.

The Muslim secularists and Pragmatists espoused the Western idea of nationalism to integrate and unify their fragmented societies, and to consolidate political power. However, nationalism has further divided the Muslim world as a whole, while the leadership of Muslim nations pursue national interests at the expense of the *umma*. In the interests of *realpolitik*, Muslim natins ignore brethren in distress e.g., whether starving in Somalia and Bangladesh, or victims of genocide in Bosnia-Herzegovina and Chechniya, or suffering oppression under tyrannical Muslim regimes such as those in Algeria and Tajikistan, or bearing Israeli assaults in the West Bank and Southern Lebanon, or suffering the indignities of being classified as "terrorist states" such as Iraq, Iran, Libya, and Sudan.

The ideology of pan-Arabism pursued by secularists to rectify the failure of narrow national interests enjoyed popularity in the 1950s and 1960s, but lost favor when Arab Muslims realized that pan-Arabism was a thinly disguised extension of secular nationalism promoted primarily by those leaders who sought to dominate the entire Muslim world. Anyway, pan-Arabism neither unified the Arabs against Israel, nor settled the Palestinian problem. Pan-Arabism was discredited first by the Arab defeat in the 1967 Arab-Israeli war, second by its failure to increase trade and commerce between Arab nations, and third by the failure of Arab governments to break the bonds of dependency with the West or, in a few cases, with the Communist bloc.

The secularists and Pragmatists have also failed to fulfill their post-independence promise of implementing liberal, parliamentary democracy. Of all Western values and ideologies, this is the first to disappear from their modernization policies. Most regimes in the Muslim world are authoritarian; some are as callous, oppressive, and tyrannical as prior colonial regimes.

Nor have the secularists and Pragmatists delivered on their promised post-independence utopia of genuine independence and sovereignty. Their desire to modernize has retarded any process of breaking dependency relationships with the West. Instead, modernization programs have reinforced dependency.

The secularization process promoted by the secularists throughout the Muslim world in the name of modernization has not brought the development they promised their citizens. Instead, secularization has merely resulted in the transplantation of alien Western institutions, laws, and procedures that have eroded the traditional and holistic system of Islam, and have thus created an acute identity crisis. Not surprisingly, in those states where secularists have most aggressively pushed secularization, Islam has become the primary idiom of political protest. For example, in Algeria, Tunisia, Egypt, and Tajikistan the Islamic backlash smolders despite, and ironically because of the efforts of, those secular regimes to crush it by force.

In brief, the Muslim secularists and Pragmatists have failed to deliver on the inflated promises they made at the time of independence. Moreover, the failure of their imported secular policies and programs is resulting in the masses demanding the "Islamic alternative" as the answer to their socioeconomic and political ills. Seeing the Islamic trend sweep their country and the rest of the Muslim world, Muslim Pragmatists are exploiting Islamic rhetoric and symbolism in domestic and foreign policy in an effort to shore up their wavering support. However, Muslim Pragmatists are not perceived as the devout "born-again Muslims" they portray themselves as, but are seen as hypocrites and opportunists not to be trusted. Therefore, instead of undermining, co-opting, and appeasing the more sincere Islamic revivalists or Islamists, the Muslim Pragmatists, with their grossly hypocritical manipulation of Islam, end up strengthening political Islam as an idiom of anti-government dissent and fanning flames of an Islamic revivalism that could very well destroy them.[2]

The simultaneous occurrence of several developmental crises

In contrast to the West where modernization, secularization, and democratization occurred gradually, modernization in the Muslim world occurred very rapidly and, occassioned five developmental crises simultaneously, namely: those of identity, legitimacy, participation, penetration, and distribution. These crises have profoundly destabilized Muslim societies and completely overwhelmed Muslim governments.[3]

Identity crisis

A major factor that has contributed to an identity crisis among many devout Muslims today is the preeminent place that the *umma* occupies in Islamic theory. The *umma* in Islam implies that Muslims all over the world are brothers and sisters despite their history, region, culture, color, language, or socioeconomic and political status. Both the Islamic notion of *umma* and the alien, Western, secular notion of territorial nationalism involve a peoples' sense of "we-ness," togetherness, peoplehood, group identity and group loyalty due to shared heritage. Both demand the prime loyalty of their followers. However, "nationalism" attempts to engender solidarity among the diverse people living within the territorial boundaries of a particular Muslim nation-state. Being indoctrinated to love one's country from an early age, people in countries all over the world are influenced, manipulated, and even coerced into being/becoming patriotic, owing their allegiance to their government, and fighting for their country's national interests. The Islamic *umma*, on the other hand, rises above narrow national interests and is concerned with improving the welfare of and forging a sense of solidarity among, Muslims all over the world. While this pan-Islamic vision seems utopian and difficult to achieve today, it nevertheless is the dream that figures prominently in the Islamist's worldview.

The apparent primacy of the identity crisis suggests a failure of nation-building and political development. Unlike Europe and America, the Muslim world was initially conceived as a single political and religious unit. The creation of nation-states from the dismemberment of this unit was an artificial and arbitrary contrivance of the colonial powers; it was not wholly consensual. Consequently, the resulting false borders were rejected as truly legitimate among Muslims. This rejection has been exacerbated by the oppressive and ineffectual leadership of Muslim secularists who regard the nation-state and national interests as preeminent and want their countrymen to do likewise. Sincere Islamists wish to unify Muslims under the universal law of the *Shariah* and the banner of the universal *umma* or pan-Islamism. At the other extreme, community units smaller than the nation-state are more likely to arise – units based on family, a religious sect, a tribe, a clan, etc. But whether the pull is toward utopian Islamic universalism or toward narrow Islamic parochialism, the pull is decidedly away from the nation-state.

The identity crisis in the Muslim world is also being fueled by the massive rural to urban migration. Muslims leaving their extended families and the familiar surroundings of their villages are experiencing a "culture shock" in the "urban jungle." Their security and identity is threatened by such problems as finding and keeping a job; paying for the high cost of living; experiencing the selfishness, materialism, anonymity, alienation, and crime prevalent in the cities. For Muslims, this identity crisis often draws them closer to the religion into which they were socialized as children. Their religion acts as an anchor in times of acute uncertainty, a "security blanket" that alleviates their terrible fears, and gives them solace, stability, direction, and hope that things will turn out well in the future.

Legitimacy crisis

A political regime and/or system that does not enjoy the trust and goodwill of the governed, enjoys no legitimacy, and is forced to resort to increasing degrees of coercion to maintain itself in power. The chronic legitimacy crisis in the Muslim world is the result of immense differences in values between the rulers and the ruled. The governing secularists and Pragmatists are often educated, Westernized, and secularized. In contrast, the masses are far less educated, far more steeped in Islam, and thus not on the same wave-length as their leaders. Islam permeates the culture of the Muslim masses and conflicts with the Western-oriented modernization, secularism, and secularization of society that the Muslim leaders have pursued since independence from Western colonial rule. Hence the secularists and Pragmatists are unable to legitimize their rule, mobilize their populations behind their policies and programs, or integrate their profoundly fragmented multi-ethnic citizenry. Lacking mass support, they are ever vulnerable to overthrow. Thus, to stay in power, they have resorted to a mixture of secular indoctrination, co-optation, and coercion. However, oppression only further polarizes the power elite from the governed and accentuates the legitimacy crisis.

Penetration crisis

The penetration crisis refers to the chronic problem faced by central governments of all Muslim countries to enforce their decisions at the grass-roots level. This process of state-building is associated with the emergence of a centralized bureaucracy with increased coercive capacity to effectively enforce national authority, secure public compliance, and govern the society.

All political systems are created and controlled by the governing elite. The problem of penetration, then, is one of identity and legitimacy. The penetration crisis can be resolved only by bridging the conspicuously wide gulf between the governing elite and the governed citizenry so that the developmental needs of the country can be met. This task in the developing Muslim world is particularly formidable as the ambitious modernization programs of the governing elite far exceed the comprehension of people accustomed to old parochial ways. The wide "cultural gap" or "cultural cleavage" which impedes any resolution of the legitimacy crisis, also impedes leaders from either developing a rapport with the people they govern, legitimizing their rule, or reaching down to the grass roots level to change old values and behaviors. Hence, the secularists and Pragmatists are unable to motivate and mobilize the Muslim masses behind their essentially secular modernization programs.

Distribution crisis

The ultimate gauge of a government's political performance is its management of the distribution crisis in terms of national security, general socioeconomic welfare, and individual liberties. The distribution crisis is compounded in the Muslim world by the population explosion which contributes to a chronic shortage of resources (such as food, drinking water, clothing, housing, education, health care, consumer goods, and electricity), leads to the chronic overcrowding of cities and towns, contributes to the sharp rise in the cost of living, greatly reduces the opportunities that job seekers will have obtaining relevant training and employment, and accelerates ecological degradation. A shortage of food, consumer goods, and services creates inflationary pressures that make the attainment of food, goods and services more expensive, and thus less accessible to the needy majority, more of whom slip into the category of the "absolute poor" every day.

Likewise, the distribution crisis is accentuated by the problem of "relative deprivation," which causes sociopolitical instability. After all, people act aggressively, and even violently, not only because they are poor and deprived in an absolute sense, but because they feel deprived relative to others, or relative to their own expectations. Rebellions and revolutions may also occur when a society, having enjoyed a prolonged period of expectations and rising gratifications, suddenly experiences a sharp reversal. A period of rapid growth may have heightened people's expectations of continuing improvement in their lives. Thus, when a sudden reversal occurs, the gap between the accelerating expectations and the realities of plummeting gratifications is far more distressing and intolerable than if the reversal had followed a period of relative stagnation. These accumulated and intolerable frustrations eventually seek violent outlets. If frustration and bitterness have been festering for a long time and are sufficiently widespread, intense, and focused on the established regime in power, violence may explode into a revolution that displaces the ruling regime, undermines the old and discredited power structure, and radically transforms the entire society through coercion and attendant bloodshed. If the outbreak of violence is not focused, intense, or widespread enough, the result may merely be a coup at the apex of power, or government oppression. In the latter case, potential rebels may choose to live with their frustrations rather than endure job loss, long prison terms, torture, or execution. Just as often, the government partially addresses the grievances of the discontented masses.

In Muslim societies today, the distribution crisis is particularly chronic because the gap separating the rich and powerful few, from the poor and powerless majority, has grown wider. Since the Islamic faith emphasizes socioeconomic equity and justice, does not separate religion from politics, and even permits the believer, under certain specific circumstances, to engage in a *jihad* against injustice and tyranny, Islam is easily politicized by the poor, disenfranchised, exploited, frustrated, and alienated Muslim masses to challenge the governing elite.

The participation crisis

Relative political deprivation, or the participation crisis, occurs when the governing elite does not accommodate the aspirations and expectations of citizens to participate in the political system. The participation crisis in the Muslim world has increased over the last decade because Muslims are politically conscious of the vibrant and prosperous democracies in the West and the democratization occurring in the non-Muslim Third World. The grass roots pressure for increased participation in the Muslim world is contributing to

Muslim regimes becoming more autocratic as they struggle to stay in power. Sometimes the participation crisis will cause a military *coup d'état* or, more rarely, a broad-based revolution.

The participation crisis is often related to the legitimacy and penetration crises. Legitimacy often becomes untenable either under conditions of severely limited participation, which is common in the Muslim world, or under conditions of widespread participation occurring outside existing political institutions. Excepting controlled forms of pluralism and democracy in Pakistan, Bangladesh, Malaysia, Turkey, Jordan, Lebanon, and Turkey, there are no other functioning democracies among the remaining forty-four predominantly Muslim countries.

These five unresolved crises have bred dissatisfaction with present governments, caused widespread unrest, and renewed faith in political Islam as an appealing alternative. The disappointed, frustrated, and alienated Muslim masses have turned away from the neo-Western ideologies of the secularists and have returned to Islam as an anchor in a turbulent and unpredictable world. Although the Pragmatists began employing Islamic symbolism to garner support, they have been perceived as hypocrites and their cynical use of Islam has only further legitimized the Islamic "backlash" to their rule.

Four case studies of the failure of secular ideologies and the five developmental crises: Iran, Sudan, Lebanon, and Algeria

Iran

Iran is a representative example of a country that experienced all five developmental crises simultaneously, and with such elevated intensity, that the compound mixture reached "critical mass" and exploded in an Islamic Revolution in 1978–79. Iran's Reza Shah Pahlavi initiated a process of very rapid modernization incompatible with the traditional Islamic way of life. In turn, the Shah aggravated the five crises of development. He permitted no political participation in his monarchical system and thus delegitimized himself and his government. The Shah fostered a revolution of rising expectations, but failed to insure the just and equitable distribution of resources and goods to all Iranians – the Shah's policies and programs benefitted the upper middle class far more than it did the masses. The rapidity of the Shah's modernization programs also caused massive dislocation in the countryside. The cities were suddenly filled with a teeming population of job-seeking peasants and ex-farmers. This dislocation, and the consequent frustration and alienation felt by most Iranians, engendered a crisis of identity that left Iranians angry with the Shah's government and looking for meaning and direction in life. Moreover, the Shah's reign was further undermined by the singular place in Iranian society of the Shi'ah clerical establishment. Overwhelmed by the developmental crises, the Shah fled and his regime collapsed. The Ayatollah Khomeini representing the "Islamic alternative," assumed power and promised to reverse the pro-Western policies of the Shah and establish a "true" Islamic state.

Sudan

Sudan, like Iran, is experiencing all five developmental crises at once. However, the identity crisis is particularly acute. Southern Sudan, which is primarily Christian and animist, does not identify itself with the predominantly Muslim north that governs Sudan. The overwhelming majority of those living in Southern Sudan resent the authoritarian control exercised by the largely Muslim army in the north and have waged guerrilla warfare for autonomy for over two decades. The situation worsened in the late 1970s when Sudan's Muslim Pragmatist President Ja'far al-Numayri imposed the *Shariah* and started an aggressive "Islamization" program. Though Numayri was overthrown in a military coup in 1985, subsequent Sudanese regimes continued his Islamization program. The current military regime headed by President Omar Hassan al-Bashir has appointed several prominent Islamists in the National Islamic Front (dominated by the *Ikhwan al-Muslimin*) to high level government positions, and is seriously committed to instituting Islamic policies and programs and making Sudan an Islamic state. Unhappy with the current Sudanese regime's Islamic worldview and its refusal to participate in Operation Desert Storm, the West and the conservative oil-rich Arab kingdoms of the Persian Gulf have stopped most of their aid to Sudan. This abrupt discontinuation of aid, coupled with the US government's efforts through the UN Security Council to isolate Sudan in the world community (like it has done with Iran and Libya) on the unsubstantiated grounds of "aiding and abetting terrorism," has further aggravated and compounded all five developmental crises in this impoverished and polarized Muslim country.

Lebanon

The two decades long civil war in Lebanon can be attributed to the convergence of the five developmental crises. First, this predominantly Muslim country has been controlled by the Christian minority since it gained its independence from the French colonialists. Over time, the Muslim population grew at a faster rate than the Christian's, while individual Muslims became more conscious of both their Islamic identity and the state of their relative deprivation *vis-à-vis* the governing Christian elite. Second, the Palestine Liberation Organization (PLO), targeted by King Hussein's army in Jordan, escaped into Lebanon after September 1970. The PLO and their families were initially treated as refugees by the Lebanese Shi'ahs of South Lebanon but, by the late 1970s, not only came to control the Shi'ah heartland of the South Lebanon, but were perceived by the Lebanese to be a state within the state of Lebanon. The identity crisis worsened after the Israeli invasion of Lebanon in 1982. Initially, the Shi'ah majority welcomed the Israeli invaders as liberators. Yet when the Israelis, like the PLO, overstayed their welcome and victimized the Lebanese Shi'ahs, the Shi'ah majority of Lebanon, emboldened by the successful Islamic Revolution in Iran, rose up and challenged an unjust *status quo*. The fact that the poor country of Lebanon is a complex mosaic of different ethnic groups has complicated its tragic fate. After all, the divided Christian elite, the fragmented Palestinians, the Sunnis, the Druze, and the polarized Shi'ah – with Muslim Modernists such as Nabih Berri, who heads the Amal (Hope) organization and even enjoys a ministerial position in the Lebanese government, on the one hand, and radical Muslim Fundamentalists, represented by the pro-Iranian, Islamic movements of the Islamic Amal and Hizbullah on the other – are all proud of their identity, highly politicized, and heavily armed. As if these divisions and rivalries were not bad enough, the Lebanese system is also deeply penetrated by large powers, such as the US and France, and regional powers, such as Syria, Israel, Iran, and Saudi Arabia. Each external power manipulates its surrogates in the Lebanese system to do its bidding, often to Lebanon's detriment. The penetration of the Lebanese system by outsider powers has greatly destabilized the fragile ethnic balance of a once peaceful and prosperous country, and has contributed to the prolongation and exacerbation of the civil war that tore the country asunder. Although the civil war subsided in the early 1990s, Lebanon continues to be plagued by all five developmental crises; they will be difficult to alleviate.

Algeria

Algeria has also been rocked by all five crises since the late 1980s. Beginning with the massive uprisings that occurred in October 1988, in which more than 600 people were killed and over 10,000 were injured, the military regime of President Chadli Benjedid relented and by February 1989, announced its decision to adopt a multi-party system. This was the first time since Algeria's independence from France in 1962 that Islamic groups were allowed to organize themselves into political parties. The Islamic Salvation Front (FIS) consistently stressed its plan to establish an Islamic state. The FIS won 55 per cent of the vote in the June 1989 regional elections, and 49 per cent of the vote in the first round of the general election held on 26 December 1991. In fact, the FIS won 188 out of 430 seats in the national legislature and needed only an additional 28 (out of 199 seats) in the second round of the run-off voting held on 16 January 1992. The secular socialist National Liberation Front (FLN), on the other hand, won only fifteen seats in the Algerian parliament because the ruling party that had governed Algeria since independence, was perceived by the Algerian masses as guilty of authoritarianism, corruption, nepotism, close ties with France (Algeria's unpopular former colonial master), and above all, the gross mismanagement of an economy suffering from 100 per cent inflation and 25 per cent unemployment. Western leaders, and Pragmatists in the Muslim world, were shocked that the Islamists walked away with almost half the national vote, despite competition from forty other political parties. Algeria's secular military elite fearing a victory by the Islamic Salvation Front would result in the loss of their positions, privileges, and comfortable lives at the very minimum, pressured President Benjadid to resign and began to crack down on the FIS. On the day Algerians were to celebrate the occasion of the Arab World's first genuine multiparty democracy, the army called on Muhammad Boudiaf – a hero from Algeria's war of independence against France, who had just returned to Algiers after three decades of exile in Morocco – to head the army-backed, five-member "collegial presidency," and run the country in place of the elected leaders until new elections were held. Boudiaf was assassinated in early July 1992 and today the country is in even worse shape under President General Liamine Zeroual. In fact, according to several sources, as many as 40,000 Algerians may have lost their lives in the civil war that erupted just after the aborted election in mid-January 1991.[4]

The Masjid's role in fostering political Islam

Since there are few democratic institutions or processes in Muslim societies through which the masses can vent their deeply felt grievances, or from which they can expect justice, the *masjid* seems to be filling this institutional void. Prophet Muhammad is believed to have strongly urged congregational prayer, especially on Friday afternoons. Disallowing Friday congregational prayers would cause a furor among worshipers. Moreover, *masjids* in the Muslim world often require no government license to operate and so authoritarian Muslim governments refrain from closing them down or sheeding blood therein. Because *masjids* are, to a certain degree, immune from blatant government repression, the *masjid* has become the focal point of antigovernment opinion in many Muslim countries. Numerous Muslim clerics, following the example of Muhammad, utilize the sacred premises of the *masjid* not only to worship God, but as a political platform from which to enlighten, influence, and mobilize the faithful to political action. Some clerics deliver sermons sharply critical of government policies, programs, and leadership. Thus, the clerics in the Muslim world have risen to positions of leadership in opposition to unpopular and tyrannical secularist and Pragmatist regimes and their corrupt and unrepresentative political institutions. This clerical class largely has not imbibed Western intellectual thought, has not traveled abroad, and can speak no Western languages. Therefore, when the clerics communicate with the people in the Islamic idiom, they are seen as sincere, unlike the Pragmatists. These Islamic revivalists have risen repeatedly throughout Islamic history, leading mass movements against foreign imperialists and domestic despots perpetuating injustice. The last two decades represent a cyclical renewal of this Islamic revivalism. The Fundamentalists and the Traditionalists, often insulated from direct government control in the *masjids*, have effectively used potent Islamic concepts of *khurooj* (the right to revolt against an unjust and tyrannical ruler), of *jihad*, and of *shahadat* (martyrdom attained in a *jihad*) to agitate and mobilize the Muslim masses against regimes throughout Islamic history.

Aware of the lessons of this history, the Pragmatists have not stood idly by in the face of *masjid*-instigated antigovernment activity. The possibility of spontaneous demonstrations, following congregational prayer, are thwarted by the ubiquitous presence of government troops within sight of the *masjid* entrance. Many Muslim regimes have taken this strategy a step further and have attempted to exercise direct control over urban *masjids* by appointing the *imams* who deliver the *khutbahs* (sermons). Despite these efforts, the dynamism of political Islam is undampened, the clerics undeterred, and the mosque remains a safe haven for antigovernment opposition.

The Arab-Israeli conflict

The Arab-Israeli conflict has also contributed significantly to the ideologization of Islam. The failure of either Arab regimes, or the secular Palestine Liberation Organization (PLO), to defeat Israel, has reinforced an inferiority complex among Arab and Palestinian Muslims, discredited secular and Pragmatist Arab regimes devoted to the defeat of Israel, and has contributed to an Islamic backlash to perceived Western neo-colonialism through the Israeli "surrogate." Thus, the conflict, still unresolved after fifty years, is fueling the ideologization of Islam by playing upon anti-imperialist feelings among Muslims, and by underscoring the incompetence of any but purely Islamic regimes in the region.

Israel's spectacular victory over Arab forces, in merely six days, during the June 1967 War was a watershed for the global revival of political Islam. After so much boasting and bravado, the Arab World's political giant, Egyptian President Nasser, in the space of a week, discredited himself and his secular ideology of "Nasserism." Islamic groups throughout the world were quick to ascribe the humiliating defeat of the Arabs to the emphasis on the fashionable secular ideologies of the Muslim world's political and economic elites. Political Islam, it was increasingly claimed, could defeat the Israelis – a conclusion bolstered by the improved showing of the Arabs against the Israelis in the 1973 War, when Islamic rhetoric and symbolism was used.

It is also rather ironic that both, explosive conflicting events, and dramatic peace agreements between the Arabs and Israelis, have contributed to furthering the ideologization of Islam on the world stage. This was especially true after the June 1967 Arab-Israeli war when the Islamic revival began in Egypt. After growing and spreading throughout the Middle East for the next six years, the revival of political Islam got much media attention during the 1973 Yom Kippur/Ramadan War. Then, the Israeli invasion of Lebanon in the summer of 1982 contributed to vigorous reassertion of Islam, particularly in Lebanon, but more generally in the entire Muslim world – as television pictures of that invasion were broadcast all over the world. Israel's periodic bombing of Southern Lebanese villages and towns by air, sea, and land, for much of the 1980s and the 1990s, has kept the ideologization of Islam in Lebanon simmering and continues to strengthen political Islam in the Muslim world.

One would think that Arab-Israeli peace agreements would dampen the rise of political Islam, but they seem to have had the opposite affect. Egyptian President Muhammad Anwar al-Sadat's trip to Jerusalem in November 1977, and the 1979 Camp David Peace Treaty between Sadat and Israeli Prime Minister Manachem Begin, were widely condemned by the *umma* as a sell-out and a betrayal of the Arab and Muslim cause. Thus, Sadat's efforts at peace with Israel may have actually reinforced the reassertion of political Islam, not only in Egypt, but in the Middle East at large. Just as Sadat lost his leadership of the Arab World, and then his life, to radical Muslim Fundamentalists, so too is Arafat in danger of losing his life to Muslim Fundamentalists as a result of the Declaration of Principles for limited Palestinian self-rule in Gaza and parts of the West Bank. Many Palestinians in the Israeli-occupied territories, and in the diaspora, see the Arafat-Rabin handshake on the White House lawn in September 1993 as a "raw deal" for the Palestinians. Thus, the Arafat-Rabin "land for peace agreement" has greatly swollen the ranks of radical Palestinian Islamic organizations such as Hamas and Islamic *Jihad*.

With the Hebron massacre of Palestinian worshippers in Ibrahimi Mosque on 25 February 1994, the revival of political Islam in the West Bank and the Gaza Strip gathered greater momentum. Prime Minister Yitzhak Rabin's assassination by a Zionist terrorist in November 1995, and the assumption to power of his predecessor Shimon Peres, did not end the cycle of violence. Hamas' military arm, the Qassam Brigades, launched a spate of suicide bombings in major Israeli cities, killing nearly sixty Israeli civilian and wounding many more. Prime Minister Peres retaliated by intensifying the Israeli government's war against Hamas. Moreover, Hizbullah's commando raids against Israeli troops in Israel's so-called "security zone" in Southern Lebanon, and Hizbullah's katusha rockets fired into Israel, evoked massive Israeli retaliation against Southern Lebanese villages. Despite Peres' attempts to create the impression that he was tough against "Arab terrorism," Israeli's gave his opponent, Benjamin Netanyahu, a victory in the May 1996 elections. Netanyahu appealed to Israeli fears and promised to be far tougher against the Arabs. This new development does not auger well for the hobbled "peace process." The overwhelmingly superior Israeli government forces will probably overtly suppress the intifadah in the West Bank. However, Israeli policies against the Palestinians are bound to undermine Yasser Arafat's Palestine National Authority (PNA) and fuel an Islamic resurgence in the Gaza Strip and West Bank. The major question is: will the Israeli Defense Forces (IDF) be able to crush the Islamic resurgence that is going to sweep the Israeli-occupied West Bank, or will the Jewish-Muslim crusade make the West Bank ungovernable and therefore an unbearable liability for Israel?

OPEC's impact

The predominantly Muslim Organization of Petroleum Exporting Countries (OPEC) established in 1960, did not flex its muscles until the early 1970s. It was Libya's leader Colonel Mu'ammar Qaddafi's success in demanding larger revenues and higher taxes from foreign oil companies operating in Libya, that was soon repeated by other members of OPEC. Then came the 1973 Yom Kippur/Ramadan War, which was soon coupled with the Organization of Arab Petroleum Exporting Countries (OAPEC) oil embargo against Israel's allies in the West. The resulting oil shortage put an upward pressure on oil prices.

The oil price explosion that the world witnessed from 1974 to 1982, when OPEC flexed its economic muscle in the aftermath of the 1973 Arab-Israeli War, fueled the fires of political Islam on several levels. First, OPEC was perceived by Muslims the world over as having broken the bonds of prostrate dependency on the West. Second, OPEC's rapid modernization resulted in rapidly escalating expectations, unprecedented socioeconomic dislocation, and immense uncertainty. Third, the Muslim member governments of OPEC (especially, Saudi Arabia, Libya, Kuwait, the United Arab Emirates, and Iran) donated much aid to poverty-stricken Muslim countries, gave a number of financially strapped Muslim countries a discount on oil, purchased food and had it distributed among starving Muslims around the world, financed a number of Islamic organizations (movements, parties, and interest groups both at the grass roots level and in the corridors of power in the Muslim world), built *masjid*s and *madrassah*s, and distributed Quran's and other Islamic literature to the *madrassah*s. The worldwide *umma* interpreted OPEC's success during the "oil boom" years as Allah coming to the assistance of His "chosen people."

However, initial satisfaction and indeed, euphoria in the Muslim world, for the apparent successes of OPEC, were short-lived and tempered by the realization that OPEC, with the exception of Iran and Libya, represented *status quo* powers uninterested in revolutionary Islam. The governments of many Muslim countries complained that they were promised far more by their oil-rich brethren than they received. Moreover, OPEC's dramatic oil price increases contributed to increased inflation, followed by higher interest rates and recession. All three of the aforementioned economic problems plagued the oil-poor Muslim countries many times more than it did the developed Western world, and resulted in the Third World becoming far worse off than before the oil price explosion. Furthermore, the glut of oil and subsequent decline in oil prices in 1982, combined with the effort by OPEC member-states to sell more oil than their OPEC-allotted quota, the Iran–Iraq War, Operations Desert Shield and Desert Storm, and the division within OPEC ranks between pro- and anti-Western member states, led to the decline of OPEC's decade-long influence on the world stage.

OIC's Role

The 1969 burning of the Al-Aqsa Mosque in Israeli-occupied Jerusalem infuriated Muslims around the world and led to the establishment of the Organization of the Islamic Conference (OIC) that same year. Dedicated to principles of Islamic solidarity, the OIC has contributed to the Islamic revival by institutionalizing the lost but never forgotten Islamic dream of the universal *umma*.

Like OPEC, however, the promise of the OIC has not yet been realized. There is a widespread perception in the Muslim world that the OIC has failed to protect and defend the rights of the *umma* by, among other things, having failed to achieve their principal objective of getting Israel to withdraw from all the Arab territories captured in the 1967 war and restoring the legitimate rights of the Palestinian people; having done nothing to stop the periodic Israeli aggression in Lebanon or the rapid growth of Israeli settlements in the West Bank; having failed to prevent two disastrous Persian Gulf wars; having been impotent to prevent the starvation of Muslims in Somalia or the massacres of Muslims in Bosnia-Herzegovina, Chechniya, India, Algeria, Israel, Burma, and other parts of the Muslim world; and finally, having failed to unite the Muslim world and improve the lot of the *umma*.

Despite its shortcomings, the very existence of the OIC is both the result of, and a contribution to, the global Islamic revival. Its affiliated institutions, like the Islamic Development Bank, have shown Muslims around the world the potential power of an Islamic bloc dedicated to Islamic politics. Nevertheless, Islamic revivalists are encouraged ever onward to fulfill the potential inherent in pan-Islamism and institutionalized by the OIC.

The Islamic revolution in Iran

The implications of Iran's Islamic Revolution extended far beyond its borders. It is a classic case study illuminating the causes of Islamic resurgence. The new Islamic regime, under the leadership of the Ayatollah Khomeini, signified a watershed in world history, and its repercussions shook both West and East. Seizing the attention of all Muslims, the Iranian Revolution became the "source of emulation" for Islamists and Islamic organizations throughout the world. Inspired by its success, stirred by its utopian appeal to pan-Islam and against both the capitalist West and the communist East, Islamists were emboldened to bring about Islamic revolutions in their countries. On the other hand, Muslim secularists and Pragmatists trembled at the triumph of the Islamic Revolution. Western analysts, in turn, perceived a new threat to Western hegemony in the "crescent of crisis" – the specter not of fascism or communism, but of revolutionary political Islam.

The significance of Iran's Islamic Revolution for the ideologization of Islam throughout the Muslim world is simple: the Iranian Revolution was the Islamic movement that toppled a secular, Western-looking government "in the name of Islamic purification." For Muslims around the world, and especially for Islamists and Islamic organizations that continue to endure the heavy hand of governmental oppression, the success of Iran's Islamic Revolution in the face of palpable Western hostility, was an inspiring and heartening experience that greatly accelerated and fortified the global Islamic reassertion.

The US embassy hostage crisis

The fall of the Shah and the "loss" of Iran was traumatizing for the West. The US government was thoroughly unprepared to deal with the new Islamic regime in Tehran, especially one headed by Shi'ah Muslim clerics. Worse than that, however, the US totally undermined the chances of US-Iranian reconciliation after the Islamic Revolution by permitting the Shah to enter the US for medical treatment on advice from Henry Kissinger and David Rockefeller. By admitting the Shah into the US, President Carter stoked the paranoia of the Iranian people who remembered the role of the US in the 1953 ousting of Mossadegh. Playing on this paranoia, Khomeini called on the Iranian people to protest the Shah's admittance into the USA. Three million Iranians marched on the US embassy on 1 November 1979. Three days later, hundreds of young Iranians militants stormed the embassy and took US diplomats hostage. So powerful was the image of Iranians attacking the US embassy that similar attacks were made against US diplomatic offices in Libya and Pakistan.

The radical Iranian youths in control of the US embassy in Teheran accused the US of spying in Iran and of supporting the Shah while he massacred protesters, tortured political prisoners, squandered and plundered the nation's wealth, and introduced Western values at the expense of Islamic values. Although originally detaining ninety persons in the US embassy, the hostage-takers released all non-US hostages, all African-Americans, and all women (except one). The remaining fifty-two were branded as spies and held prisoner for 444 days. The "hostage crisis" enraged and humiliated the US and became a lesson in the limits of US power. The inability of the US, the world's foremost military and industrial power, to expeditiously resolve the crisis or pressure a mere Third World Muslim country into submitting to its demands, sobered Americans. The world watched, captivated and bewildered, as the drama of the "hostage crisis" dragged on and on. Never before had the US appeared so absolutely helpless, particularly when, in April of 1980, the Carter administration bungled a military rescue attempt to free the hostages. America itself was held hostage by militants in Teheran. The sight of US powerlessness, in turn, encouraged Islamists around the world and terrified Muslim Pragmatist leaders. The realization dawned that if the radical ideologization of Islam could paralyze the US, imagine what it could do to "un-Islamic" regimes in the Muslim world itself.

The hostage crisis poisoned Iranian relations with the outside world. The USA and its Western allies successfully used the United Nations and the Western mass media to portray Iran as a "pariah state", and isolated it in the world community for its breach of international law. Nevertheless, the spectacle of the hostage crisis amazed Muslims throughout the world as they saw the Khomeini regime act courageously (some say "imprudently"), defiant in the face of a preeminent superpower equipped with the most advanced military technology, and perhaps nuclear arsenal, in the world. Khomeini's gamble, by supporting the hostage-taking, was a big one. However, when the US attempt to free the hostages failed, in an Iranian desert sandstorm, Islamists were convinced that the tide was turning against the West at last and that God was fighting in Iran's corner.

The Soviet invasion of Afghanistan

Another dramatic international event in the late 1970s that contributed to the ideologization of Islam, was the Soviet invasion of Afghanistan. The armed struggle of the Afghan *mujahidin* (holy warriors) against the Soviet colonizers, for the entire decade of the 1980s, did much to discredit both the Soviet Union and their ideology of Marxism-Leninism, in the Muslim world.

The Soviets were perturbed and concerned about Iran's Islamic Revolution and Ayatollah Khomeini's revolutionary Islamic message spreading among the over forty million Muslims who inhabited the vulnerable underbelly of the Soviet Union. They were also worried that the Communists who had come to power for the first time in Afghanistan's history, in April 1978, were endangered by another radical Islamic movement. Therefore, in order to prevent the downfall of the Communist regime, and to crush the budding Islamic revolutionary movement in Afghanistan, the Soviets sent some 80,000 troops into Afghanistan in late December 1979.

Much of the world united in condemning the Soviet invasion of a poor and weak Third World Muslim country. The Afghan *mujahidin* were treated favorably in the Western and Muslim mass media as a group of devout Muslims fearlessly resisting a ruthless, atheistic superpower's attempts to subjugate them, bravely matching their inadequate and antiquated weapons against the modern brute force and sophisticated weaponry of the Sovjets. by brute force and sophisticated weaponry. Their crusade gave birth to an Islamic resurgence in Afghanistan and inspired Muslims all over the world.

The Rushdie affair

Even the publication of Salman Rushdie's *The Satanic Verses* in 1988 and Ayatollah Khomeini's subsequent death sentence on the author contributed to the ideologization of Islam. The Muslim world was infuriated by Rushdie's novel because the Muslim author, among other things, used the name "Mahound," the insulting epithet given by medieval Christians to Prophet Muhammad to discredit Islam; insinuated that the "businessman-turned-prophet" manufactured the Quran for his own benefit under "Satanic" influence; and, thus, that the holiest book of Islam was not the revealed word of God, but a work of clever forgery. He also named twelve prostitutes after Prophet Muhammad's wives. Rushdie's novel was an affront to devout Muslims because it violated Islam's core beliefs and defamed its last prophet.

To Westerners and Muslims alike, the Rushdie controversy warranted outrage, but for different reasons. Westerners viewed Muslim attempts at censorship as an affront to principles of freedom of speech and expression. While an overwhelming majority of Muslims perceived Rushdie as a traitor, and wanted his book banned on the grounds that it was an obscene attack on the central beliefs of Islam and the *umma*. After all, the two worlds have different conceptions of treason: in a secularist's worldview a traitor is someone who betrays his country and its citizenry, while in an Islamist's religiopolitical worldview, a traitor is a Muslim who betrays Islam and the umma. While the Western mass media, with an eye to the sensational, portrayed all Muslims as narrow-minded and anti-democratic religious fanatics demonstrating against Rushdie and even burning his book, Islamists perceived Western attempts to glorify Rushdie and promote his novel as the continuation of a 1,400 year-old cultural crusade against Islam. In fact, the Islamists were incensed that the West bestowed upon Rushdie the right to blaspheme Islam and slander its one billion believers, while the right of those one billion believers to apply their community standards against Rushdie's heretical, hate-inspiring book, were denied.

Evidently, Rushdie's *Satanic Verses* represented only the latest in a series of perceived Western-instigated affronts to Muslims and their Islamic faith. Just as the West had used the Rushdie controversy to vilify Islam and ridicule its alleged "medievalism," so did radical Islamists on the same basis justify their rejection of Westernization and secularization as evils inherently incompatible with the "straight path" of Islam. The Rushdie controversy did not occur in a vacuum, but must be considered in the context of the growing ideologization of Islam. In fact, Muslim Fundamentalists, like Khomeini, utilized the Rushdie book to galvanize mass support against Western influence and against the Muslim secularists and Pragmatists governing Muslim societies. By extrapolation then, the Rushdie controversy is not merely a manifestation of the ideologization of Islam, but has positively contributed to its strength and popularity.

Conclusion

The ideologization of Islam is not the "green peril" or dangerous specter that the sensationalist Western mass media has made it out to be. In fact, the Muslim world – which is developing, divided, weak, and vulnerable – has much more reason to feel threatened by the West's economic, technological, political, military, and mass media dominance.

Western analysts and policy makers often overlook the curious history of good relations with Islamists, even with Muslim Fundamentalists. Sadly, when Westerners think of Islamic fundamentalism, their memories inevitably focus on Iran in the first years of its revolutionary rage or on Lebanon in thick of its civil war. The West forgets its good relations with Zia-ul-Haq's Fundamentalist regime in Pakistan, with several Fundamentalist Afghan *mujahidin* factions fighting Soviet colonialism during the 1970s in Afghanistan, with Sadiq al-Mahdi's moderate Fundamentalist Sudanese regime, and with the moderate Wahhabi Fundamentalists of Saudi Arabia and Qatar. Even Iran, under President Hashemi Rafsanjani – a Moderate Fundamentalist Shi'ah cleric – has made positive steps to improve relations with the West. Rafsanjani pressured Lebanese hostage-takers to release all Western hostages, maintained Iran's neutrality during Operation Desert Shield and Operation Desert Storm, and is opening Iran to Western multinational corporations. Is fundamentalism that terrible or frightening an enemy? Is it inherently an enemy at all?

In any event, radical fundamentalism, in the name of any religion, is historically short-lived after its empowerment. Sustaining revolutionary fervor, when the revolution has already succeeded, is all but impossible. Cultural revolutions, whether on the Chinese or Iranian models, become tiresome to the average citizen and are a drain on popular support. However, when external or internal forces threaten the regime, as Iraq threatened Iran during the 1980s, the revolutionary spirit is prolonged. Furthermore, when external forces crush fundamentalist movements as a matter of policy in the Muslim world, such movements are proportionately popularized and radicalized. Religion and nationalist passions are easily inflamed when "imperialist" powers meddle in the Muslim world. Sadly, this has been exactly the policy of the US. The Iranian revolution burned hotter and brighter directly as the result of US meddling and a war of aggression, supported by the US among others, perpetrated against Iran by Iraq. There was no better way to guarantee that the revolution would be radicalized, uncompromising, and militantly anti-American.

The Cold War with the communist world has ended, but the West is inexplicably embarking on a new Cold War against not communism, but Islamism or Islamic fundamentalism. Any authoritarian regime that promises to do the West's bidding and keep the fundamentalists at bay, receives Western aid. During the 1980s when Iraq invaded Iran, Western policy was blatantly pro-Iraq. After all, the West wanted to contain and undermine revolutionary Iran. However, the moment Saddam Hussein invaded non-Fundamentalist Kuwait, the West turned against the "Butcher of Baghdad." Saddam Hussein had not changed. He was the same old butcher that the West knew and supported. Yet when he fought Iran at least he was "our" butcher. When he invaded pro-Western Kuwait, he became "the new Hitler." We wonder why the people of the Muslim world decry the Western double-standard?

In the short run the West must "rehumanize" the Muslim world. Only through education is this possible. High schools and universities throughout the Western world often give short shrift to the Muslim world in educating its young. Both Western schools and the Western mass media need to dispel stereotypes of Muslims, not perpetuate them. After all, the West is barely knowledgeable about Islam, a religion whose adherents account for one in five human beings on the planet. For this reason alone, a closer and more equitable treatment of Islam is warranted. It is in school and through television that Westerners form negative opinions of Islam and thus, it is through school and television that these opinions can be tempered by the realistic portrayal of Muslims as human beings, not as terrorists, oil-sheiks, and religious fanatics.

To create better understanding between the West and the people of the Muslim world, Western governments should employ experts on Islam and the Muslim world. Employing Muslim citizens of Western countries might also improve relations with the world of Islam. In any event, recognizing the central place of Islam in the cultures of Muslim countries, and in the Islamic revival, will avert unnecessary misperception and misinterpretation of a region strategically so important to the West.

The West must stand up for human rights not only by turning its back on tyrannical regimes that oppress its own people, but by applying standards evenly and without regard to short-term interests. By condemning all who violate human rights and perpetrate abuse on their neighbors and countrymen, the West can better serve its long-term interests; that is, it can earn the trust and the friendship of the people of the world.

The foreign policy agenda of Western powers must be more in line with post-Cold War reality. The West must abandon the possibility of getting into a new Cold War with the Muslim world. Instead, the West must attack some of the real problems facing mankind in the twenty-first century: appalling poverty, starvation, disease, and inequality in the Third World; serious environmental hazards, drug smuggling and addiction, proliferation of weapons of mass destruction, radical ethnonationalism, and terrorism around the world. These enemies are truly worthy adversaries against which we must struggle. By concentrating on the new Cold War against Islam we lose time, money, and energy. Such a Cold War, unlike the last one, is purely a figment of our collective imagination, a bogeyman with which to scare children.

Notes

1 The example of secular socialism implemented in the Communist world has disappointed the Muslim masses because they have learned more about the lack of political, economic and social freedoms prevalent in the Communist bloc. Moreover, Muslim elites have also stopped looking at Socialism and Communism as ideologies to emulate because the former Soviet-dominated Communist bloc itself has renounced and repudiated Communism. The Muslim masses, however, have been equally disappointed by the example of secular capitalism practiced in the West. Many Muslims feel that capitalism breeds excessive greed, exploitation of man by man, individuality, materialism, hedonism, and inequality, while lacking compassion for the poor and needy.

2 Fouad Ajami, *The Arab Predicament: Arab Political Thought and Practice Since 1967.* (Cambridge: Cambridge University Press, 1981), p. 171.

3 Lucien W. Pye. *Aspects of Political Development.* (Boston: Little, Brown and Co., 1966); Lucien W. Pye and Sidney Verba. *Political Culture and Political Development.* (Princeton: Princeton University Press, 1965); Lucien W. Pye. *Politics, Personality and Nation Building: Burma's Search for Identity.* (New Haven: Yale University Press, 1962); Leonard Binder, James S. Coleman, Joseph LaPalombara, Lucien W. Pye, Sidney Verba, and Myron Weiner, eds. *Crises and Sequences in Political Development.* (Princeton: Princeton University Press, 1971); Raymond Grew. "The Crises And Their Sequences," in Raymond Grew, ed. *Crises of Political*

Development in Europe and the United States. (Princeton, New Jersey: Princeton University Press, 1978).

4 Alfred Hermida, "Algeria: Fundamentalists Sweep to Near Victory," *Middle East International,* 10 January 1992: 7–9; "Algeria: An Alarming No Vote," *Time,* 13 January 1992: 28; "Fundamentalist Leaders Reported Arrested in Algeria," *The New York Times,* 20 January 1992: A-3; Stephen Budiansky, "Democracy's Detours: Holding Elections Does Not Guarantee that Freedom will Follow," *US News & World Report,* 27 January 1992: 49; Howard La Franchi, "Algeria's Leadership Chooses Head of Ruling Council," *The Christian Science Monitor,* 16 January 1992: 3; "Algerian Islamic Parties," *The Minaret,* Vol. 10, No. 3, Summer 1989: 36.

Chapter 6

Islamic activism in Egypt, 1974–1996

NematAllah Adel Guenena

Introduction

The title of the conference "Islam in a Changing World", and of this chapter confirm the interactive nature of the relation that exists between the world as a whole and each of the events and phenomena that together form the sum of its parts. Islam, or rather "Islamic activism", is the subject of concern here. It is affecting the world order, shaping it, and being affected by it. While the religion as a belief system is not the issue, its use as an idiom to express social malaise and discontent is causing quite a stir among the international community. This is evidenced over the past two decades by the abundance of literature which has emerged and the number of colloquiums that are being held to discuss the possibilities and modalities for a rapprochement between cultures and religions.

A main difference between Islamic activism and other "so-called" fundamentalist movements or related incidents which have occurred in the USA, Europe, Japan, and elsewhere, is that the manifestations of Islamic activism have transcended national and regional boundaries and are perceived to have infringed on values and rights related to civil society, democracy, and even on the sovereignty of individual nations.[1] Consequently, in most of the countries having experienced repercussions of the phenomenon, people are being called upon to revise their world view and to question many of its givens.[2]

The call for the mobilization of international efforts to combat terrorism is an acknowledgement of the need to band together to confront such intrusive ideological manifestations. Moreover, while focusing on security measures, this rallying call invokes the necessity for collaboration on more than one front, namely diplomacy and economic aid. On the diplomatic front, greater transparency is envisaged in the dialogue between nations as a result of depersonalizing the enemy, i.e., terrorism and terrorists instead of Islam and Muslims, and linking collaborative efforts to peace and prosperity.[3] On the economic front, the issue linked to development entails sustained commitment to aid, often accompanied by a more accommodative schedule for debt repayment. Furthermore, the rising numbers of permanent migrants, especially Muslims, in America and Europe entails significant political, economic, social, and cultural implications that are forcing a number of countries in these continents to revise their laws particularly those relating to citizenship – as well ways to establish a more harmonious relationship between co-existing cultures. Germany, the United States of America, and France are cases in point. To accommodate the ever-increasing influx of migrants, Germany has been obliged since the 1990s to revise its hard-core citizenship requirements; and both the US and France are currently revising their citizenship laws. In addition, in both the USA and France (long-known as immigrant nations), a debate is taking place concerning the need to integrate migrants as opposed to assimilating them. This has come to be considered by many as constituting cultural aggression.

Finally, it is becoming increasingly clear that further knowledge and understanding are needed in order to diffuse the tension and turmoil that characterizes the relationship between the North and the South. While comparing expressions of Islamic to other forms of religious activism at local, regional and international levels would contribute to demystifying much of what is believed to be the impending "advent" or "march" of Islam,[4] the findings hereby presented refer mainly to the Egyptian case (the reason being that while such comparisons are necessary, they should nevertheless be based on a recognition of the differences characterizing such movements in the region and elsewhere). Consequently, the objective of the research endeavour behind these findings is to examine the behaviour and intellectual discourse of Egyptian Islamic activists, thereby adding to the empirical knowledge base related to the phenomenon and reducing the information gap that often curtails attempts to engage in the aforementioned comparisons.

Background: Islamic activism in contemporary Egypt

Activists who have raised Islamic banners in their quest for power do not represent a new phenomenon, but one that has existed since the end of the first "hijra" century (eighth century). The rise and fall of the ruling dynasties in the Islamic world has, for the most part, been associated with reform-oriented and radical Islamic movements. The Abbassids and Fatimids early on, and the Wahabi's, the Mahdists, and the Sanussis in the eighteenth and nineteenth century, are all cases in point. Moreover, modern Egypt has witnessed three major waves of Islamic activism. Linked to periods of instability and uncertainty, these waves have occurred at the turn of the century, towards its middle, and near its end, and have resulted in the assassination of top political figures such as Prime Ministers Boutros Ghali, Ahmed Maher, Mahmoud El Nokrashy, and more recently, President Sadat. The role of religion as an idiom of discontent has therefore been a constant in the twentieth century. However, Sami Zubaida points out that: "These groups are not new to the political scene, except, perhaps that their situation now is more transparently desperate, they have emerged on to a new political conjuncture of repeated failures of leaders and ideologies, and crucially, have witnessed the triumph of the Islamic revolution in Iran" (Zubaida, 1992: 159).

The assassination of Egypt's president Anwar Al Sadat in October of 1981 was a turning point at which Islamic activism veered from its predominantly violent orientation of the 1970s, to a period of relative accommodation throughout most of the ensuing decade. The period of grace ended in 1988, and was followed by two years that witnessed escalating pressure on the part of the government aimed at curbing the popularity and influence of the Islamic movement. First, there was the government's crackdown on the Islamic investment companies (*sharikat tawzif al amwal*). The promulgation of Law 146 (of 1988) was detrimental to these companies because it required that their activities be regulated by the central bank, as opposed to their previous mode of operation, which depended on contractual agreements with clients. The law also had a negative impact on Islamic businesses, and on the various Islamic associations which epitomized the "Islamic Alternative" in its moderate form.[5] Second, there was the government's refusal to respond to the demands made by Islamists and other political forces regarding the reformation of the electoral system, which prompted a boycott of the 1990 parliamentary elections. Consequently, Islamic activism in its moderate form suffered a temporary setback.

The continued viability of the Islamic alternative, and its reversion to hostile forms of expression after 1988, was to be expected, given that the political and socioeconomic conditions that had been conducive to its articulation still prevailed, and that no competing alternative had emerged to replace it. It was therefore not the credibility of the Islamic alternative which was at stake after 1988, but rather that of its moderate expressions.

The escalation of violence and hostility characterizing Islamic activism during the period from 1990 onwards, together with the public space it has monopolized, indicates that the "Islamic alternative" in its militant form has gained momentum. This momentum is fed by the regime's ineptitude in addressing internal needs; its ineffectual strategy in coping with Islamic activism; and by a number of regional and international factors. Moreover, an explanation of the dynamics of Islamic activism in Egypt can only be attained through an understanding of the historical process, in juxtaposition with the interplay of internal, regional, and international events.

At the local or national level, the increasing religiosity of Egyptian society provides a support system upon which Islamic activism feeds and thrives. The end product is a polarization of the political and social discourse between " islamicists", and "secularists" (*elmaniyin*), with the former being perceived by a sizeable number of people as role models (*qudwa*), and the latter as deviationists (*munharifin*). Such polarization has led to an increasing number of confrontations between the regime and proponents of the Islamic alternative, between islamicists and secularists; and, between Muslims and Christians. These confrontations, which have transcended Egyptian boundaries, have become more protracted and are accompanied by increased violence and a significant rise in the number of targets and casualties. Whereas in the 1970s, which is the period during which Islamic activism resurfaced after years of suppression, militant acts were targeted primarily at government officials, selected representatives, or specific "enemies of Islam", the 1990s, on the other hand, are witness to violence that is much more pervasive. Banks have been targeted, and tourists attacked in a declared attempt to destabilize and discredit the government. In addition, the perpetration of such violent acts is no longer confined to Egypt or to Egyptians, neither is it for that matter confined to any one country or nationality. The 1995 bombing of the World Trade Centre in New York is an example of the globalization of Islamic activism. The operation was blessed by a representative of Egyptian Islamic activism, Sheikh Omar Abdel Rahman, engineered by Ramzi Youssef a Pakistani, funded by the Saudi Ossama Ben Laden, and committed by a multinational group of Islamic activists.

To conclude, the Islamic movement in Egypt has experienced a number of changes since the 1970s. Understanding the nature and magnitude of these changes will pave the way towards effecting a rapprochement between the West and Egypt which, apart from being a major player in the region, is the seat of the most prestigious Islamic institution, Al Azhar. It is also the country of origin for "The Muslim Brothers" (*Al Ikhwan Al Muslimin*) who as Zubaida pointed out, took the articulation of the Islamic Alternative beyond the realm of an intellectual endeavour to that of organized politics and popular agitation (Zubaida, 1992: 47).

Islamic activism in Egypt today

Islamic activism in Egypt today is characterized by a high level of fissiparousness. While divisive tendencies have always existed, particularly in times of stress, the magnitude of these tendencies has increased during the past two decades. The banner of the Islamic alternative was carried in the 1970s by four main groups: the then newly organized Ikhwan; Al Faniya al Askaria (Military Academy), Jamaat al Muslimin (otherwise known as Al Takfir wal Hijra – Repentance and Holy Flight, and Al Jihad (the group responsible for carrying out the assassination of president Sadat). Nowadays, the quest for replacing the existing secular regime with an Islamic one is carried out by factions of these same groups together with numerous new ones.[6] This quest, which was a shared aim among the groups in the 1970s and now those of the 1990s, seems to have become the only commonality between the earlier and latter Islamic activists. Their profiles have changed; so too have their strategy and tactics. Finally, despite the fact that the third wave of activism is still in motion, the dynamic nature of the phenomenon is exemplified through the following milestones.

The first milestone: 1974–81

In the 1970s, Islamic activism was mainly represented by organized groups that varied in their strategies and tactics. The Muslim Brothers' vision appeared to be characterized by a commitment to long-term change mainly through proselytization. The issue of Jihad was approached cautiously. While a continuous struggle of the soul (Jihad Al Nafs) is a must for Muslims all over the world (so as to free their souls from evil), armed struggle, on the other hand, was confined to situations where the Muslims would be denied their right to preach. Because such denial was usually associated with foreign powers, the relationship of the Ikhwan with Sadat's regime was, for the most part, one of mutual acceptance. This was not the case with the other groups whose quest for change was more immediate, and who expanded the scope of the armed struggle to include "corrupt regimes". Most of these groups envisioned the actual status quo of Muslims as being weak and decadent, a situation reminiscent of the "Jahiliya" or the pre-Islamic era. Removal of corrupt regimes was the first step towards redressing the situation. Because society at large was believed to have been led astray by their rulers, once these were removed, society would revert to the right path, that of Islam. The only group that did not have such an indulgent view of society was Al Takfir Wal Hijra. They considered their rank and the only true Muslims. Consequently, their eventual struggle was against corrupt, if not infidel, societies.[7] The "Da'wa", or advocacy which was the Ikwan's declared means of achieving the desired change, was perceived by these groups as ineffectual. In addition, the Muslim Brothers were viewed as having become weak-hearted as a result of the repression they had suffered under President Nasser.

Looking back at the period following the October war of 1973, up until 1981, one concludes that it is these groups' articulation of the Islamic alternative which seemed to prevail. The Ikhwan's long-term strategy for change was neither relevant nor appealing to a volatile segment in Egyptian society: young, university-educated, middle- and lower-middle class urbanites who represented the raw nerves of Egyptian society, and who had become a vulnerable group under the economic open door policy of Sadat.[8]

The second milestone: 1981–88

The assassination of President Sadat in 1981 marked a shift in favor to the moderate end of Islamic activism.[9] The Muslim Brothers assumed a more active role in the political, social and economic spheres, thereby imputing their rallying slogan "Al Islam Howa Al Hal" (Islam is the Solution) with a significant measure of credibility. Setting aside their initial reluctance to play politics as usual, they participated in the parliamentary elections of 1984 in coalition with the Wafd party, and in those of 1987 with the Labor party (Al Amal): they respectively won twelve and thirty-eight out of a total of 445 seats.

The establishment of the Islamic investment companies in the early 1980s was attributed to the Ikhwan. The impact of these companies was only felt in the mid-1980s when the realization dawned that a large portion of Egyptian savings was entrusted to their care.[10] However, until the issuance of Law 146 (of 1988), repeated warnings concerning the shadowy transactions of these companies remained largely unheeded both by the government and the public. For their clients, return on investment of over 20 per cent constituted a significant supplement to their monthly or annual income; and, even in the rare instances when the client was not in need, the opportunity to substantially increase capital was too good to be missed. For the government, these companies were part of a web of services which gave it breathing space, by virtue of catering to the less fortunate.[11] However, by the time the government cracked down on Islamic businesses, it had little, if anything, to show for the time it was allotted. More serious was the fact that the accommodative articulations of the Islamic alternative had suffered a severe blow.

It is noteworthy that during the period from 1981 to 1988, the appeal of the more hostile groups was undermined. In the absence of any credible secular alternative, the setback suffered by moderate Islam, while not posing a threat to the viability of the Islamic alternative per se, was bound to entail, as it did, a reactivation of the appeal of its more radical articulations.

The third milestone: 1988 onwards

The 1990s have witnessed the rising violence and aggressive proliferation on the part of militant groups, in both urban and rural governorates.[12] Ibrahim confirms the shift towards shanty towns and rural areas, pointing out that while "there were no rural residents among the arrested activists of the 1970s, the Egyptian public has now begun to hear of villages as small as Sanabou, Walidiya, and Salamoun in the governorate of Assyut having become the scenes of sustained armed confrontations between Islamic militants and state security forces" (Ibrahim, 1996: 36). This shift is not only reflected in the behaviour of Islamic militants but also in the ongoing discourse of Islamic activists, which has become more rigid and less tolerant of the other. An example in point is the widely publicized case of Nasr Hamed Abu Zeid, a professor at the faculty of arts at the university of Cairo, who in addition to having been denied promotion as result of his writings, was pronounced unfit to remain married to a Muslim, thereby resulting in the issuance of a court order separating him from his wife.[13] Moreover, the amorality of shanty-town dwellers is also a feature that is increasingly observed in the ideas, attitudes, and behaviour of the rank and file of Islamic militants. Field research among the militants of Imbaba revealed, for example, a noticeably casual attitude towards sex, marriage, and the family that is very characteristic of the environment of informal settlements.[14]

Most of the actual militant groups have splintered from the groups of the 1970s and 1980s. However, as previously mentioned, the only factor they seem to share with the former groups is their quest for an Islamic alternative; the profile of their members is different. They are both younger and less well educated than their earlier counterparts. Whereas the average age of Islamic activists arrested in the 1970s and 1980s, ranged between 25–27 years old, the average age of the present day activist is 21 years old.[15] Education levels also differ greatly: 64 per cent of those arrested in the 1970s were university graduates as opposed to 48 per cent in the 1980s, and only 30 per cent in the 1990s. The class background is another change. This downward tilt towards lower-middle class, was less prevalent in the former distribution of Islamic activists. In addition, the change in their strategy and tactics has resulted in a broader range of targets and an increase in the number of casualties. The Ibn Khaldoun Centre for Development Studies (ICDS) count indicates that, while the death toll did not exceed 250 fatalities during the period from 1974 to 1987, during the period from 1988 to 1995 approximately 1,400 fatalities occurred as a result of Islamic activism; the casualty count, which includes the wounded, is of course higher.[16] Moreover, most of the incidents of violence related to Islamic activism have occurred in Upper Egypt, particularly in the governorate of Assiut; in Lower Egypt, most confrontations took place in Cairo. It is worth noting that there are significant numbers of Copts residing in Upper Egypt, and that the development process is generally lagging in Upper Egyptian governorates.

Together with the rise in violence, the recent period has witnessed a significant upsurge of "Social Islam". While the birth of what Denis Sullivan refers to as "the Private Islamic Organisations" (PIOs) dates back to the 1980s, nevertheless, their wide-scale proliferation is a product of the 1990s. So, while "Political Islam" may have captured the limelight, it is "Social Islam" which has impacted more significantly on the lives of people. Social Islam consists of a web of welfare services and developmental activities that have emerged to fill the void caused by the government's absenteeism from the development process. Sullivan describes the situation as being one in which "the government is, by necessity, involved more in conflict management than in development" (Sullivan, 1994: 65). The government's recent focus on developing slum areas in Cairo is a case in point. Its concern came about only after these areas were identified as breeding grounds for the rank and file of Islamic militants. Moreover, Ghassan Salame' points out that Islamic activism feeds on the government's failure to live up to people's expectations. The appeal of Islamists, according to Salame', lies in their endeavour to deliver on the promises of the nationalist regimes (Salame', 1993: 22).

Migration and the globalization of Islamic militancy

Islamists claim that there are over 120,000 Islamic militants in Arab prisons, while various governments only admit to approximately 60,000 prisoners (El Hayat, 14-5-1996). The significance of these numbers is that they are symptomatic of the schizophrenic behaviour of most Arab governments. On the one hand, there is a tendency to downplay the importance of the phenomenon; on the other hand, these same governments sometimes resort to extreme measures in order to stifle Islamic activism, regardless of whether its expressions are militant or not. In Egypt, for example, this tendency is exemplified by the fact that while the official statements issued by various ministries such as Tourism and the Interior claim that terrorism has been eradicated, security measures are stepped up and military trials are constantly being held to try cases related to Islamic activism. There are thirteen members of the Muslim Brotherhood (supposedly the representatives of moderate Islam) currently on trial for conspiring to overthrow the government. In addition, during last year's parliamentary elections, it was observed that the Islamists were prevented from even reaching the constituencies where they had candidates (which meant that they were denied the opportunity to vote) and hence, to participate legitimately in the decision-making process. In the meantime, the PIOs are given an edge over their secular counterparts who, under Law 32 (of 1964), which is the law of associations, operate in a restricted field of action which prevents them from being effective.[17] This lack of consistency on the part of the Egyptian government, coupled with the regional and international developments of the past decade, has contributed to the globalization of Islamic activism and made migration one of its main channels.

At present, over ten million Muslims live in Western Europe, and their number is still growing despite the various governments attempts to curb migration. Many of these incomers are first generation migrants, and according to a *Newsweek* article, a number of these are "rebels in exile", involving leaders of outlawed organizations mainly from North Africa and the Middle East. By establishing or joining existing networks, these migrants proceed, according to Gilles Kepel, to build in Europe a kind of Islam which, despite its minority status, has important implications for the Muslim world. Being close to the centres of power, and to the international media, they are able to organize and communicate with increasing efficiency. Moreover, the impact of Muslim migration to Europe and elsewhere is not confined to the Muslim world. Without detracting from the positive and enriching cultural, economic, and demographic aspects of migration, the fact remains that before arriving in Europe or the USA, many of the present-day migrants have transited in countries such as Afghanistan or Bosnia (where they fought side by side with other Muslims), thereby acquiring a sense of purpose in addition to various warfare skills. Upon migrating, these people often tend to join the ranks of the discontented. Consequently, their disenchantment is often expressed through affiliation to a collectivity and to a cause for which their skills are put to use.

In addition to migration, the globalization of Islamic activism and militancy has also been furthered by the media. Modern means of communication has an outreach capacity that extends not only to the most remote areas, which are unfortunately the ones that are forgotten by governments and planners alike, but also to the widest and most diverse audiences. The success of the Irani revolution in 1979 for instance, was broadcast worldwide and celebrated by Islamic activists all over the world. Despite their declared differences with Shiite Islam, this event was perceived as a first step towards reinstating the "Khilafa" or the universal Islamic state under the banner of which the "Umma" would unite. Daily broadcasts of the plight of Palestinians, Afghans, and more recently that of Bosnians and Chechen Muslims confirm the idea that there is a conspiracy against Muslims and that there are double standards and particular-istic interests governing the manner in which these conflicts are handled. The USA's absolute support of Israel, its immediate and swift reaction to the gulf crisis, and its unrelenting sanctioning of Iraq is held in comparison to a perceived apathy or nonchalance in reacting to the Serbs treatment of Bosnian Muslims, or to Russia's handling of the Chechen issue. Muslims all over the world are constantly exposed to the controversial and often contradictory norms and practices governing the relationship between the West and the Muslim world.

Finally, the grounds upon which Islamic activism and militancy feed, are fertile ones. On the one hand, the political rhetoric employed by the governments of most developing countries is constantly undermined by their inability to deliver on promises related to the equitable access to opportunities and consequent distribution of resources. On the other hand, there is a universal moral rhetoric which is being discredited by the political stances and choices that the governments of developed countries (and other formal representatives of the international community) have opted for. Bridging the gap between what is expected from national governments, civil society, and international organizations, and what is actually being delivered, might constitute the biggest challenge of the twenty-first century.

Conclusion: problems and prospects

The globalization of Islamic activism and militancy is a matter of concern to the international community for a number of reasons. First, the disruption and loss of lives and property that militant acts cause are, certainly and understandably, a main factor of such concern. However, Islamic militants are a minority among Islamic activists (the majority of whom do not condone the acts perpetrated by militants). Also, militant acts are still, despite increased difficulty, containable through security measures. Mainstream Islamic activism, on the other hand, is much more elusive and definitely more pervasive. The intellectual discourse of Islamic activists is generally moderate and therefore, appealing to the masses. The personal behaviour and public practices of most Islamic activists are perceived as consistent with their utterances and with the precepts of the Koran. However, despite widespread recognition of the ingenuity displayed by the representatives of Islamic activism, and their effectiveness in addressing real needs through the PIOs, there remains a concern among civil rights advocates as to both the declared goal and undeclared implications of Islamic activism. The possibility that there could be some degree of "Dissimulation" (*taqia*) behind the discourse espoused by the Muslim Brotherhood and other Islamists, is being considered by detractors of the Islamic alternative as well as by impartial observers.[18] The possibility that the services provided for by the PIOs do not serve interest or necessarily fit within the framework of civil society, is also a matter of concern. Zubaida, for one, believes that social Islam (or the Islamic model) falls short of a framework for civil society in which the exercise of human rights and social autonomies are paramount. "Islamic associations", according to Zubaida, are the instrument or means by which the Islamists control and direct the masses (Zubaida,S, 1992: 9–10). Sullivan and Ibrahim, on the other hand, have a more benign view of social Islam. They see it as a positive force for change that should be supported. They see no other alternative for the state but to co-operate with Social Islam, which Sullivan describes as a potent socioeconomic and political force. The reality falls somewhere in between. While indiscriminate, repressive measures are certain to produce negative consequences, the government's reluctance to relinquish its hold over the institutions of civil society, and its attempts at stressing Islamic credentials through the manipulation of Islamic symbols, are proving detrimental to change in the direction of civil rights and democracy.

The Egyptian case has its particularities. However, like Algeria, Jordan, and the other countries of the region, the secular state continues, and will continue, to prevail – at least in the near future. The prevalence of the state in each of these countries is due to a number of factors that are specific to the socioeconomic and political environment, as well as to the nature and performance of the Islamic movement in each country. However, the common factors shared by these states, as Willis points out, are the lack of unity and cohesiveness among the Islamic activists in each country, and the strong hold that the states continue to maintain over their military apparatus. A recent example of the divisiveness characterizing the Islamic movement in Egypt, is the conflict among the ranks of the Muslim Brothers, resulting from the announcement that a new party, El Wassat, was being established by a number of the organization's members. While this party has been accused by the government of being a front for the Muslim Brothers, its initiators are being blamed by the Muslim Brothers for compromising the unity of the organization. In addition, in Algeria, the GIA's (Group Islamique Arme) recent murder of seven French monks has resulted in further estrangement, not only from the FIS (Front Islamique du Salut) but also from the Islamic groups of other Arab countries.[19] Consequently, it can be said that despite the growing appeal of the Islamic alternative, an Islamic takeover in the countries of the region is not imminent at this particular juncture in history, nor is the mass migration feared by the West (Willis, M. 1996: 24–25). However, terrorist acts, whether committed within or outside domestic boundaries, will persist as long as the states of the region continue to think in terms of security measures, thereby disallowing the participation of Islamists in the political process.

Finally, in order to demystify the phenomenon of Islamic activism, it is important to note that while the potency of secular ideologies seems to be dwindling in favour of religious and other primordial forms of expression, radicalism is not an endemic feature of this shift of appeal. In the case of Islamic activism, such radicalism is usually commensurate with the worldly concerns and aspirations of its proponents. However, in order to survive and remain relevant, radical ideologies, regardless of whether they are secular or religious, have to become more moderate. Once they do, they are contained through incorporation into the sociopolitical mainstream.

Notes

1 Aside from Iran's position *vis-à-vis* Salman Rushdie, who is a British citizen, an example of sovereign rights having been invoked would be the accusation that was made recently by the Pakistani authorities, more specifically by the Pakistani Minister of Interior, concerning the involvement of the Muslim Brothers in Egypt in an attempt on Mrs Bhutto's life. The alleged involvement was denied by the group (*El Hayat* daily newspaper – 23 April 1996, no. 12112, p. 7). Another example is the accusations levied by various governments against Sudan and Iran as harboring Islamic activists on the run, as well as encouraging attacks perpetrated by Islamic activists. A case in point are the accusations made in the aftermath of the attempt on president Mubarak's life during his visit to Ethiopia in 1995 for the OAU (Organization for African Union) summit. Also, noteworthy is the fact that the millionaire Ossama Ben Laden, reputed to encourage Islamic militancy through the establishment of training camps and funding, was until recently living in Sudan.

2 Professor Anne Marie Schimmel admitted in 1995 during an interview published by the daily newspaper *El Hayat* in May 1996, that Germany's hostile attitude towards Turkish migrants may stem from a subconscious association between Turkish migration and the Ottoman expansion in the Balkans and their siege of Vienna in the sixteenth century.

3 The depersonalization of the enemy is a recent phenomenon that is mostly apparent in political statements. Until quite recently, Islam, or rather radical Islam, was described by certain Western politicians and high ranking officials, namely NATO Secretary General Willy Claes and Stella Rimington of Britain's M.1.5, to constitute the "geo-political menace of the future" (*Newsweek*, 29 May 1995, p. 13). It still remains to be seen whether such depersonalization is depictive of a newly revised perception of Islam, or if it is just a politically more diplomatic way of handling the issue.

4 The different and often variant terminology used to desribe Islamic activism is indicative of its complexity. R.H. Dekmejian observes that "The heightening of Islamic consciousness has been variously characterized as revivalism, rebirth, puritanism, fundamentalism, reassertion, awakening, eformism, resurgence, renewal, revitalization, militancy, activism, millenarianism, messianism, return to Islam, and the march of Islam" (H.R. Dekmejian, 1985 p. 4).

5 The Islamic alternative is an ideological construct that is used to describe the objective behind the activities and writings of Islamic activists. This alternative, which is the replacement of the secular state by an Islamic one, is generic, meaning that its modalities and mechanisms of implementation differ according to its proponents.

6 The issue of group affiliation is sometimes confusing owing to the fact that the militants themselves refer to their groups differently from the way that the government and the media do. Apart from resorting to different names, recently Islamic militants are often referred to as the returnees from Afghanistan, the Afghan Arabs, and the returnees from the Sudan. This referral system reflects not only the factual occurrence of their having spent time in these countries; but also places on foreign countries, and sometimes governments, the responsibility of encouraging terrorist/militant activities.

7 Al Takfir Wal Hijra was the group headed by Shoukry Mostafa a former member of the Ikhwan. It was implicated in the murder of Sheikh Al Dahabi, a former minister of Religious Endowments in 1977. The group believed in emulating the prophet's Hijra (Flight) from Mecca to Medina to return only when they had organized their ranks and were strong enough to engage in the necessary struggle. Consequently, Al Takfir Wal Hijra isolated themselves from mainstream society and took refuge in the desert

8 The Open Door economic policies of the Sadat era were widely criticized for having marginalized the professional middle class in favour of the remnants of the old upper class, together with a new entrepreneurial class which was after quick profit.

9 On a continuum devised by Saad eddin Ibrahim, the apolitical Muslim Brothers, i.e. the sympathizers and the Muslim Brothers organization occupy a moderate end, while the anti-regime organizations and the anti-society groups occupy its more radical end.

10 Islamic investment companies operate on the basis of contractual agreements with clients. These companies operate on the basis of dividends rather than interest, which, being fixed is likened to "Riba" (usury), which is repugnant to Muslims.

11 These services are provided by nurseries, schools, clinics, and hospitals which are usually affiliated to mosques. They are offered at affordable prices and are renown for their good quality.

12 Saadeddin Ibrahim suggests that the mounting urgency characterizing Islamic activism in Egypt and elsewhere in the Arab world as due to the adverse consequences of populist policies which are rapid population growth, urbanization, and bureaucratization. Consequently, Ibrahim views the conflict as due to the regime's increasing inability to effectively manage their society and state.

13 This court order was issued based on Islamic law or Jurisprudence which gives to any "Upright" Muslim under the conditions of the "Hisba" (accountability), the right to press charges against other members of the community or "Umma", who commit acts that are threatening or repugnant to Islam.

14 Imbaba is a low income district which has rural fringes which are consistently being encroached upon as a result of population growth. The resulting configuration is that of a neighborhood saddled with all sorts of socioeconomic distortions and environmental ills. This district which came to be known as the republic of Imbaba, was the scene of dramatic events perpetrated by Islamic militants during the late 1980s, early 1990s. It was only in 1992 when the government cracked down on the district that it regained control of the situation.

15 Some of the activists recently arrested for attacks on tourists were as young as 16 years old.

16 This count was compared to that of the state security department, published in Al Ahram newspaper on 3 May 1996, for the years 1993 to 1995, for cross-checking purposes. While the broad trends were the same, ICDS's count was approximately three times higher than the official one; however, it should be noted that the official count, while including the casualties among security forces, civilians and tourists, did not include the usually larger number of casualties among militants. This omission, together with the tendency of the government to downplay the importance of the phenomenon, should account for the gap between the two counts.

17 This lack of effectiveness is specially apparent during times of crises. The 1993 October earthquake is a case in point. The government decreed that all relief funds were to be funneled through the Red Crescent association. The limited outreach capabilities of this association were complemented by those of the PIOs which, as they are not constrained by the terms of Law 32 regarding receipt of donations, were actively engaged in providing support to the needy, unlike the secular associations that stood by as mere bystanders.

18 The concept of Takia is embedded within the shiite tradition of Islam allowing Muslims to conceal their beliefs in times of danger.

19 Statements condemning the act perpetrated by the GIA have been issued by the Jihad group in Egypt and by representatives of the Libyan and Syrian Islamic groups (*El Hayat*, 10 June 1996, issue No. 12159).

Bibliography

Abdel Nasser, Walid M. (1994) *The Islamic Movement in Egypt*. (London, Kegan Paul International.)

Halpern, Manfred (1963) *The Politics of Social Change in the Middle East and North Africa*. (New Jersey, Princeton University Press.)

Ibrahim, Saadeddin (1988) "Egypt's Islamic Activism in the 1980s," *Third World Quarterly*, Spring issue.

—— (1994) "Political Islam – Past, Present, and Future," Symposium Keynote speech, February.

—— (1996) "The Changing Face of Islamic Activism," in Robert Aliboni, George Goffi and Tim Niblock, eds. *Security Challenges in the Mediterranean Region*. (London: Frank Cass.)

Kepel, Gilles (1984) *Le Prophet et Pharaon*. (Paris, Editions La Decouverte.)

Mostafa, Hala (1992) *Al Islam Al Siyasi Fi Masr*. (Cairo, Al Ahram Center for Political and Strategic Studies.)

Willis, Michael (1996) "The Islamist Movements of North Africa," in Robert Aliboni, George Goffi and Tim Niblock, eds. *Security Challenges in the Mediterranean Region*. (London: Frank Cass.)

Zubaida, Sami (1992) "Islam the State and Democracy," *Merip*, November–December.

—— (1993) *Islam, The People and The State*. (London: I.B. Tauris.)

—— (1995) "Is there a Muslim society? Ernest Gellner's 'Sociology of Islam,'" *Economy and Society*, Vol. 24, No. 2, May.

Sullivan, Denis J. (1994) *Private Voluntary Organizations in Egypt*. University of Florida.

Salame, Ghassan (1993) "Islam and the West," *Foreign Policy*, Number 90, Spring.

Stark, R. and Bainbridge, W. (1985) *The Future of Religion*. (Berkeley: University of California Press.)

Chapter 7

Civilizations: clash or co-operation?

Anders Jerichow

This chapter is a collection of reflections on a Muslim-European conference in which participants were promised closed doors and anonymity. Behind this veil of sincerity, however, a whole range of sensible issues centering around identity, representation, evolution as well as power and image projections were raised, with more questions than answers. Firstly, are Muslims, and Muslim societies, necessarily exceptions in history in terms of popular, democratic rights?

Civilizations do develop and change. So too, do their relationships with the interpretation of the letters of God and human law. For instance, certainly a dialogue between Arab-Muslim and European intellectuals takes on a different color and shape in, say, 1920, 1950, 1990 and 1995. This is due not only to changing power structures in the local and interrelated worlds of Europe, and the Muslim Middle East and North Africa but, it is fair to say, due as well to the changing patterns of Muslim politics in the years in between.

When the great powers of Europe, in all their imperialist might, put up new borderlines in Arab sands following the defeat and decline of the Ottoman Empire, neither the mosque nor the local power structures would envisage a future debate on popular participation, electoral democracy or the protracted rivalry between politics of the state, the people and that of the mosque itself. After four centuries of Ottoman rule, the Middle East was just beginning to grasp the emergence of modern nation-building, while final national sovereignty of old nations like Syria, Egypt and Iraq – tribal powers still competing for power in the Arab Peninsular – could only slowly comprehend that independence would be a fact of life.

Thirty years later, in 1950, these central powers were still well established, each of them with its own brand of Arab-Muslim rule, each of them partners in a newly shaped Middle East facing what would become a main determinant for future Middle Eastern politics: the newborn Jewish/Israeli state situated right in the heartland of the Arab world. By 1990, all Arab nations (apart from the Palestinians) had long since won their independence. However, after decades of almost constant Arab-Israeli wars, the Arab nations were confronting not their former colonial powers, but an aggressor within the Arab family itself: Arab governments who sided with the 'so-called' West in the defense of Saudi Arabia and the liberation of Kuwait. Although a substantial part of the Arab populations may have sympathized otherwise, this crisis marked not only new alliances in the Middle East, but paved the way for an open inter-Muslim/inter-Arab competition on government policies and the very right to power.

A matter of representation?

Today, post (if not pre) the Desert Storm Gulf crisis, the Arab-Muslim world and Europe (i.e. 'The West'), is caught in an identity battle of sorts. Some historians, like Samuel Huntington, expect 'A Clash of Civilizations' between the Arab/Muslim East and the Christian Democracies of the West. Others read it as a local Middle Eastern/ Muslim revolutionary development, entailing a final power struggle between palace and parliament, reflecting as well the rivalry between mosque and government might. In either case, it leaves open for debate the question and prospect of Muslim reformation and in particular, when calling for such debate in the Muslim communities with Europeans situated on the other side of the Mediterranean, one must ask: who is to debate, who represents the Muslim nations, and who, in fact, represents Islam?

A non-Muslim participant at the Copenhagen conference had this to say: "To look for democratic prospects in the Arab World is like asking a blind man to search in a dark room for a black cat that's not there." And this response came back: "Why would Arab nations be exceptions in history? Democratization is on its way all over the globe and certainly in the Middle East. Just look back – what kind of autocratic regimes ruled the Middle East decades or just years back? Only in the last very few years have a substantial number of countries – like Jordan, Palestine, Kuwait and Yemen – experienced fairly free elections. All along the Arab Gulf Coast, 'Shuras' or consultative assemblies have been established, and all over governments and peoples talk about popular participation."

As amply demonstrated by the participation and presentations at the Copenhagen Conference, Muslims – scholars and intellectuals – differ in interpretation as do Christian Europeans. Perhaps just an academic exercise, yet the question of interpretation and the right to the interpreted tradition of the holy book remain. However divine, the Koran, like Muslim tradition itself, did not foresee certain questions raised if only because of material developments. Cars, satellite dishes, shortwave radios and faxes were not invented, nor were popularly elected parliaments introduced or international human rights instruments established when the Koran was given from above. Yet the people of the Muslim world need workable answers and new interpretations to help them incorporate modern society's social and material developments into their traditional Islamic readings.

Politically and religiously, representation falls to the heart of the matter. Who governs? Who issues the fatwas and leads the prayers? Is power to be elected, selected or inherited?

Though Western academics would probably be eager to offer answers, obviously it is only Muslim decisions that will provide the traditions of the future. As the Copenhagen conference proved, a balance between Islam and democracy is still sought. While countries like Saudi Arabia, Kuwait and Iran all would lay claim to operating within the framework of Muslim law, the character of popular participation has taken hold in distinctly different forms, e.g., with quite open, though theoretically controlled electioneering in Iran; absent elections, a royally selected shura in Saudi Arabia; and an fairly free, male-elected but still government controlled democratic process in Kuwait.

Image projections

Are any of these societies "more or less" Muslim than others? Who will decide? The ulema in Saudi Arabia? The emir in Kuwait, or the shia-seminars in the holy Iranian city, Qom? According to Danish permanent Secretary of State Henrik Wlhk, the participants at the Copenhagen conference were invited to "dismantle misconceptions" and seek co-operation and dialogue not only between governments, but between the people of the Muslim and European worlds. The Danish Minister for Foreign Affairs, Niels Helveg-Petersen, in his large essay on relations with Muslims, wrote: "They won't disappear."

Quite certainly, they will not. But though a fifth of the world's population today is Muslim, Islam, in the projections of the West, is still characterized by an often violent, non-participatory political culture, distanced from universal values, difficult to comprehend and just as difficult to negotiate with. In the forefront of Western projections, a growing Muslim revivalism, falling under the pretext of "fundamentalism", continues to puzzle and scare, and confronts the West with a sense of an impending cultural clash. The West, however, is not alone in its fear of a religious revivalism that questions local and international law. The Muslim world, itself, is looking for answers as to whether the "so-called" fundamentalists represent an enlightened, or misguided revivalism of Islam. Muslim revivalism clearly is not one phenomenon, but many political expressions, ranging from political radicalism to more violent movements, leaving frequent concepts of "a" revolutionary Muslim fundamentalism as an ill-founded enemy of limited use. So who is the Muslim, and who are the Muslim people?

"Take care," advised one scholar, "for there is no such thing as the people. Whenever someone is talking about the people, one usually has their own plan for what they consider to 'be' the people but which, in reality, consists of highly different sociological and economical interest groups." Yet, the notion of "the people" is what is frequently used by rulers and rival opposition groups alike.

Fig leafs and fundamentalists

Another common feature of power and opposition is the use of Muslim symbolism and various sorts of "Islamisms" as a fig leaf for legitimizing existing power or as a trademark in rival calls for influence or overthrow of old structures. "What we are facing is the ideologization of Islam", said Professor Mir Zohair Husain. Islam, a historic and organic religion, has become a vehicle for change and as such, contains many references to justice, fairness and equity. Jihad, another fearsome word in the international vocabulary, traditionally represents a struggle for social justice. In the new Muslim revivalism however, it has become a catch phrase for a power struggle sometimes, but certainly not always by, violent means.

To the violent supporters of this radical Islam – in its many forms – *jihad* has attained another of its historic meanings, the promise for the *mujaheds* to become *shahids*, or martyrs. Thus Islam has lent itself to politization, just as eagerly used or misused by the existing rulers, as by the revivalist struggling to replace them. "A medium of legitimacy" is a powerfully mobilizing ideology of the masses.

The Muslim revolutionaries have succeeded in setting a new

agenda, forcing the use of an encompassing Islamic symbolism upon the present rulers of Arabia. Although by instinct secular in administrating power, the rulers increasingly cling to Islamic symbols, remembering to subscribe to Koranic verses when legitimizing new legislation, remembering visits to local mosques when touring the countryside, and remembering the religious institutions when setting aside financial contributions.

"Still, power is the bottom line," said a Middle Eastern Scholar. "Power is what it's all about." "Islam is neither the problem, nor the solution," reminded another scholar. "We are, after all, dealing with countries that do not function very well. Previous political movements in the Middle East, from pan-Arabists to baathist to communists have all failed in ensuring the same social development and political transformation as seen in other parts of the world. The political ideologization of Islam has offered new hope, but being used by both ruler and the ruled, side by side, not everything can be Islamic that pretends to be."

Nowhere in the Muslim world, not in secular countries, not in officially Islamic states like Iran and Sudan have rulers provided answers to social problems of society. Even more so, as often with revolutionary ideologies, political Islam frequently has divided, rather than united, nations and populations. It has had a rhetorically uniting effect as a cultural reference point. Yet the Muslim Middle East has lived through one crisis after another, from wars to internal strife, social frustration and political uncertainty. "Crisis?" asked one. "Can an almost permanent row of crisis at all be termed 'crisis'?"

Another problem, common to governments and oppositions alike, is a lack of focus. "We hardly know what Arabs or Muslims want from their future," a speaker noted. "We have few fair elections and no free elections, we have few opinion polls. Almost all over the Middle East and North Africa, states are not getting stronger, but weaker."

Universalism and islamism

The notion of a separate Muslim version of democracy calls for attention, but has not been followed by concrete alternatives to popular voting along party lines and a competition for parliamentary majorities. [It is] "worthwhile to remember," a Danish scholar said, ". . . that universal human rights were established to limit the abuse of state power – period. Human rights are a tool in the hands of the most vulnerable groups in a community. And that is where they stand to a test."

Western or universal values? Muslim scholars seem to differ. Not suitable for the Muslim world? "Now that would be the ultra-imperialist plot, not to offer democracy for Muslims. The world could export food, technology, weapons, but hold democracy, account-ability and demands of transparency back," commented one.

Troubles and triangles

The concept of "civil society" is at the core of the debate, translating into a society with well-founded civil institutions, governmental as well as non-governmental networks, and legally founded political institutions set up to minimize governmental abuse, maximize popular participation in decision-making and ensure governmental accountability and transparency.

Promising democratic development in Muslim countries like South Asian Bangladesh, semi-European Turks refute accusations that democracy and the Muslim society are not compatible. Indeed, looking into the recent past of the Middle East reveals that, in fact, political development has indeed changed into more participatory political systems. Similarly, Europe less than two decades ago, had several nations that were ruled by autocratic, semi-fascist dictator-ships (one being Greece, the perceived cradle of democracy, and the others being Spain and Portugal). To be perfectly fair, it was only fifty years ago that two other key European countries – Germany and Italy – cast most of the world into war. In the decades since then, Muslim nations in The Middle East and North Africa have won their independence; presently one government after another is opening its systems to a larger system of popular participation.

"Democracy has never come as a gift, but always as a result of popular demand or, indirectly, as an offer from rulers, who brought about some degree of popular participation to deal with criticism," said a Middle Eastern activist. "The Middle East and North Africa are facing a three-angle conflict," according to Egyptian scholar, Said Eddin Ibrahim. "Three forces are competing for power: first, autocratic regimes attempting to stay in power; second, the growing forces of civil society; and third, extremist, often times religious forces, trying to bring about the downfall of present regimes and, in the process, preventing secular, pluralistic forces from having a chance to introduce parliamentary democracy.

Governments of the surrounding world are, to some extent, dependent on the stability of some of the autocratic regimes, in particular Saudi Arabia. They confront a number of other autocratic, radical regimes like Sudan and Iran. Quite a few of the Western/ European governments are trying to bolster the more vulnerable governments, most notably in Egypt, which are otherwise destabilized by a population boom, the lack of sustainable social institutions, and by a growing Muslim revivalism.

A reformation of Islam

So far, Muslim revivalism has succeeded in changing the agenda of the Middle East and North Africa but, apart from Iran and Sudan, it has failed in reaching its ultimate goal of seeing the secular regimes out. As the focus of the Copenhagen 'Islam' conference debate, this presented at least two dilemmas for revivalist movements and societies alike. First, will revivalist movements or parties necessarily remain alternatives to the development of pluralist societies, or will they accept their own place in a predominantly secular society under present and future democratization? Second, will the Middle Eastern and North African societies, gradually transforming into civil societies with a larger degree of popular participation, be open to an accommodation of revivalist movements? And will they have the courage to test the democratic capacity of revivalist parties?

Bearing Algeria in mind, both revivalists and secularists find an argument to avoid an answer. True to the facts of the Algerian elections in 1991/92, Islamists doubt if they would ever have the chance to win a fair parliamentary election. Only the military intervention in Algiers prevented a revivalist democratic takeover while Arab regimes elsewhere, whether by law or by decree, have so far prevented Islamist parties from taking part in a contest to the liking of the voters. Secularists, on the other hand, find strong reasons not to trust a democratic posturing by Islamists in light of the ensuing and massive bloodshed in Algeria, where revivalist radicals cut the throats of not only soldiers, but of women, as well as writers, journalists and other intellectual proponents of civil democratic society.

Ironically, as the Copenhagen conference was taking place, yet another test of Islamist takeover occurred – in the secular, democratic (Muslim) society of Turkey. Having suffered through military takeovers three times in the past – in 1960, 1971 and 1980/82 –

Turkey this time prepared itself to see an extraordinary coalition between the Islamist Refah ("welfare") party and the secular, kemalist True Path Party. Now, the questions were: To be trusted or mistrusted? To be "allowed" or prevented? By new elections or another military intervention? After all, democracy depends on the voters willingness to accept the result of their own decision – as well as the willingness of winning party/power to face a new election in due time.

Acknowledging a far greater popular participation in Iranian political life than in Saudi Arabia, both systems still rely on regime-appointed ulema to decide. In Iran, it is decided by who is religiously credible, and worthy for democratic candidacy; in Saudi Arabia, it is decided by which royal decrees are in accordance of Islamic law. In both countries and systems, the present rulers are given the last word, deciding on the composition of the upper religious councils.

Muslim scholars elsewhere maintain, nevertheless, that a pluralist democracy, based on the will of the people and the voters, and not on the verdict of rulers, may be in full accordance with the book of Islam. Others use the word "reformation" quite openly, not just to remember what was necessary in Europe to gradually separate state and church (developing slowly as it did into a pluralist, civil and democratic society), but forcefully to set course on a new interpretation of Islamic law and Muslim tradition. Until that event occurs, however, the secularists call for a revivalist promise that the killings of civilians, e.g., as in Algeria, cannot be justifiable and or in accordance with Islam. "In fact," reminded Arab scholars at the Copenhagen conference, "a central, and for this century, early Islamist, Hassan al-Banna, sought a reinterpretation of Islam as well as of Western values, in effect trying to create a new set of values, feasible for changing an Arab society."

The role of mosque: playing by the rules

Be reminded, the Muslim Middle East and North Africa are not waiting for a future clash of secular and religious revivalist civilizations. The two competing paths taken by Muslim societies are in the midst of an everyday fight for the backing of people and future "voters". Directly in the center of this competition is the Mosque, the most forceful and vital civil institution of modern Muslim society.

In most, if not all societies of the region, only the mosque is free to assemble people and spread religious as well as political messages. It is no coincidence that state power is doing its utmost to control the mosques by keeping an eye on Friday prayers, putting preachers on the government payroll and increasing the ban on whatever actions it may deem to be a political use of the mosque, be it in Egypt, in Saudi Arabia, in Algeria or in Palestine.

Religious institutions on the periphery of the mosque increasingly offer alternative social networks to that of the state. Religiously sponsored health clinics offer better and cheaper service for the poor than do national institutions. Religious foundations offer alternative schooling, based on Koranic classes, and often are well into social sciences and the like.

What is happening is the evolution of alternatives to the state, with the Mosque at the center. This is posing an even greater challenge to the state and secular society at a time when the region is experiencing increasing fragmentation.

"The Hizbollah's and Hamas" of the Middle East and North Africa have certainly proved able in their adaption from sheer political opposition to the practice of political power," a Copenhagen conference scholar said.

> They have realized and accommodated to the power of institution building. It becomes all the more important since most of the states in the region are still in a process of nation building, and many are facing severe economic difficulties as well. Where the state fails, the religious networks pop up, often as the best alternative – or the only one. Islamists quite convincingly have learned from communists and trade unions what it takes to organize an opposition.

The religious – or revivalist – alternative may, out of government control, be a revolutionary risk. On the other hand, a government controlled, semi-independent religious network may as well serve to keep the lid off the pressure, leaving room for the ruling government to maneuver.

But serving as alternative networks, whether tolerated as part of a government plot to keep the opposition at bay, these religious networks and revivalist movements behind are only tested for their non-governmental capacity, and not for their ultimate capacity and ambition: to govern.

Genetics and democratics

While scholars and philosophers in the Muslim world and the West elaborate at length on the compatibility of Muslim culture and universal human rights – and democracy – Muslims in their daily lives have long since proved they are no different from the rest of the world. "Why would they be," asked an Egyptian scholar. "For genetic reasons or . . .?"

"Note the difference," another scholar said while pointing at the podium. "Three Muslim speakers in the panel – and three opinions, as should be! Don't ignore that the Middle East is deep into a robust debate on the future political system and, addressing the demands of a stable, civil society."

This same scholar once traveled to Sudan on for the Arab Organization of Human Rights to appeal on behalf of three people in Khartoum, who were sentenced to death. Sadly, the Sudanese leader, Ibrahim Turabi had them executed anyway. Later, when Turabi himself was jailed, the AOHR-delegation went back to Khartoum, this time to appeal on Turabi's behalf. This, I argue, is what human rights are for (although Profeesor Turabi has not quite accepted the idea).

Nevertheless, several Muslim countries, with Turkey, Bangladesh and Pakistan in forefront, have directed its citizens to the polls and accepted the voice of the people. In the same fashion, citizens of a growing number of Arab nations show up at opportunity to make their case.

People cannot be fooled into democracy by bogus electioneering. In fact, some 90 per cent of the people voted in Egyptian elections after its independence. Nowadays that figure is only 45 per cent. Why? In 1924, people hoped that the innovative democracy would work. In 1995, they were confident it did not. "The proof," said the Egyptian scholar, "is that in rural districts the participation is far bigger, because there, it matters. And that is what makes democracy work – popular confidence that voting can make a change."

The Middle Eastern and North African states are clearly in a process of accepting the institutions of civil society and human rights. At the time of AOHR's establishment in the mid-1980s, the founders of the organization had to meet in Cyprus. Today, the AOHR has sixteen branches all over the Arab world.

Indeed, it does give reason for hope. "Do remember however," another scholar reminded his colleagues that at present, democratization right across the Arab world is at the mercy of the present rulers. They can do what they like, and they do. None of them have left their own fate in the hands of the people. Contrary to the democratic societies of Europe, this in a sense has rendered far more stability to the Middle East and North Africa. While Europe keeps changing governments, the Arab world is characterized by the same rulers for decades.

Societies of the Middle East are certainly not static. Seen across the last decades rather, they are in a dynamic process of change – politically, at least. While nations in the Far East have transformed democratically along a present 10 per cent economic growth rate, a number of Arab nations have witnessed economic crises and setbacks, experiencing some of the worlds lowest economic growth rates; some countries even having negative rates of growth.

Crisis management: state and NGO

Seemingly in a state of permanent crisis, five central challenges were identified by an Egyptian scholar. The Middle East and North Africa remains a conflicting environment, not only *vis-à-vis* Israel, but inside the Muslim world as well. It faces a heavy population boom, an exploitation of natural resources and lack of fresh water for drinking purposes as well as for agriculture, food security is threatened, resources (including oil) are being depleted, while other sources of income, in particular employment-giving work places, are not established instead. Democracy, or at least some sort of popular participation, is developing, but far from securely to avoid renewed autocracy, civil strife or confrontation between rulers and revolutionary religious revivalists.

Most importantly perhaps, the perpetuated crisis is threatening the credibility of state and government and, in turn, lends new credibility to other forces – be they traditional networks of tribe or mosque, or the alternative of the religious revivalist movement.

Very few revivalist movements have concentrated on solving the problems of inflation, the debt dilemma or have offered viable solutions to declining growth rates. It need not be necessary to pose as an alternative to the fragmenting power of present rulers. Most powers in the Middle East and North Africa, though, are still in the process of nation building, in contrast to European states, where state power is superseded by transnational regulating institutions, most importantly the European Union.

But the Muslim Middle Eastern world is experiencing a 'mushrooming' of new associations and institutions eager to take on a role in nation building. In fact, wherever licenses for non-governmental unions and associations are issued, new organizations are established. Civil society is on its way.

Old blame, new ways

The Muslim Middle Eastern world is still entrenched in crisis, however, and all sorts of blames are highlighted, some which are useful for governments, some for the secularist, and some for the religious revivalists.

Only few decades removed from colonialism, much of North African and Middle Eastern states willingly find reasons for their present disarray in the past. To the contrary, others find it more appropriate to accept local responsibility, using the same explanation – several decades, after all, have passed.

Apart from the burden of previous colonialist rule, the region has been involved in numerous wars. Almost all states have suffered from authoritarian rule, bureaucratic waste, widespread corruption and nepotism. Individual states, as well as the entire region, have confronted immensely uneven distribution of resources and welfare.

In material and social terms, the present is not much better. Infrastructure has almost been completed in the Oil states along the Arab Gulf Coast. Few wars persist, although sources of more wars continue to threaten: most of the Palestinian territory, just like South Lebanon, is still under Israeli occupation; the rest of Lebanon is still controlled by Syria; the northern part of Western Sahara is occupied by Morocco; Sudan is still in a state of civil war in the south and Iraq in the kurdish North; while a civil war is tearing Algeria apart.

The uneven distribution of resources has found no solution, nor has the authoritarian rule of most countries faced the final call for democracy or other forms of popular partition (should they exist). Economically, all of North Africa, and most of the Middle East, is still tied up in a structural crisis. Transparency, let alone accountability, continues to be a feature for the coming days.

So what kind of future can they expect, looming or promising? Just as new interpretations of Islam cannot, and should not, be forced upon the Muslim nations, democracy and universal values of human rights should not either. Though it is part of the universal concept not to make any distinction between European and Muslim rights, the outside world will expect religious reinterpretation to come from within. Yet a democratization of the Muslim communities is called for – and is partly a prerequisite to – the future cooperation between the two civilizations, Europe and the Muslim Middle East and North Africa.

In this respect, the balance is uneven with strong economies from the North, meeting fairly weak economies on the southern shore. According to the Barcelona declaration, the envisaged co-operation will set its roots in the dialogue not only between governments, but between peoples and non-governmental organizations. Partnership is what is called for. Economic growth and social development is what is needed – apart from a settlement of conflicts and the avoidance of potential tension.

If private organizations and investment is indeed welcomed in the South, it may not be attractive to the North – for governments seeking a stabilization of the Mediterranean area, certainly, but not for private investors looking for a proper return and a safe outcome. In the eyes of European governments, North Africa represents an even larger challenge and risk to their investment, although the need for such is well recognized in order to reach the basic goals of political and social stability.

As one observer from the conference dryly phrased it: "Poor Mexico, so close to the US, but so far from God. But even worse for the Arab Middle East and North Africa: close to God, but so far from the US." According to the same humorous witness to history, European investments in the South Asian country of Sri Lanka have even exceeded those in needy Egypt.

The called-for partnership is still hampered by trade barriers put up by the EU. If for no other reason, this might tempt Arab and other Middle Eastern nations to increase their internal trade and cooperation. Today, most external trade is bound to nations outside the Middle East and North Africa. According to a non-Arab participant in Copenhagen, "this tradition has the extraordinary result that just as the Israeli economy turns its back on Palestinians, most Arab economies turn their back on other Arabs."

Perhaps this is a hint of the Muslim dilemma: in a changing world, the local setting of Muslim societies and the questions of identity, the interpretation of Islam, the aspirations for the future and the co-operation with outside partners require a whole lot of basic choices: the courage to look back and to look forward, and the courage to choose between universal values and past traditions, or the possible adaption of the two.

Annex 1: Conference Speech

The Euro-Mediterranean partnership

Juan Prat

In November of 1995, the Barcelona Conference launched a new form of co-operation and spirit of partnership between the European Union and its twelve partners in the South and Southeast Mediterranean. The Conference was an event of major political and symbolic importance. The parties involved agreed on the establishment of an ambitious Euro-Mediterranean partnership, one at least equal, in terms of scope and dimension, to other regional co-operations in Europe such as the intensive co-operation we are achieving with the Eastern and Central European countries.

For the first time, this Conference, and this partnership with our neighbours to the South, was prepared for, and decided on, *together*. Until now, our Mediterranean policy had been created within Europe for the benefit of our partners, since we had to provide them with policies. I think it is also very important to underscore the fact that this is the first time the Declaration was unanimously approved and the Programme of Action were all achieved by joint initiatives. Once again, it was prepared together and so there is a common feeling of ownership.

The Euro-Mediterranean partnership, though, is not the only framework for co-operation between the European Union and countries of the Islamic world. We maintain important contractual relations with many leading Islamic countries and we have institutionalized relations with several Islamic blocs. Through our long-standing relationship with the Gulf Co-operation Council Countries of the Middle East, we now have a new co-operation underway with the ECO countries (Economic Co-operation Organization) founded by Turkey, Iran and Pakistan and joined recently by many others from the Caucasus. This is an economic co-operation organization which, for the first time, is based on culture and religion. What must be recognized is that the Euro-Mediterranean partnership provides the most innovative and most comprehensive partnership to date.

Let me explain in more detail the architecture of the partnership agreed in Barcelona, which is based on two fundamental ideas:

- First, that efforts to create a zone of peace, stability and security in the Mediterranean must go hand in hand with the promotion of more balanced economic growth and development between the North and the South of the Mediterranean. This is both evident and absolutely necessary.
- Second, that the Euro-Mediterranean partnership will only succeed if accompanied by a cultural dialogue between the two sides of the Mediterranean based on the principles of equality and mutual respect.

To fulfil these fundamental ideas, there are two tracks and three pillars. The two tracks are regional and bilateral in nature, whereas the three pillars are:

- political and security
- economic and financial
- social and cultural.

In order to efficiently cover all three main pillars, the European Union has promised to devote significantly increased financial resources. This funding is essential to the credibility of a common plan of action.

Political and security co-operation

Under this first pillar, a declaration of political principles forms the basis for co-operation. The achievement of this joint political declaration is, in itself, very significant not only, because it was decided upon unanimously, but because it sets out commonly held principles of democracy, respect of human rights, the rule of law, pluralism and tolerance as the basis for Euro-Mediterranean political dialogue and co-operation.

The achievements of the Copenhagen Conference will indeed make an important contribution to furthering this process of identifying and adhering to commonly held and interpreted fundamental values. In the security sphere, many principles were also adopted to guide co-operation, the most important ones being the sovereign equality of states; non-interference in internal affairs; respect for the territorial integrity of states; peaceful settlement of disputes and the renunciation of force. In addition, common commitments were agreed upon, in particular to combat terrorism, organized crime and the illegal trafficking of drugs as well as common objectives such as the disarmament and the non-proliferation of weapons of mass destruction.

Though it was not easy to achieve this declaration, the most interesting aspect of the negotiations were that, up until the late hours the day before the Conference, it was not the so-called North–South confrontation that was difficulty, but the fact that for the first time, an open South–South dialogue emerged. This was unfamiliar territory for our partners and that called for the adaption of common positions, something to which we are more used to in the EU.

Economic and financial co-operation

This is the key to combatting political, economic and social instability in the Mediterranean. To this end, it was decided that a vast Euro-Mediterranean free trade zone would be established as a framework for the economic growth and development of Mediterranean partner countries by the year 2010. The important point here is this: a specific date was set to achieve these goals rather than leaving it "open-ended".

The building blocks for the establishment of a Euro-Mediterranean free trade zone will be the bilateral association agreements between the European Union and Mediterranean countries, allowing each Mediterranean Country to make the economic transformations necessary for a sound development in accordance with its own requirements. A multilateral free trade agreement was out of the question at this point; just working for a free trade agreement on a one-by-one basis with each of the countries of the South, taking into consideration their specificity and needs, was a large enough task knowing that the outcome meant the creation of a huge new network of agreements. This, together with the introduction of specific elements such as the "cumul of origin" for the products originating in those countries will also provoke South–South trade and agreements on cross-investments. This should contribute to decloistering these economies, too heavily reliant on the Northern markets, and help to achieve a better balance of prosperity between the two sides of the Mediterranean. With the planned expansion of the European Union, the Euro-Mediterranean free trade zone can, in the future, reach the dimension of 600–800 million people.

This new, dynamic market will be reciprocal in nature. Afterall, the whole idea of these free trade agreements is to contribute to the integration of the economies of the Southern Mediterranean countries to the global world and, we hope by doing that (by integrating them within Europe first), that these countries will be more attractive to capital from other regions of the world.

The achievement, by the target date of 2010, for a Euro-Mediterranean free trade zone between the Barcelona 27, is indeed an ambitious objective. Although the transition periods will be quite significant, economic, social and political difficulties will no doubt be encountered. To counter these difficulties and help support the vital transitions needed, the European Union has made available a very important financial package in favour of its Mediterranean neighbours. For the period 1995–1999, in both the bilateral and multilateral tracks, almost 5 billion ECUS (US$6 billion) will be provided in grant aid to our partners. An equal amount should be provided in the form of advantageous loans from the European Investment Bank. In this way, these amounts, together with the efforts of individual Member States, as well as the international community, which will at least be equally significant, the EU has affirmed its commitment to the ambitious aims of Euro-Mediterranean economic and financial partnership.

But aside from the economic and political aspects, the inclusion of a *socio-cultural dimension* in the Euro-Mediterranean partnership is extremely important. Without it, the other two dimensions (political/security and economic/financial) could not be complete and would not symbolize, in the same way, a relationship based on mutual respect and equality. The inclusion of a socio-cultural dimension also provides us with a way of combating a new sort of historical pessimism concerned with the possibility of reconciling different cultures and religions (Samuel Huntington's *Clash of Civilisations* has contributed significantly to this view which I do not fully share).

In the case of a Euro-Mediterranean partnership, the commitment to dialogue, and the co-operation of all parties are sufficiently strong for us to be convinced that we can succeed in promoting peace and prosperity in a region of vital importance to the European Union.

If the United States is so interested in the Middle East peace process, it is because they are a global power, and globally speaking, they cannot be absent of such important issues. If Europe is participating, it is because it is our region and therefore, a regional concern for us. Consequently, it is important to understand that because the

Mediterranean is our geopolitical region, it is our own business to talk about the business of the other countries of this region.

The point here is that we must ensure that Euro-Mediterranean cultural co-operation materializes as soon as possible. Already this year several activities have been jointly organized, within the multilateral framework of Barcelona, mainly in the form of conferences, seminars, experts meetings and exhibitions (the highlight so far was a ministerial conference held in Bologna in April, with the participation of the EU fifteen, plus twelve Mediterranean, on the value of the Euro-Mediterranean cultural heritage).

A further programme of activities is planned for the second half of the year, including support for the production and distribution of cultural works. A statistic concerning the publishing of books will illustrate the potential of such an initiative: of the 125,000 books published each year in the Euro-Mediterranean region, three-quarters (or nearly 100,000), were published in the North Mediterranean EU countries. Only 7,000 were published in Turkey; 5,000 in Egypt and 2,000 in the five Maghreb Union countries together.

The Euro-Mediterranean partnership will assist in the increase in concrete forms of cultural co-operation. However, a quantitative increase will not, by itself, solve the problems of our cultural relations. A dialogue between religions will be very necessary. There is no doubt that the future of Euro-Mediterranean relations will, to a large degree, depend on establishing understanding between people of the Christian, Islamic and Jewish faiths. Cultural and religious dialogue must recognize the prejudices and misunderstandings which are prevalent in our societies, both North and South of the Mediterranean. We must look to the problems of the "image" we have of each other. This requires that we examine carefully the content of history books, weaknesses in regional and language studies and, above all, the stereotypical images purveyed by television.

The Barcelona Declaration encourages dialogue between religions. Important meetings have already taken place in Stockholm (1995), and Toledo (1996). The Conference in Copenhagen will continue this process of reflection. Beyond confrontation, and in a spirit of tolerance, across the different major religions, we should also encourage reflection on the conflicts between the values in our societies based on reason and those based on belief.

Renewal of cultural and religious dialogue cannot ignore the fact that a significant part of the population of the EU is now Muslim. There are more than 10 million Muslims resident in the European

Union (the exact figures are not known because the policies followed by the different countries are not the same regarding the social integration, insertion or assimilation and make it very difficult to achieve good and reliable statistics on the subject but one thing is clear: the figures are well above 10 million). The majority have, or will become, European Muslims, and we should discuss the place in European society of our citizens of Muslim culture and religion. We can even imagine that a "European Islam" could one day contribute to the development of Islamic thought generally. Recall how, during hundreds of years in Europe, in Al Andalous, it was Islam that irradiated culture to the rest of the World.

If a dialogue between cultures and religions is essential in the context of our Euro-Mediterranean partnership, it will not be accomplished simply and without difficulty. Let me illustrate some of the problems we may encounter.

First, there is a close relationship in the region between politics and culture. Discussion of the values of our respective civilizations cannot be purely an academic exercise. It will inevitably raise questions of conflicts and injustices. The Middle East conflict is a case in point. We cannot ignore the fact that the outcome of the Middle East Peace Process will determine the future of a Euro-Mediterranean dialogue in which Arab countries and Israel both participate. The fundamental aims of peace and stability in the Mediterranean cannot be achieved without a permanent and just solution to the Middle East conflict. Although the Middle East Peace Process and Euro-Mediterranean partnership are two distinct and separate processes, the latter cannot fully succeed without the success of the former.

Already in 1980, in its Venice declaration, the European Union was the first to set out the principles of a just and lasting peace in the Middle East. Since its inception in Madrid in 1991 we have resolutely supported the Peace Process. We are active supporters of its multilateral track and the European Union is the single most important source of financial assistance for the Palestinian people and the new Palestinian Authority.

The Peace Process has once again reached a crucial turning point. The EU, our Mediterranean partners, the United States and the rest of the international community must all use their influence to ensure is not interrupted and that it continues to move forward in the direction of achieving just and permanent solutions.

Other problems which we will encounter in our cultural dialogue will include:

- How to overcome the fact that it will take place between institutional representatives from two sides of the Mediterranean?
- How can we widen the circle of participants?
- How can we avoid a dialogue between elites from becoming euro-centric, dominated by European concepts and inputs?

We must find means of widening and decentralizing the dialogue. Fortunately, the EU has growing experience in decentralized co-operation and we shall put these experiences and programmes such as Med-Campus, Med-Democracy and other Mediterranean programs that we are already experiencing, at the disposal of our society and our dialogue.

Another apparent contradiction stems from the fact that our socio-cultural dialogue will deal with real problems relating to organized crime and illegal drug trafficking which inevitably focus on the problems of controls, borders, frontiers and emigrations. Cultural co-operation, however, requires increased exchanges, meetings, mobility and the opening of frontiers. There will be, therefore, important but essentially practical problems to be resolved.

In this illustration of difficulties which our cultural dialogue will encounter, let me stress the need for reciprocity. If the efforts we make in the EU to remove barriers of ignorance, prejudice and mistrust are to succeed and contribute to stability and understanding, they must be reciprocated by our partners. Ignorance, prejudice and mistrust are not found only on one side of the Mediterranean. They constitute a common danger to the objectives of partnership. The Barcelona Declaration is based on common commitments and an implicit desire to identify, from the best of our two civilizations, the elements which can be shared and considered universal. This requires efforts from both sides.

Finally, I would like to close on this point: if the historical experience and geographic proximity of the Southern EU member countries enables them to play a key role in the implementation of a Euro-Mediterranean partnership, it will not be without the interest of other EU member countries. Relations with our neighbours to the South are of interest to all EU member countries. Nothing illustrates this point better than the present Conference here in Copenhagen. Northern EU countries member states, as well as new member countries and future member countries, are all needed and involved in the process of Euro-Mediterranean partnership.

Annex 2: Conference Speech

Challenges and opportunities

Ellen Margrethe Løj

Europe and the Middle East share a common history that dates back centuries. During the last decade, the scene on which we interact has been reset. The end of the Cold War, the increasing visibility of radical Islamic movements in Muslim countries, the Middle East Peace Process and the Muslim migrant communities in Europe are important factors in this process.

New economic, political and cultural relations are being shaped. On the one hand, this provides the potential to profit fully from our regional differences. On the other hand, there is an inherent risk that misperception, prejudice and lack of respect for differences will estrange our regions; that we will drift apart instead of growing together. We face a unique historical situation, and we have to make very important choices on the content and format of our future co-existence.

The complexity of the situation, and the resulting challenge, have been realized by both the EU and the Mediterranean countries. Last year in Barcelona we established *the Euro-Mediterranean partnership*, essentially a very broad and comprehensive policy response to the perceived challenge.

The objective of the partnership is to turn the Mediterranean basin into an area of dialogue, exchange and co-operation guaranteeing peace, stability and prosperity. The mutually agreed requirements are a strengthening of democracy and respect for human rights, sustainable and balanced economic and social development, measures to combat poverty and promotion of greater understanding between cultures.

The adoption of the declaration implied a political commitment by all parties to implement and adhere to the ambitious goals and principles within it. Certainly, a historical achievement in itself.

As a policy instrument, the partnership concept combines three equally important and closely interrelated dimensions: *the political and security aspect, the economic and financial aspect and the cultural, social and human dimension.* Furthermore, the need for interregional co-operation among the countries in the region is emphasized, and support for the Middle East peace process is a fundamental element. Finally, co-operation on and between all levels of our societies, institutional, as well as non-institutional is strongly encouraged.

The challenges that the Partnership seeks to answer are multiple. From a European perspective one of the most visible challenges is that of Islamic radicalism. The perceived threat of Islamic radicals to Europe as well as to the Middle East are sometimes only too real. Acts of terror, internal instability within Muslim countries, a possible increase in migration and the export of radical ideas to migrant communities outside the Muslim world.

Some observers, Muslims and non-Muslims alike, consider Islamic radicalism inherently anti-democratic because it does not recognize separation between the secular and religious sphere and thus, constitutes an impediment to democracy and pluralism.

The discussions during this Conference have clearly demonstrated that this it not necessarily so. Many scholars have stressed the wide margin of interpretation and the need to distinguish between the Koran itself and later traditions.

The tragic results of radical Islamic terrorism make headlines all over the world. If left unqualified, front page stories add to the stock of prejudice and result in mistrust and rejection, not only of radicals, but of Islam itself.

There are a number of reasons for the revival of radicalism; distorted economic and social development, very high levels of unemployment depriving major parts of the younger generation of any prospect of the future; a population increase exceeding the economic growth rate; widespread disillusionment with post-colonial governments in their implementation of Western modernization strategies (be it capitalism, socialism or nationalism); lack of access to the political process and widespread corruption, i.e., crippled credibility of governments and administrations; And in the midst of an age of globalization, a tendency by the younger generations to strive for an identity founded on traditional cultural roots, rather than those of the West, can be observed. The role played by charismatic and highly skilled ideological leaders should also be acknowledged.

Furthermore, as a result of the impact of colonialism in the region, Europe is perceived as the source of present malaise. In addition, Western governments are being accused of holding double standards as regards to principles such as human rights and democracy that they themselves characterize as universal.

The complexity of the challenges creates a big potential for instability both within and between the countries of the Mediterranean region. We must ask ourselves how the partnership can be used to address this situation?

The political dialogue between governments constitutes an important forum within which Europe can insist on the obligation taken on by Mediterranean governments to develop the rule of law and democracy in their political systems. Partners can be encouraged to make room for pluralism and to include the non-violent opposition into the political process rather than exclude it.

Concerning the opposition, however, a distinction must be made between moderate fundamentalism and radical fundamentalism. Because it takes two to tango and partners must agree on the rules of the game. There are limits to dialogue. If radicals – either in the shape of nation states or political movements – reject the concepts of dialogue and democracy, or do apply or justify violence and terror as a political means, dialogue simply is not an option to be considered.

At any time and place, terrorism in all its forms, must be condemned and fought from within the limits of fundamental human rights and guarantee of fair trial. European countries will persistently maintain that respect of human rights will not impede the struggle against terrorism. On the contrary, it reduces the support for terrorists.

Those in power must be able and willing to face opposition and criticism. Hence, the importance of fundamental freedoms and individual rights. In the 1960s, philosophers such as Jean-Paul Sartre very loudly voiced strong criticism of Western culture. Islamic radicals have used such arguments as evidence of lack of spiritual content in Western societies and bankruptcy of materialism, etc., whereas in Europe, this discussion is perceived as part of the strength of the system.

Also in the Islamic world, pluralism could reduce the frustration which nourishes radicalism. Opposition, be it political or cultural, can be a source of inspiration and development. Moreover, although at times annoying to rulers, it is an essential tool for holding those in power accountable and to circumvent corruption and administrative misconduct. Furthermore, an uncensored public debate on contemporary problems would force responsibility upon the opposition. Both in terms of suggesting solutions to social and economic problems and to the complex question of how to come to terms with modernity in a Muslim society.

The Partnership should of course not be a one-way street. It must be a channel through which Mediterranean governments can also communicate their views and dissatisfaction, e.g., when they perceive the political behaviour on the European side as based on double standards.

The partnership, however, offers no clear-cut answers to a dilemma which touches directly upon fundamental political philosophy: What if the people in a free and fair election prefer a political party or movement which is not democratic? Would it be acceptable if a fundamentalist Islamic government, based on its moral conviction, make institutional changes which would negate the possibility of a transfer of power? This difficult question is not only of academic interest. Soon enough, we may have to find an appropriate answer to it.

Existing power structures often use the threat of Islamic takeover to perpetuate basically authoritarian political systems and to disenfranchise even non-Islamist opposition groups. But experience from several countries demonstrates inclusion of non-violent opposition to be more constructive than exclusion.

Social and economic development of the Mediterranean countries is an essential element in the quest for political stability. Economic history demonstrates beyond doubt that trade liberalization is the most efficient engine of economic growth. Therefore, the long-term vision of the economic partnership is the establishment of a free trade area.

It is evident that necessary structural adjustments may hurt in the short run, but the sacrifices required are necessary investments in the future. And the European Union has committed itself to providing considerable financial assistance for facilitating the adjustment process. Improved access to European markets is important and will gradually be provided. But increased integration and co-operation within the region south of the Mediterranean sea is as important.

Concerning economic vision, our twelve partners are much too oriented towards Europe. One of the big challenges in this regard is how to contribute to the promotion of interregional economic links?

Finally, it must be remembered that challenges are not only perceived through governmental eyes. Various views are prevalent. Valuable input and knowledge of causes and effects regarding the challenges can be channelled to governmental levels from an informed public, including the academic world.

In all countries, and especially in parliamentary democracies, governments have to take public opinion into account. But often public opinion is shaped by misinterpretations of the press and the electronic media. The answer to this challenge is not censorship or curtailing freedom of expression. The answer is to get to know each other better at all levels of society. This conference is an example.

We can see that the cultural, social and human aspects of the partnership are extremely important. There is an urgent need to develop co-operation within all levels of our civic societies and to enhance contacts between our citizens. Only through increasing our mutual knowledge of different cultures, religions, values and traditions incorporated into the partnership, will we be able to conduct a fruitful dialogue and profit fully from the existing variety.

Annex 3: Newspaper Chronicle, published in the daily *Politiken*, 17 June 1996

The Muslim world and the West – a need for dialogue

Niels Helveg Petersen

The other day at the library I noticed a small leaflet about Islam which illustrated more profoundly than many a long and complicated article, the increasing Danish curiosity regarding Islam presently observable. The leaflet listed three summer exhibitions on Islam presented by leading Danish museums as well as a number of new publications on Islam and Muslim immigrants in Denmark.

The exibitions at the National Museum and at 'Davids Samling' clearly demonstrate that fascination with the Orient but do not in themselves constitute a new phenomenon. What has changed is the perspective from which Islam is being studied. Whereas traditionally Islam has been perceived as something remote and exotic, today, it has moved right into our living rooms.

A number of our fellow citizens are Muslims. Thus, when children are having a birthday party, the traditional Danish pork sausage, dearly loved by the children, will not – as it previously did – do as the main course. The birthday party example is but one to illustrate that Islam has become a factor close to our daily lives. The public debate about Islam and politics is about to take up more space in Danish media than does the question of the influence of Christianity on political life and the development of our society. Recently at the national convention of the Danish Christian People's Party, one of the main issues discussed was whether or not the party would accept a Muslim party member to run for Parliament; and only two weeks ago, my own Social-Liberal Party hosted a well-attended conference on challenges and opportunities connected to the relations between the Islamic World and the Western world.

Every now and then we feel that aspects of Islam affect us a bit too directly. While under the auspices of the UN, Danish soldiers have been caught in cross-fire between Bosnian Serbs and Bosnian

Muslims. And we have all been deeply upset by photos of innocent victims of fundamentalist acts of terror whether in France, Israel or Algeria, knowing that Denmark will not necessarily remain un-touched.

Our knowledge of Islam often relates to terrorism and violation of human rights, thus images of scimitar-wielding hordes easily spring to mind when the concept of Islam is mentioned. Even the European debate on Islam is excessively characterized by such images. On the other hand, we obviously cannot just sit on the fence watching the fundamentalist wave sweep through the Muslim world.

Consequently, the Ministry of Foreign Affairs hosted a seminar last spring during which questions on how fundamentalism can best be understood and dealt with were discussed by leading Danish experts on Islam. As was expected, contrary to drawing up clear cut conclusions or answers to the questions, we found that the more the variety of existing Islamist movements and Muslim countries is examined, the more evident the complexity of the phenomenons becomes.

Even though the seminar did not produce unambiguous answers, a lot of useful information and reflections emerged, and I therefore decided to host a large international conference with the view to further developing our understanding of Islam. And today, in Copenhagen, leading international experts and representatives of Islamic movements and Muslim countries meet with Danish experts, politicians and civil servants to continue the debate.

As a starting point, one has to be aware that in Muslim countries the influence of religion on political life, the judicial system and everyday life of citizens is much more direct and decisive than the influence of Christianity in Europe supposedly ever was. Due to valid historical circumstances, the principle of giving Caesar his due and God what befalls him is unknown to the Muslim way of thinking. Whereas Christianity was rooted in the well-developed Roman society, Islam itself constituted the backbone in the Arab nation-state building process. Thus, not only does Islam prescribe a code of conduct regarding the way in which the individual is to relate to God. But in addition, Islam embodies prescriptions on the relationship between the individual and the nation-state as well as on the relations between believers.

When the West attempts to promote Western ideas of parliamen-tary democracy, the rule of law and equality between men and women, the beforementioned prescriptions embodied within Islam

170

cause conceptual difficulties. The reason being that while the Western line of argument is based on the rights of the individual as well as on international standards such as the Charter of the United Nations and the International Convention on Human Rights, even moderate Islamists conduct their discourse in the framework of the Koran. Thus we often speak different languages. This, however, far from implies that dialogue is out of the question. The fact that a vivid discussion on the beforementioned central questions is being conducted among Muslims, illustrates that the Koran is subject to a wide variety of interpretations.

Moderate Muslims are prepared to interpret the concept of the Shura – the Muslim principle of consultation – as the basis for a system of parliamentary pluralism. Being opposed to this line of thinking, the fundamentalists rejects the compatibility between political parties, democracy and Islam, the argument being that Islamic law – the Sharia – does indeed encompass every necessary rule of conduct related to human society, thus leaving no conceptual room for the necessity of a legislative body.

Clearly, such wide room for interpretation demonstrates that common ground can be found concerning values shared between Westerners and Muslims. To come to a consensus will require a lengthy and thorough dialogue because our points of departure are very different and on some issues, such as that of women in society, a concensus might be characterized by the lowest possible denominator.

Even moderate Islamists are of the opinion that the right place of women is that of a housewife tied to the home and the family. A number of the rules, to which Muslim women must submit themselves, can only be perceived by Westerners as being oppressive and humiliating. Quite often it is argued that Muslim women do themselves prefer the traditional role to be maintained. However, I refuse to believe that but a few women prefer being forced to refrain from driving a car, being forced to cover themselves up, being forced to obtain the permission of husbands to be able to join the labour market or being subject to a legal system in which the word of a man is considered superior to the word of a woman. It should of course be acknowledged that these rules are not applied with the same severity everywhere. Unfortunately, however, women being deprived of rights equal to those of men seem to be the normal state of things, rather than the exeption.

On occasions when I have met with well-educated and moderate Muslim leaders, I have have often been struck by how difficult it can be to understand that they can defend positions and conditions as those described above. Understanding the more extreme Islamic movements is even more difficult. During the last fifty years in Europe, we have been accustomed to a development pointing towards increasing tolerance, and internationalism, wider scope for individual freedoms and increasing equality between sexes. To a large extent this development has been promoted by groups of young people and students. Thus, to Westerners everything seems to be turned upside down when, for instance in Algeria; young students are fighting for an Islamic republic that leaves very little room for tolerance and in which women are deprived of the right to work outside the home without prior permission of her husband, as well as deprived of the right to choose their own dress code.

One of the ambitious goals of the conference is to be able to understand better how young people can wish for such a society. Already, elements of an explanation are at hand. The desperation and frustration of young people are easy to understand. In a stagnating economy characterized by soaring unemployment, the prospects of a future life based on reasonable material standards of living are desperately poor. Following decades of failed state management of the economy, socialism has lost its credibility. Too often, the reluctantly introduced liberalization of the economy has been beneficial to only a small elite while, so far, the large majority has but experienced the negative side effects such as rising prices and reduced social benefits. At the same time, political and economic liberalism is often associated with Western dominance and hence, contempt for non-Western cultures and values.

I believe that corruption also constitutes an important explanatory factor. Most Muslim countries are plagued by an almost institutio-nalized corruption absorbing many of the resources which could have been allocated for social welfare programmes, and thus undermining the credibility and authority of the state *vis-à-vis* the citizens. Hereby a vacuum is created which is often filled by Islamic organizations such as Hamas and the Muslim Brotherhood. These organizations skillfully carry out a comprehensive piece of social work and have proven to be very resistant to the temptations of corruption. In many areas the citizens have more confidence in such alternative structures than in governmental institutions.

The struggle between Islamic movements and regimes in power present us with many difficult dilemmas. In what way are we to react, when the only realistic alternative to an undemocratic regime which violates human rights is that of an even worse religious dictatorship? What would have been the comprehensive policy towards Algeria, when the military took power after the Islamic fundamentalists won the elections, in order to prevent the country from turning into an Islamic republic? In any case, hardly the line chosen at the time. And how are we to react, when the military engages in brutal counter-insurgency operations against the Islamic groups, while they on their side commit outrageous crimes such as cutting the throats of school girls, female journalists and French monks.

At times the most tempting response would be to just close your eyes while the fretful pictures are shown on TV. But neither the violent fundamentalists, the undemocratic regimes nor the enormous social problems will have gone away when you open your eyes again. We simply have to face these issues.

My own position is clear. Although not an easy one, dialogue is the only answer to the challenge of fundamentalism. The critical dialogue with Iran illustrates better than anything how frustrating dialogue with Islamic fundamentalists can be. We do not, however, have any better alternative, and fortunately this position is not only a Danish one. The EU co-operation carries sufficient weight to secure that our common position cannot be ignored. When talking to Middle Eastern governments, our most important message to them must be to broaden the political process and make room for the involvement of the responsible parts of moderate Islamic movements. Involving the moderates will, of course, neither eliminate the extremists nor prevent terror, but it may be able to reduce popular support for the most extreme groups. At the same time, we ought to stress that respect for human rights does not prevent an effective fight against terrorism. On the contrary, it is one of the essential means to prevent terrorists from gaining sympathy and winning new supporters.

An important framework for such a dialogue was established last November when the foreign ministers of the European Union and the twelve Mediterranean partners adopted the so-called Euro-Mediterranean partnership. The partnership combines important financial support from the EU with commitments from the Mediterranean partners as regards improved mutual cooperation between themselves as well as dialogue with the EU about security building measures and sensitive questions such as human rights, democracy and the status of women. We have not yet come quite as far in our relations with the Gulf states, which have been more reluctant to accept our invitations to genuine dialogue on these issues.

But our dialogue should not be limited to take place between governments. An urgent need exists for dialogue with the Islamic movements. As long as contacts are limited, the gap grows deeper and deeper. It is a task that I and the civil servants of the Ministry for Foreign Affairs can handle only partially. That was clearly demonstrated when we looked for representatives of the Islamic movements for our conference: it was incredibly hard to find relevant persons whom "official" Denmark would be able to host.

Here is a great task for many organizations and individuals in Denmark engaged in the struggle for human rights and democracy around the world. Some tend to find the possibility for action is limited to signing manifestoes to governments or writing angry letters to editors. But why not be active? Find these groups and engage them in a discussion about tolerance, pluralism or the rights of women. Why not make use of the funds of the Danish Democracy Fund to finance study trips, seminars and related activities? And why not actively support those courageous Algerian women journalists who walk a tightrope between a government which does not tolerate criticism and the murderous threats of extremist Islamist groups?

Foreign policy, of course, is the prerogative of the government. However, all efforts are needed when promoting human rights. And "civil society" is more capable of undertaking certain tasks than is "official" Denmark.

My desire for dialogue has been interpreted by some as weakness, lack of resolve or a caving in to business interests. Anyone who would take the trouble to look at the government's annual report on Danish exports can ascertain that exports to the countries in question is of marginal importance. Money is by no means a deciding factor in our policy in this area. So the easiest thing for me would be to follow the line of least resistance, demanding the use of the stick rather than the carrot.

But the thing is we get nowhere by means of threats or sanctions. Sanctions can be a justified measure. Obvious examples are South Africa, Iraq and Serbia. However, certain decisive conditions have to be fulfilled. The most important are clearly defined goals and wide international support. This does not necessarily mean that Denmark cannot take the lead as we did in the case of South Africa. Bear in mind that this was a special case. A case where we had the support of both the "second" and "third" worlds in the fight against apartheid. Those we needed to convince of the usefulness of sanctions were our democratic partners in the Western world. The moral example then set by Denmark was judged to have an impact. And indeed it did. But neither isolated bilateral Danish, nor Western sanctions, would have any constructive effect on the Islamic countries, including Iran.

Even if we cannot close our eyes to the challenges and problems the Islamic world presents to us, we should not forget the enormous potential open to us as well. As our own Muslim immigrants enrich Danish society and contribute to cultural diversity, Muslim countries can be a source of cultural and social renewal. The West can learn a lot from the Islamic movements in their focus on spiritual rather than material wealth and the strong social conscience. A sort of social conscience which is not merely reflected on the income tax form, but which is translated into individual and concrete solidarity with the disadvantaged members of society.

This is why I do not attend this conference in order to teach but to listen, learn and discuss. I do not expect us to agree. But if we leave the meeting room knowing more about each other, this conference has been a worthwhile effort.

Annex 4

Stereotypes and prejudice
Henriette Rald

The conference 'Islam in a Changing World – Europe and the Middle East', received its share of thoughtful and necessary coverage by most of the Danish newspapers. Focus on the event ranged from daily articles concerning the conference itself to more lengthy chronicles by Danish Middle Eastern experts regarding the complexities of Islam in the modern world.

It was a pleasure to read these pieces. The views expressed were not only contemporary, but also progressive in nature. Classic myths portraying Islam as "*strictly the religion of fundamentalists*" or being "*the major threat to Western Europe*" were well-challenged by detailed analysis e.g., the oppression of Women in one Islamic country, Saudi Arabia, was seen in the context of countries such as Pakistan and Turkey selecting women as State leaders; and the all too familiar pictures of a violent Islamic world, when held up to the frail and fragmented light of Arab unity, suggested an often *overexposed* threat to the security of Western Europe.

As Conference Coordinator I was pleased to find that by organizing a serious and substantive discussion on the subject of Islam, there existed the possibility to exert a constructive influence on the level of public debate, i.e, *awareness*. However, as a European citizen still sorting truth from myth, my enthusiasm for the results was quickly tempered by several of the illustrations accompanying the newspaper text.

Take, for example, a drawing that depicted a naked women with her hands and feet bound underneath the cloak of the Muslims' traditional black dress (Figure 3). Sadly, this severe stereotype appears to have been a *reflex* choice of its editor rather than a suitable response to what the reader learned: namely, that Muslim feminists are making inroads, and establishing influence, in the Iranian opposition party. Another illustration painted a classic picture of the African, i.e., Islamic masses, throwing themselves against Fort Europe (Figure 2), while a third rendering caricatured the Ayatollah with a *bomb* for a turban (Figure 1). Where black and white photos substituted, shots of the stereotypic Islamic fundamentalist/activist male were favoured (Figure 4).

What is the motive of *only* presenting these one-sided images, when new understandings and co-operations are emerging – albeit slowly – right on our very soil?

What struck me as tragic as I viewed these illustrations is how the power of a few ill-chosen images can perpetuate the wrong message and thus, undermine any intent or progress made by the spoken word, i.e, the Copenhagen Conference or by the written word i.e., Danish newspaper coverage.

Imagine if the topic of debate in an Middle Eastern country was the Danish Welfare State, and the submitted articles carried nothing but pornographic illustrations emphasizing stereotypically liberal notions about Denmark?

If new prejudices were born out of the conference "Islam in a Changing World", they were indeed raised in the direction of those "tired-old" editorial messages.

Figure 1

Figure 2

Figure 3

Figure 4

Conference programme
Eigtveds Pakhus, Asiatisk Plads 2, Copenhagen
June 16–18, 1996

SUNDAY, JUNE 16th

18.00–19.00 *Registration at the Radisson/SAS Royal Hotel Copenhagen*

19.30 *Buffet dinner at the Radisson/SAS Royal Hotel Copenhagen*

MONDAY, JUNE 17th
Eigtveds Pakhus, Asiatisk Plads 2

08.30 *Bus service from Radisson/SAS Royal Hotel to Eigtveds Pakhus, Asiatisk Plads 2*

Official Opening
Open to the press

09.00–09.15 *Opening Statement*
Henrik Wøhlk, Minister for Foreign Affairs, Denmark

09.15–10.00 *The Euro-Mediterranean Partnership*
Juan Prat, Vice President of the European Commission

10.00–10.30 *Coffee break*

Hereafter closed to the press, except journalists invited as participants. "Chatham House" rules will be applied.

Conference Chairmen:
Svend Aage Christensen, Director, Department of Analysis, DUPI
Michael Zilmer-Johns, Deputy Head of Department, Ministry of Foreign Affairs

Contemporary Islam

Current Islamic movements: A survey and a presentation of differences and common features. Special attention will be given to the different ideas presented by the various political Islamic groups throughout the Middle East.

10.30–11.15 *The Ideologization of Islam: Causes and Consequences*
Mir Zohair Husain, Associate Professor, University of South Alabama

An introduction to political developments in the Arab Peninsula, the Middle East and North Africa; the character and expression of governmental power, the influence and development of opposition movements and the background, inclination and involvement of Islamic movements.

11.15–12.00 *Multiple Faces of Islam*
R. Hrair Dekmejian, Professor, University of Southern California

An analytical approach to the various active Islamic political groups in the Arab Middle East, and the way in which such groups influence social and political life.

12.00–12.15 *Short break*

12.15–13.00 *Human Rights in Muslim Interpretation*
Ahmad S. Moussalli, Professor, American University of Beirut

Islamic Fundamentalist Discourses on Human Rights and Pluralistic Democracy

13.00–15.00 *Lunch*

15.00–17.00 *Debate: Islamic Values, Human Rights and Democracy*
Sadik Jalal Al-Azm, Professor, Damascus University
Massoumeh Ebtekar, Assistant Professor, Tarbiat Modarres University, Tehran
Morten Kjærum, Director, The Danish Centre for Human Rights
Walid Saif, Associate Professor, Jordan University
Chairman: **Niels Barfoed,** Dr.phil., Writer, Denmark

17.00–17.30 *Coffee break*

181

17.30–18.30 *A Pan-Islamic Movement – Unity or Fragmentation?*
Shahram Chubin, Executive Director, Research, Graduate
Centre for Security Policy, Geneva

An insight into the patterns of conflict and co-operation among
divergent Islamic groups and a highlighting of the differences.

18.30 *Bus service from Eigtveds Pakhus to Radisson/SAS Royal
Hotel*

19.45 *Guided walk from Radisson/SAS Royal Hotel to Restaurant Divan II, Tivoli*

20.00 *Dinner, Restaurant Divan II, Tivoli*

TUESDAY, JUNE
18th Eigtveds Pakhus, Asiatisk Plads 2

08.30 *Bus service from Radisson/SAS Royal Hotel to Eigtveds
Pakhus, Asiatisk Plads 2*

Civil Society

A presentation of the development of civil society in the Middle East; the
development of pluralism, popular participation and accountability in a
current Muslim context

09.00–10.00 *The Troubled Triangle*
Saad Eddin Ibrahim, Professor, Ibn Khaldoun Centre, Cairo

Populism, Islam and civil society in the Arab World.

10.00–10.30 *Coffee Break*

10.30–12.30 *Debate: Civil Society*
Toujan Faisal, Member of Parliament, Jordan
Saad Eddin Ibrahim, Editor, El-Watan, Algeria
Sami Zubaida, Reader in Sociology, University of London
Ziad Abu-Amr, Professor, Member of Palestinian Elected
Council
Chairman: **Jørgen Bæk Simonsen,** Dr.phil., University of
Copenhagen

12.30–14.30 *Lunch*

Challenges and Opportunities

A discussion of the post-1989 challenges and the opportunities for co-operation in the Mediterranean region, with an emphasis on social and economic issues in the light of a developing partnership

14.30–15.15 *Islamic Activism in Egypt 1974–1996*
Nemat Guenena, Director, Socio-economic Development Department (EQI), Cairo

A survey of Islam or Islamic activism as affecting the world order, shaping it, as well as being affected by it.

15.15–15.30 *Europe and the Middle East – the Need for Co-operation*
Ellen Margrethe Løj, State Secretary, Ambassador, Denmark

A survey of the potential and actual co-operation patterns between Europe and North Africa and the Middle East.

The conference will now be open to the press

15.30–17.00 *Debate: Regional Challenges and the Euro-Mediterranean Partnership*
Abdel Monem Said, Director, Centre for Political and Strategic Studies, Cairo
Uffe Østergaard, Professor, University of Århus
Aicha Lemsine, Writer & Columnist, Algeria
Nemat Guenena, Director, Socio-economic Development, Cairo
Chairman: **Ellen Margrethe Løj**, State Secretary, Ambassador, Denmark

17.00 *Closing remarks*
Niels Helveg Petersen, Minister for Foreign Affairs, Denmark

17.15 *Bus service from Eigtveds Pakhus to Radisson/SAS Royal Hotel*

Evening free

Danish Institute of International Affairs (DUPI)
and the Danish Ministry of Foreign Affairs

List of participants

President, Director General **Hanan A. Awwad**
PEN centre for Palestinian writers, Jerusalem

Middle East Writer **Charlotte Aagaard**
The Independent Danish Daily, Information, Copenhagen

Professor **Ziad Abu-Amr**
Palestinian Elected Council, Birzeit

Professor **Sadik Jalal Al-Azm**
University of Damascus

Head of Department **Lars Erslev Andersen**
Odense University

MP **Elisabeth Arnold**
The Danish Social-Liberal Party, Copenhagen

Dr. phil. **Niels Barfoed**
Politikens Hus, Copenhagen

Chef de Bureau **Djamel Benabi**
El-Watan, Alger

Chairman **Saïda Benhabylès**
Mouvement Féminin Algérien de Solidarité, Alger

First Secretary **Aliza Bin-noun**
Embassy of Israel, Copenhagen

Minister Counsellor **Sven Bille Bjerregaard**
The Royal Danish Representative Office in Jeriko

Ambassador **Peter Branner**
Royal Danish Embassy, Rabat

Head of Department **Torben Brylle**
Ministry of Foreign Affairs, Copenhagen

Editor **Ilnur Cevik**
Turkish Daily News, Ankara

Director **Svend Aage Christensen**
Danish Institute of International Affairs, Department of Analysis, Copenhagen

Executive Director **Shahram Chubin**
Geneva Centre for Security Policy, research, Geneva

Head of Section **Dorthea Damkjær**
Ministry of Foreign Affairs, Copenhagen

Journalist **Ole Damkjær**
Berlingske Tidende, Copenhagen

Professor **Hrair Dekmejian**
University of Southern California, Los Angeles

Secretary General **Jean-Michel Dumont**
Parliamentary Association for Euro-Arab Cooperation, Bruxelles

Assistant Professor **Massoumeh Ebtekar**
Tarbiat Modarres University, Tehran

Programme Coordinator **Said Essoulami**
Article 19, London

Parliament Member **Toujan Faisal**
Jordanian Parliament, Amman

Professor **Mhamed Fantar**
Institut National du Patrimoine, Tunis

Ambassador **Jamal Eddine Ghazi**
Embassy of the Kingdom of Morocco, Hellerup

Senior Lecturer **Erik Gram**
Army Specialist Training School, Copenhagen

MP **Jonna Grønver**
The Danish Liberal Party, Copenhagen

Director **NematAllah Adel Guenena**
Environmental Quality International, Socio-economic Development
Department, Cairo

Professor **Dr. Bozkurt Güvenc**
Office of the President, Ankara

Minister Plenipotentiary, **Faud A. Hafiz**
Royal Embassy of Saudi Arabia Chargé d'Affaires, Copenhagen

Assistant Professor **Birthe Hansen**
University of Copenhagen

Ambassador **Herluf Hansen**
Royal Danish Embassy, Tunis

Chairman of the Board of Danida **Holger Bernt Hansen**
Ministry of Foreign Affairs, Copenhagen

Freelance Journalist **Jørgen Harboe**
Rungsted

Professor, Dean of the Faculty of Arts **Manuel S. Hassassian**
Bethlehem University

Ambassador **Niels Helskov**
Royal Danish Embassy, Ankara

Head of News **Flemming Dan Heltø**
Danish Broadcasting Corp., Frederiksberg

Ambassador **Poul Hoiness**
Royal Danish Embassy, Riyadh

Research Fellow **Ulla Holm**
Centre for Peace and Conflict, Research, Copenhagen

Head of Department **Robert Houlisto**
European Commission, Bruxelles

Associate Professor **Mir Zohair Husain**
University of South Alabama, Mobile

Chairman **Saad Eddin Ibrahim**
The Ibn Khaldoun Center for Development Studies, Cairo

Professor **Raphael Israeli**
Hebrew University, Jerusalem

Research Assistant **Martin Vive Ivø**
University of Copenhagen

Head of Section **Michael Irving Jensen**
Danish Immigration Service, Copenhagen

Foreign News Editor **Anders Jerichow**
Politiken, Copenhagen

Associate Professor **Norman Kanafani**
Royal Agricultural University, Frederiksberg

Ambassador **Ingmar Karlsson**
Swedish Ministry for Foreign Affairs, Stockholm

Ambassador **Taher A. Khalifa**
Embassy of Egypt, Copenhagen

General Manager **Rami George Khouri**
Al Kutba Publishers, Amman

Secretary of Embassy **Marianne Balling Kiil**
Denmarks Permanent Representation to the EU Bruxelles

Director **Morten Kjærum**
The Danish Centre for Human Rights, Copenhagen

Director **Martin Kramer**
Tel-Aviv University

Writer and Columnist **Aicha Lemsine Laïdi**
Women's World, Alger

Ambassador **Sten Lilholt**
Royal Danish Embassy, Cairo

Ambassador, Counsellor **Ludwig Linden**
German Foreign Ministry, Bonn

Dr. **O. Faruk Logoglu**
Embassy of Turkey, Copenhagen

Ambassador **Lars Lönnback**
Ministry for Foreign Affairs, Stockholm

Director **Torben Lundbæk**
The Danish National Museum, Copenhagen

Project Coordinator **Marc Luyckx**
European Commission, Bruxelles

State Secretary, Ambassador **Ellen Margrethe Løj**
Ministry of Foreign Affairs, Copenhagen

Vice President **Manuel Marin**
European Commission, Bruxelles

MP **Arne Melchior**
The Centre-Democrats, Copenhagen

Student of Political Science **Trine Mogensen**
Danish Institute of International Affairs, Copenhagen

Director **Peder Mortensen**
Prehistoric Museum, Højbjerg

Professor **Ahmad S. Moussalli**
American University of Beirut

MP, Dr. phil. **Per Stig Møller**
The Conservative Party, Copenhagen

Director **Niels-Jørgen Nehring**
Danish Institute of International Affairs, Copenhagen

Deputy Head of Department **Ole Neustrup**
Ministry of Foreign Affairs, Copenhagen

Ambassador **Erling Harild Nielsen**
Royal Danish Embassy in Tehran

Professor **Augustus Richard Norton**
Boston University

Research Director **Gorm Rye Olsen**
Centre for Development, Copenhagen

Foreign Editor **Kent Olsen**
Morgenavisen Jyllandsposten, Viby J

MP **Vibeke Peschardt**
The Danish Social-Liberal Party, Copenhagen

Mag.art. **Jakob Skovgaard Petersen**
University of Copenhagen

Minister for Foreign Affairs **Niels Helveg Petersen**
Ministry of Foreign Affairs, Copenhagen

Vice-Chairman, Professor **Nikolaj Petersen**
Danish Institute of International Affairs, Copenhagen

MP **Gert Petersen**
The Socialist Peoples Party, Copenhagen

Ambassador **Mohammad Pourmohammadi**
Embassy of the Islamic Republic of Iran, Copenhagen

General Director **Juan Prat**
European Commission, Bruxelles

Senior Correspondent **Herbert Pundik**
Politikens Hus, Copenhagen

Programme Editor **Birgitte Rahbek**
Danmarks Radio, Copenhagen

Conference Co-ordinator **Henriette Rald**
Danish Institute of International Affairs, Copenhagen

Ambassador **Jakob Rytter**
Royal Danish Embassy, Tel Aviv

Director **Abdel Monem Said Aly**
Centre for Political and Strategic Studies, Cairo

Associate Professor **Walid Saif**
University of Jordan, Amman

Counsellor **Niels-Jørgen Schelde**
Royal Danish Embassy, Riyadh

Dr. phil. **Jørgen Bæk Simonsen**
University of Copenhagen

Managing Director **Dr. Nabil Sukkar**
The Syrian Consulting Bureau for Development and Investment, Damascus

Journalist **Jesper Sørensen**
Denmarks Radio, Frederiksberg

Vice-Chairman **Christian Wittenkamp**
Confederation of Danish Industries of OPEC and Middle East Business
Club, Copenhagen

Permanent Secretary of State for Foreign Affairs **Henrik Wøhlk**
Ministry of Foreign Affairs, Copenhagen

Deputy Head of Department **Michael Zilmer-Johns**
Ministry of Foreign Affair, Copenhagen

Reader in Sociology **Sami Zubaida**
University of London

Professor **Uffe Østergård**
University of Aarhus